Intermediate Teacher's Math Activities Kit

Includes 100 ready-to-use lessons and activity sheets covering six areas of the 4–6 math curriculum

Stephen J. Micklo

JOSSEY-BASS
A Wiley Imprint
www.josseybass.com

Published by Jossey-Bass
A Wiley Imprint
989 Market Street, San Francisco, CA 94103-1741 www.josseybass.com

Design and Production by Navta Associates, Inc.

Jossey-Bass books and products are available through most bookstores. To contact Jossey-Bass directly, call our Customer Care Department within the U.S. at 800-956-7739, outside the U.S. at (317) 572-3986 or fax (317) 572-4002.

Jossey-Bass also publishes its books in a variety of electronic formats. Some content that appears in print may not be available in electronic books.

Library of Congress Cataloging-in-Publication Data
Micklo, Stephen J.
    Intermediate teacher's math activities kit : includes 100 ready-to-use lessons and activity sheets covering six areas of the 4–6 math curriculum / Stephen J. Micklo.
        p.   cm.
    ISBN 0-471-64910-4 (pbk. : alk. paper)
        1. Mathematics—Study and teaching (Elementary) 2. Mathematics—Study and teaching (Elementary)—Activity programs. I. Title.
QA135.6.M52 2005
510' .71'2—dc22   2004002219

Printed in the United States of America
PB Printing   10 9 8 7 6 5 4 3 2 1

About This Resource

The *Intermediate Teacher's Math Activities Kit* is designed to support any intermediate grade teacher (grades 4, 5, and 6) in implementing a professional mathematics program. Included are illustrated activities and teacher directions to help supplement other mathematics programs. The book is divided into six sections. Each section includes detailed lesson plans, activity sheets for the lessons, objectives for the lessons, material lists, answer keys, and related activities for each mathematical topic. The specific mathematical topics include symmetry, geometry, measurement, statistics, probability, and algebra. Problem solving is included in all of the topics.

These lessons and activities are designed to be used with intermediate students. Each activity has specific teacher directions for presenting the information to the students and a related activity to reinforce the knowledge. The lessons can be taught to the entire class or to small groups of students. Each lesson includes a reproducible activity sheet that is designed to involve students working individually, in pairs, or in small groups.

The activities and lessons are divided into levels of knowledge.

- *Beginning Level* activities introduce mathematical content and related vocabulary. Much of this knowledge has already been introduced in the primary grades and needs to be built upon in the intermediate grades.

- Once the content has been introduced, it is reinforced with activities at the *Learning Level*. Many of these activities and lessons involve the students with hands-on, concrete materials since this is still the best way that children learn. It is assumed that the students possess the beginning knowledge of the topics. If this is not the case with your students, introduce the concepts and then reinforce them with the activities in this book.

- Finally, activities at the *Challenging Level* ask students to use the content knowledge in a different way. These activities lend themselves to students working cooperatively in small groups, helping one another master the content.

A unique feature of this book is the appendix of teacher resources. This section includes pictures, grids, tables, graphs, figures, and much more to make it easier for you to teach the activities. These resources are designed to be reproduced for teacher and student use and made into overhead transparencies for lessons, and are incorporated into many of the lessons. This means no more hunting for resources. This book provides them for you.

Also included is a glossary of the mathematical vocabulary used in this book.

I hope you enjoy the *Intermediate Teacher's Math Activities Kit* as you explore the world of mathematics.

About the Author

Stephen J. Micklo, Ph.D. (Florida State University), is an associate professor of Childhood Education at the University of South Florida, St. Petersburg. He currently teaches Early Childhood Education courses and Elementary Education mathematics methods courses.

Dr. Micklo has been a teacher of young children from prekindergarten through the primary grades, an elementary school assistant principal, and was an elementary school principal. He has written several articles dealing with mathematics for young children for leading professional journals, is the author of the *Primary Teacher's Math Activities Kit* (The Center for Applied Research in Education, 2002) and is the coauthor of the *Elementary Math Teacher's Book of Lists* (Jossey-Bass, 1997).

Contents

Section 1

SYMMETRY

Activity	Concept	Knowledge Level
1-1. Turn, Flip, or Slide	Turn, Flip, Slide	Learning
1-2. Draw the Ways	Turn, Flip, Slide	Learning
1-3. Turning and Turning	Turn, Rotational Symmetry	Learning
1-4. Turn Around	Turn	Challenging
1-5. Flip Me Over	Flip	Challenging
1-6. Flip Me to Read Me	Flip	Challenging
1-7. Mirror Lines	Bilateral Symmetry	Learning
1-8. Mirror, Mirror	Bilateral Symmetry	Challenging
1-9. Pentomino Search	Turn, Flip, Bilateral Symmetry	Challenging
1-10. How Many Times?	Rotational Symmetry	Learning
1-11. Rotate and Color	Rotational Symmetry	Challenging
1-12. Alpha Time	Bilateral and Rotational Symmetry	Challenging
1-13. Will It?	Tessellation	Learning
1-14. Flip Rows	Tessellation	Challenging

Teacher Directions

© 2004 by John Wiley & Sons, Inc.

■ **1-1. TURN, FLIP, OR SLIDE (Learning Level)**

Objectives: To determine how a figure was moved
To draw the resulting figure after a move

Materials: Book with a colorful cover
Plain sheets of paper
Crayons or markers
Turn, Flip, or Slide activity sheet

Directions: "When figures are moved there are usually three ways it can happen. One is a flip." (Write "Flip" on the board.) "Another is a turn." (Write "Turn" on the board.) A third is a slide." (Write "Slide" on the board.) Have the students describe each move as best as they can. (*Flip—to turn a figure over. Turn—to rotate a figure. Slide—to move a figure in one direction.*)

Hold the book so all can see. "A flip occurs when a figure is turned over. There can be a horizontal flip." (Flip the book horizontally to demonstrate. Move the book back to its original position.) "Or there can be a vertical flip." (Flip the book vertically to demonstrate.) Repeat the horizontal and vertical flips of the book several times to reinforce the different positions. Have the students identify if the flip is horizontal or vertical as you move the book.

"A turn occurs when a figure is rotated." Turn the book ¼ of the way around. "We can turn a little, like this one-fourth turn." (Move the book back to the original position and then turn it ¾ of the way around.) "Or we can turn it a lot, like this three-fourths turn. As we turn it, the book looks a little bit different until we get back to where we started."

"A slide occurs when a figure is moved in a straight path. It could move horizontally." (Move the book horizontally.) "Or vertically." (Move the book vertically.) "Or diagonally." (Move the book diagonally.) "Each time, the figure moves in a straight path."

Distribute a sheet of paper to each student and have each write the numeral "3" on the piece of paper. Then have the students turn the paper over and trace the 3 from the front onto the back of the paper. Have them turn the paper over again and place it on the desk so the numeral "3" is shown correctly. Call out movements ("Flip your paper. Now turn your paper," etc.) and have the students demonstrate the movement. It will be easy to observe the students, since all of the papers should have the same orientation.

Review the concepts of vertical flip, horizontal flip, and ¼ turn. Continue to call out directions as you circulate around the room observing the students. ("Flip the figure horizontally. Turn the figure one-fourth of the way around. Flip the figure vertically," etc.) Since all of the students began in the same position and are making the same moves, it will again be easy to spot a student who has made an incorrect move.

Distribute the Turn, Flip, or Slide activity sheet. The students can use their paper as an aid if they wish as they identify how figures have moved and then interpret the moves and draw the resulting figures.

Flip
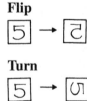

Turn

Slide

Answer Key: 1. horizontal turn; 2. slide; 3. vertical flip; 4. horizontal flip or a turn; 5. turn or a vertical flip; 6. slide; 7. Ɛ; 8. Ƙ; 9. ꓷ; 10. X, X, X, X

Related Activity: Pair the students and provide each with paper, pencils, and stencils of letters. Each student will choose a letter and will trace the letter on the paper. Then, without their partners seeing, the students will make five turns, flips, or slides, tracing each move and numbering the moves as 1, 2, 3, 4, and 5. The partners will exchange papers, then interpret and label each other's moves (1 slide, 2 flip, etc.). If the move can be accomplished two ways, the students will label both moves.

■ 1-2. DRAW THE WAYS (Learning Level)

Objective: To draw the resulting figure after specified moves

Materials: Trapezoid pattern block for each student (if not enough trapezoids are available, use a variety of pattern blocks)
Scissors, paper, and pencil
Draw the Ways activity sheet

Directions: Place a trapezoid on the overhead and use it to review the concepts of flip, turn, and slide, especially horizontal and vertical flips. Distribute the trapezoids. Review and model ¼ turns ⌒↘ and ½ turns ⤵ as the students follow along. Emphasize that turns could go in either of two directions, but for now all turns will be made in a clockwise manner, or to the right from the original position (⟳). Have the students place their trapezoids on their paper with the longest edge of the trapezoid at the bottom, and trace around it. "Flip the block horizontally." The students will complete the move with their trapezoids and draw the new position by tracing around the block. Each student can check with a neighboring classmate to determine if he or she moved the block correctly.

Instruct the students to place the trapezoid below the drawings with the longest edge still on the bottom, and trace it again. "Move the block one-fourth turn." The students will move their block, trace it, and then check with a neighbor for agreement. Continue the procedure with "Flip the block vertically" and "Move the block one-half turn." Finally, give a two-step direction, "Flip the block horizontally, then flip it vertically. Draw its new position."

Distribute the Draw the Ways activity sheet and scissors. The students will follow the directions and draw what the figure looks like in its new position.

Answer Key: 1. ▷ 2. ◁ 3. ◁ 4. ◁ 5. ◁ 6. ▷

Related Activity: Pair the students. Provide a cutout of the letter L (approximately 3 inches) for each student and a die for each pair. The partners will sit back-to-back and place their L in front and to the left of where they are sitting. The students in each pair will take turns rolling the die and following these moves, without looking at what their partners are doing. Each number on the die determines how both students should move their Ls, but only one student at a time will be rolling the die and calling out the number.

1 = ¼ turn	4 = flip vertically
2 = ½ turn	5 = slide horizontally
3 = flip horizontally	6 = the student calls a move

After each student in the pair rolls the die three times and the moves are made, the students will pick up their Ls and sit *next* to their partners (not opposite). One partner's L should be in the same position as the other partner's. If not, one or both of the pair made an incorrect move. They can go back and recreate their moves, checking each other. Then the students can change partners with another pair and perform the activity again.

■ **1-3. TURNING AND TURNING (Learning Level)**

Objective: To draw a symmetrical pattern using turns

Materials: Triangle pattern block and square pattern block
Overhead transparency of a Symmetrical Pattern and an Asymmetrical Pattern
    (see appendix)
2 blank transparencies
Paper and pencil
Turning and Turning activity sheet

Directions: Write "symmetry" on the board and ask the students to define the word. (*A figure or design that has balance. When the figure is balanced, it appears to be orderly and pleasant.*) The students may respond with the idea of one half of an object looking like the other half, which is bilateral symmetry. That type of symmetry will be covered later. Write "rotational symmetry." "Rotational symmetry is the result of turning, or rotating a motif (a design) around a point. The result is a pattern, and that pattern can be balanced, or symmetrical." Display the Symmetrical Pattern transparency. "Here we see balance. A motif (point to the top ellipse of the pattern) was turned around the circle and drawn again. Each turn was equal. This gives it the balanced and pleasant look. It is symmetrical." Display the Asymmetrical Pattern. "This pattern is not balanced. The motif was not turned equally. It is not symmetrical."

   Place a blank transparency onto the overhead. Position the triangle pattern block at the top of the transparency with the square below it and touching it, making a "house" motif: ⌂ Trace around the motif and draw a point approximately ½ inch below the square. Turn the motif approximately ⅛ turn (clockwise) around the point and trace it. Then turn it so it shows about a ⅔ turn and trace the motif again. "Is this a balanced pattern?" (*no*) "Is it symmetrical?" (*no*)

   Place another transparency on the overhead. Position the motif the same as before and trace it. This time move it ¼ turn and trace it. Move it another ¼ turn and trace it, followed by a last ¼ turn and trace. "I moved the motif one-fourth turn, then another one-fourth turn, then another one-fourth turn. I moved it the same each time. This pattern has balance, or symmetry. It is symmetrical." Place both patterns on the overhead at the same time to use as an example of symmetrical and nonsymmetrical patterns.

   Instruct the students to write a manuscript capital C on their paper and draw a point under it. Have them picture what the C would look like after a ¼ turn around a point and draw it. (⌒)

   Use other letters (not the letters B, F, A, or X, which are on the activity sheet) to practice the orientation of ¼ and ½ turns around a point. Distribute the Turning and Turning activity sheet. The students will create patterns using turns and explain the orientation of the motif.

Answer Key: 1. ᗺ; 2. ⊣ꟻ ᖴ⊢; 3. ⊲ᐯᴀᐳ ; 4. X; 5. straight up, on its right side, upside down, on its left side; 6. looks like an X in every position, an X looks like an X when it is moved ½ turn; 7. a design or figure

Related Activity: Pair the students and provide each student with a geoboard and geobands. Without the partner seeing, one of the pair will create an irregular figure on the geoboard with a geoband. The creator will then turn the geoboard either a ¼, ½, or ¾ turn, show the figure to the partner, and state, "I moved the figure ___ turn." The partner will then attempt to interpret the move, use his or her mind to picture the figure in its original position, and show the original figure on the geoboard. The partners will then switch roles.

   If this proves too difficult for some students, they can copy the figure on their geoboards after they have been turned, and then turn their boards back to the original position. This still allows them to see the result of turning a figure.

■ **1-4. TURN AROUND (Challenging Level)**

Objective: To draw or create a symmetrical design using turns

Materials: 16 red, 8 blue, and 4 yellow (or any three colors) 1-inch-square overhead counters
Overhead transparency of Four Regions (see appendix)
4 square, 4 blue rhombus, and 4 white rhombus pattern blocks, or cutouts of
   square and blue and white rhombus pattern blocks for each student
Turn Around activity sheet

Directions: This activity can be completed in two different ways depending on the abilities of the students. The students can follow the directions on the activity sheet and glue pattern block cutouts to show the turns, or they can use pattern blocks to reproduce the pattern, turn the pattern, and then trace its new position. When finished, the students can then color the design the corresponding colors. The second method would probably be more difficult for most of the students.

   If necessary, quickly review the concepts of turn, flip, and slide. Display the Four Regions overhead. Add the counters as shown.

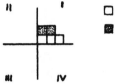

Point out the four regions, the horizontal and vertical lines, and the pattern. Ask the students to try to picture moving the pattern ¼ turn from region I to region IV. Ask several students to describe what that might look like. Place three red counters and two blue counters on top of the red and blue counters in region I. Move the counters one by one, moving the pattern ¼ turn into region IV, leaving the original counters in region I.

Have the students describe why this correctly shows a ¼ turn. Ask the students to describe what the pattern in region IV would look like if it was moved ¼ turn into region III. Place counters in region III to show the turn as individual students describe the move.

The final step is to describe a ¼ turn from region III to region II.

Have the students describe the completed design and the procedure used to develop the design.

Remove the counters and create a new pattern in region I by adding a yellow counter to the design. The task is still to move the pattern ¼ turn through the regions. Ask individuals to come to the overhead and make the different turns as they describe the process.

Decide if it will be better for the students to use cutouts or the actual pattern blocks. Distribute the Turn Around activity sheet and the materials. The cutouts are provided on the activity sheet. The students will turn a pattern to create a design. Save the completed Turn Around activity sheets for use in Section 1-5, "Flip Me Over."

Answer Key:

Related Activity: Provide additional copies of Four Regions (see appendix). The students will choose pattern blocks or other materials in the room (base-10 blocks, Cuisenaire rods, etc.), create a pattern that encompasses most of region I, and then turn the pattern through regions IV, III, and II. The designs can be colored accordingly and displayed throughout the school.

■ **1-5. FLIP ME OVER (Challenging Level)**

Objective: To draw or create a symmetrical design using flips

Materials: 16 red, 8 blue, and 4 yellow (or any three colors) 1-inch-square overhead counters
Overhead transparency of Four Regions (see appendix)
4 square, 4 blue rhombus, and 4 white rhombus pattern blocks, or cutouts of
   square, blue rhombus, and white rhombus pattern blocks for each student
Flip Me Over activity sheet

Directions: This activity, like the previous Turn Around activity, can be completed in two different ways depending on the abilities of the students. The students can follow the directions on the activity sheet and glue pattern block cutouts to show the flips, or they can use pattern blocks to reproduce the pattern, flip the pattern, and then trace its new position. When finished, the students can then color the design the corresponding colors. The second method would probably be more difficult for most of the students.

If necessary, quickly review the concepts of turn, flip, and slide. Display the Four Regions overhead. Add the counters as shown.

Point out the four regions, the horizontal and vertical lines, and the pattern. Ask the students to try to picture flipping the pattern vertically from region I to region IV. Ask several students to describe what that might look like. Place three red counters and two blue counters on top of the red and blue counters in region I. Move the counters one by one, flipping vertically into region IV, leaving the original counters in region I.

Have the students describe why this correctly shows a flip. Ask the students to describe what the pattern in region IV would look like if it was flipped horizontally into region III. Place counters in region III to show the turn and ask the students to describe the move.

The final step is to describe a horizontal flip from region III to region II.

Have the students describe the completed design and the procedure used to develop the design.

Remove the counters and create a new pattern in region I by adding a yellow counter to the design. The task is still to move the pattern by flipping through regions IV, III, and II. Ask individuals to come to the overhead and make the different flips as they describe the process.

Decide if it will be better for the students to use cutouts or the actual pattern blocks. Distribute the Flip Me Over activity sheet and the materials. The students will flip a pattern to create a design. Make the students' Turn Around activity sheets available. They will be asked to compare the design resulting from turning the motif to the design resulting from flipping the motif.

Answer Key: ✳   The resulting designs are the same.

Related Activity: Provide additional copies of Four Regions (see appendix). The students will choose pattern blocks or other materials in the room (base-10 blocks, Cuisenaire rods, etc.), create a pattern that encompasses most of region I, and then flip the pattern through regions IV, III, and II. The designs can be colored accordingly and displayed throughout the school.

■ **1-6. FLIP ME TO READ ME (Challenging Level)**

Objective: To interpret words that have been flipped vertically

Materials: Blank transparencies and overhead pens
1 copy of Flipped Words (see appendix) for each student
1 mirror for each student
Flip Me to Read Me activity sheet

Directions: Write the word "Hello" on a transparency, flip it horizontally, and place it on the overhead. Turn on the overhead and see if the students can identify the word. Then ask how the word was moved from the normal way that we write. (*flipped horizontally*) Show "Hello" as it is normally written and demonstrate the horizontal flip for all to see. Turn the overhead off, put "Hello" in its normal position and move it ¼ turn. Ask the students to identify the move. (*¼ turn*) Continue the process using a ½ turn and flipping vertically.

Write "number" on another transparency, flip it vertically, and place it on the overhead. Ask the students to identify the word and how it was moved. (*vertical flip*) Ask how the students were able to identify the word, and take several explanations. Distribute a copy of Flipped Words to each student along with a mirror. Have the students determine how to use the mirrors to identify the words and then write the words correctly. (*rectangle, covering, rhombus, vertically*) Some may flip the paper and hold it up to the light. This will work, but also encourage them to use the mirrors.

Distribute the Flip Me to Read Me activity sheet. The students will use the mirrors to read the questions and then answer the questions. The answer to question 1 should be written flipped vertically.

Answer Key: 1. their name flipped vertically; 2. answers will vary; 3. to rotate a figure; 4. to turn a figure over; 5. to move a figure in one direction

Related Activity: Pair the students and have them sit next to each other. Provide each student in the pair with approximately eight assorted one-inch cubes, the same variety of colors for each student in the pair. One student will use the cubes to create a motif. The other student will mentally flip the motif vertically and then show the flip using her or his cubes. Once the two students agree that the flip is accurately shown, they can switch roles and do the activity again.

■ 1-7. MIRROR LINES (Learning Level)

Objective: To determine the number of mirror lines for different figures

Materials: 1 copy of Mirror Lines and Figures (see appendix) for each student
Mirrors and scissors for each student
Mirror Lines activity sheet

Directions: Write "bilateral symmetry" on the board and ask students to define the term. "Bilateral symmetry is also called mirror symmetry. Bilateral symmetry occurs when a design or figure has two or more regions that are equal, but flipped. We call it mirror symmetry because it is like looking at one of the regions with a mirror."

Distribute a copy of Mirror Lines and Figures to each student along with a mirror. "Some figures have bilateral symmetry. Look at figure 1. This figure has bilateral symmetry. We can tell by using our mirrors. Place your mirror along the vertical line. You should be able to see one-half of the original figure plus a mirror image of the other half. Do the halves of the figure and the mirror image look the same?" (*yes*) "Together do they look like the original figure?" (*yes*) "The vertical line is called a mirror line. It divides the figure into two equal or identical regions. Use a pencil and the edge of the mirror to finish drawing the mirror line on the figure."

Continue, "Now look at figure 2. Place your mirror along the horizontal line." The halves of the figure and the mirror image should be identical. Instruct the students to complete the mirror line by using the bottom edge of the mirror as a straightedge. "You have drawn one mirror line for figure 2. Some figures have more than one mirror line. See if you can find another mirror line." There is also a vertical mirror line. Have the students make sure that the region of the figure and the mirror image are identical and then draw the vertical mirror line. Then have the students explore figure 3 and draw the two mirror lines. (*horizontal and vertical*)

Distribute the scissors and instruct the students to cut out figure 3. "Another way to determine mirror lines is to fold the figure into equal regions." Demonstrate folding on the mirror line and unfolding the figure to reveal two equal and identical regions. The students will fold their figure on both mirror lines, one at a time, to show the equal regions. Have the students cut out figures 4 and 5, and find their mirror lines by folding. Remind them that the regions must be identical on both sides of the mirror line. Give them a little time to explore and fold the figure. Then stop them and stress that not every figure will have a mirror line. Some figures do not have bilateral symmetry, such as the parallelogram they had been exploring.

Distribute the Mirror Lines activity sheet. The students will determine the number of different mirror lines for the various figures.

Answer Key: 1. 2; 2. 4; 3. 3; 4. 5; 5. 6; 6. 8, it has eight sides 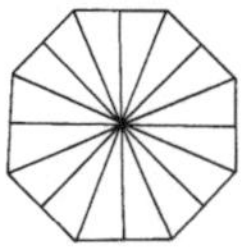

Related Activity: Display an overhead transparency of What Comes Next? (see appendix). Place the students in small groups and provide a copy of What Comes Next? to each student. Each group will study the pattern and draw the next figure. When the group correctly identifies the next figure, have them draw the next five figures to correctly complete the pattern. (The next figure in the pattern is ᖶ4.) There is a vertical mirror line in each figure. On the right side are the numerals 1, 2, 3, and 4. The left side is flipped horizontally. The next five figures are ƨ5, ∂6, ⅂7, 88, and ϱ9.

■ 1-8. MIRROR MIRROR (Challenging Level)

Objectives: To interpret words that have been flipped vertically
To create a symmetrical design

Materials: Blank transparencies and overhead pens
Overhead pattern blocks
1 mirror for each student
Mirror Mirror activity sheet
Crayons

Directions: "Bilateral symmetry is also known as mirror symmetry. The mirror line divides the design into two regions. You see both regions, but one is flipped. People show bilateral symmetry very nicely. Look at my face." Use your finger to draw an imaginary line vertically down your face. "My finger is showing where a mirror line would be. The mirror line would divide my face into two regions. They are the same but one side is flipped. One eyebrow is not identical to the other. One is flipped." Emphasize the difference by tracing your eyebrows with your finger or using two fingers to show how they are opposite. "One side of my mouth is like the other side except that it is flipped. In fact, we could draw a mirror line down the center of the torso. One side would be the same as the other, only flipped." Use hand gestures to emphasize the mirror line and the opposite sides of the torso, arms, hands, etc.

"The flip can be horizontal or vertical. With either kind, if the design is symmetrical, there would be at least one mirror line." Place a transparency on the overhead and four square pattern blocks in the middle.  Have the students identify the mirror lines. For now, work with only the vertical mirror line. Place a different pattern block on one side of the squares so that it touches the squares, for instance, . Ask a student to add a pattern block to the other side to keep the design symmetrical across the vertical mirror line.  Add another block and ask a student to add a block to keep the design symmetrical. Repeat the process several times until you feel sure that the students understand the concept.

Distribute the Mirror Mirror activity sheet and mirrors to the students. The students will use the mirrors to read the directions and add regions to the design so that it remains symmetrical.

Answer Key: Answers will vary.

Related Activity: Provide each student with an 8½-inch by 11-inch piece of white paper. Have the students fold the paper into four regions. ⊞ In the upper left region have the students use black chalk or charcoal to draw several lines that go from edges to folds and overlap some. Make sure they use pressure to produce a dark line. Fold the paper vertically and rub the paper to transfer the lines to the next region. Open the paper to observe the bilateral symmetry. Trace the lines in the mirror region with black chalk or charcoal and then fold the paper horizontally. Rub the paper again to transfer the lines. Open the paper to observe the symmetry. A motif was produced in the upper left region. It was flipped horizontally across the vertical mirror line. The new motif was then flipped vertically across the horizontal mirror line. Instruct the students to color the first region and then color the other regions to show the flips. The finished product will be an example of bilateral symmetry.

■ **1-9. PENTOMINO SEARCH (Challenging Level)**

Objectives: To show the 12 different pentomino nets
To identify the 6 pentomino nets that have bilateral symmetry

Materials: 60 1-inch-square cutouts or 60 1-inch counters for each pair of students
20 1-inch-square overhead counters
Pentomino Search activity sheet

Directions: Write "pentomino" on the board and ask the students to define the term. (*five squares joined at their edges to create a figure* ⊞ *or* ⊞) If students are not familiar with the term, give clues such as "It has the same prefix as pentagon." Place five counters on the overhead and explain the rules about determining pentomino nets. The five squares must be joined together. The full edges must join one another. This is allowable ⊞, this is not ⊞, and this is not ⊞. Once a net has been created, a flip, a turn, or a slide of that net is not a different net. It is the same net with a flip, a turn, or a slide.

Arrange the five counters into a net such as ⊞. Arrange five more counters into the same net and turn the net. "Is this a different net?" (*no*) "Why not?" (*It is the same net, only turned.*) Rearrange the counters to look like the original net, and this time flip the net. "Is this a different net?" (*no*) "Why not?" (*It is the same net, only flipped.*) Repeat the process using a slide. It is not a different net. Keep the ⊞ and place five additional counters on the overhead. Arrange the squares into the net ⊞. Turn the net, flip the net, and slide the net, each time determining that it is not a different net. It is still the same net in spite of the movement.

Leave the two nets on the overhead and add five more squares. Invite a student to come to the overhead and attempt to create a third net. Then invite a different student to create a fourth net. As each net is created, review the rules for forming a pentomino net to make sure it is in compliance. Pair the students. Distribute the Pentomino Search activity sheet to each student and 60 square cutouts to each pair. The students will form the squares into 12 different pentomino nets, each containing 5 squares. Each net must follow the rules concerning the edges of the squares and may not be a turn, a flip, or a slide of any previously formed net. As the students discover each new net, they will draw and shade it on their activity sheet. After they have found all 12 pentomino nets, they will identify the six nets that have bilateral symmetry and draw the mirror lines on those nets.

Answer Key:

© 2004 by John Wiley & Sons, Inc.

Related Activity: Pair the students. Provide each pair with a set of pentomino pieces, some yarn or string, and scissors. The pairs of students will choose two or more pentomino pieces and join them so that the resulting figure has at least one line of symmetry. The rules for joining the pieces are the same as for making pentominoes: the edges must join fully and the pieces may not be joined at the vertices. The students will then cut a piece of yarn and place the yarn on the figure to show the mirror line. They will then join other pentomino pieces so the resulting figures have at least one mirror line, and show the mirror line using a piece of yarn. After some time, the students can tour the room to see what figures other pairs have created.

Here are some solutions:

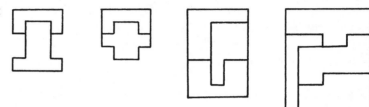

■ 1-10. HOW MANY TIMES? (Learning Level)

Objective: To identify and draw the number of times a figure can be turned and still look like its original position

Materials: Blank transparency
Overhead pattern blocks
1 triangle, square, trapezoid, and hexagon pattern block for each student,
    or pattern block cutouts
How Many Times? activity sheet

Directions: Place a blue rhombus pattern block on the overhead in the same position as shown in the following figure and have the students place a blue rhombus on their desks in the same position. "Sometimes figures can be moved, and you cannot tell if you did not see it move." Turn the overhead off and move the figure ½ turn but without the students seeing what you do. Then turn the overhead back on. "Was the figure moved or is it still in its original position?" To either answer: "How can you tell? You cannot really tell unless you saw what happened. Look at your blue rhombus and use your imagination to see the numbers 1 and 2."

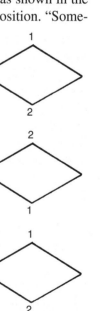

"Now slowly turn the rhombus and stop when it looks exactly like the way that it started. It looks the same, but something is different. What is different?" (*The numbers have changed places.*) "Correct, the rhombus still looks like it did in the original position but it was actually turned. Vertex 2 is where vertex 1 was, and vertex 1 is where vertex 2 was."

"Now turn the rhombus again and stop when it looks exactly like the original position. We are back to where we started. Vertex 1 is back in its original position and so is vertex 2."

Write, "A rhombus can be turned _____ times and still look like its original position" on the board. Ask a student to fill in the answer (*2*) and explain why it is correct.

Distribute the How Many Times? activity sheet. Instruct the students to place a green triangle pattern block on top of the triangle on the page. Place a blank transparency on the overhead and display a green triangle. Write the numbers "1," "2," and "3" on the transparency in the same order as they are on the activity sheet. "Slide your pattern block to the right so it is not on the drawn triangle. Use your imagination to follow the numbers. Turn your pattern block and stop when it looks like the drawn triangle, its original position. Trace the triangle and show the numbers of the turned triangle for each vertex." Slide the triangle to the right, turn it until it looks like the original, trace it, and show the numbers for each vertex. Now slide the triangle, turn it until it looks like its original position, trace it, and number the vertices. How many times did we turn the equilateral triangle and still have it look like its original position?" (*3*) Some students may answer *4* since they see that many triangles. Allow students to state why they believe their answer is correct. They may see 4 triangles but there were only 3 turns. Instruct the students to fill in the answer for number 1 (*3*) and then determine the number of turns for each of the other figures. They should draw and number the vertices for each turn.

Answer Key: 1. 3; 2. 4; 3. 1; 4. 6

Related Activity: Distribute the Find Those That Match sheet (see appendix). There are five pairs of identical figures, except that one has been turned. The students will determine and record the matching pairs of figures. (a matches e; b matches f; c matches j; d matches g; h matches i)

■ **1-11. ROTATE AND COLOR (Challenging Level)**

Objective: To color a turned figure and demonstrate rotational symmetry

Materials: Transparency of Rotational Symmetry (see appendix)
Overhead color pens
Crayons
Rotate and Color activity sheet

Directions: Write "Rotational Symmetry" on the board. "Rotational symmetry is also known as turning symmetry. A motif is turned around a point. If each turn is the same as all of the rest of the turns, there is balance, or symmetry. It is important to picture the motif turning and how each part of the motif would look when it is turned."

Display the Rotational Symmetry transparency. Color each circle in the motif (figure 1) according to the diagram (substitute colors as necessary). In figure 2 the motif has been moved ¼ turn. Have the students state the color of each circle in figure 2 so it would show what figure 1 would look like if it was moved ¼ turn. If the students experience difficulty, move the transparency ¼ turn to let them see what the result would look like. Then move the transparency to the original position. Color the circles in figure 2 as the students name the correct color.

Repeat the process as the students name the colors in figure 3 to show what figure 2 would look like moved ¼ turn.

Then move figure 3 ¼ turn to figure 4.

The result should be a balanced design. A motif was rotated around a point (show the point) ¼ turn each time. The result is a symmetrical design.

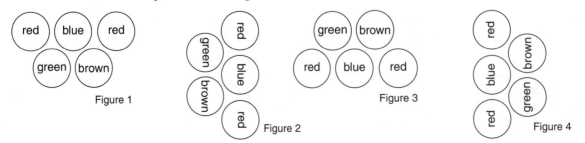

Figure 1   Figure 2   Figure 3   Figure 4

Distribute the crayons and the Rotate and Color activity sheet. The students will color the motif (figure 1) according to the directions and then color the other figures to show the motif moving through ¼ turns.

Answer Key:

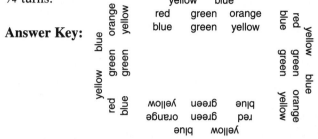

Related Activity: On a computer with a drawing program (AppleWorks or Microsoft Word are two that can be used), have the students create a motif. Highlight the motif, duplicate it, rotate the duplicate 60 degrees, and move it to show a turn around an imaginary point. Highlight that motif, duplicate it, rotate the duplicate 60 degrees, and move it to show a turn around an imaginary point. Continue the process until a symmetrical design is created from 60-degree turns. The students can also explore 90-degree and 120-degree turns to create a symmetrical design. The completed designs can be categorized by the number of turns and can then be displayed in the room.

■ **1-12. ALPHA TIME (Challenging Level)**

Objective: To demonstrate bilateral and rotational symmetry

Materials: Alpha Time activity sheet

Directions: Review the concepts of bilateral and rotational symmetry by having the students define each. (*bilateral, mirror, or flip symmetry; rotational, turning symmetry*) Ask several students to show examples of each type of symmetry either with materials or drawing on the board. Write the numerals "0, 1, 2, 3, 4, 5, 6, 7, 8, 9" on the board. Ask the students to identify the numerals that have one or more lines of bilateral symmetry and come to the board to draw the lines. (0, 3, 8) Ask which of the numerals has rotational symmetry and have the students demonstrate why they believe it is correct. (*0, 8*) Finally, have the students determine which numerals have both bilateral *and* rotational symmetry. (*0, 8*)

Write "808" on the board and draw a mirror line to the right of the number. "The motif is 808. What would this motif look like on the other side of the mirror line?" (*808*) Have a student write the number on the right side of the mirror line. (*808 | 808*) "The number eight hundred eight has bilateral symmetry. It looks exactly the same on both sides of the mirror line. Let's try three hundred three." 303 | ƐOƐ "Does three hundred three have bilateral symmetry?" (*no*) "What other numbers besides eight hundred eight show bilateral symmetry?" Allow the students to try different numbers either at their desks or at the board. The only numbers that will work are combinations of 8 and 0. (*8008, 80808*, etc.) If you show the numeral one as having a line of symmetry (|), then you can add it to the numerals that have bilateral symmetry, rotational symmetry, and both. You can also use it in numbers that have bilateral symmetry. (101, 181, 818, etc.)

Distribute the Alpha Time activity sheet. The students will identify rotational and bilateral symmetry.

Answer Key: 1. A, B, C, D, E, H, I, M, N, O, T, U, V, W, X, Y, Z; 2. H, I, O, X; 3. answers will vary

Related Activity: The students will, in their own words, answer the following questions and use illustrations to add to their descriptions:

■ What is symmetry?

■ How can you tell if a figure is symmetrical? (Describe two types of symmetry.)

■ **1-13. WILL IT? (Learning Level)**

Objective: To cover an area with a figure

Materials: Several regular octagon cutouts approximately 1 or 1½ inches in size
Overhead transparency of Will It? Frame (see appendix) and overhead pen
Figures for Will It? activity sheet (see appendix) copied onto card stock for each student
Will It? activity sheet

Directions: Place the Will It? Frame transparency onto the overhead. "I want to cover the area of this square and I want to do it using only one figure. I will place a figure in the middle and then add more of those figures until I cover the area. There can be no gaps and no overlapping pieces." Place an octagon cutout in the middle of the square. "I am going to place several more octagons in the square. Do you think I will be able to cover the area with no gaps and no overlaps?" Take several responses and ask the students to justify their answers, but do not acknowledge the correctness of the answer yet.

Place another octagon in the square so the two are touching along one side. "Would anyone like to change their answer or give an answer?" Allow students to give their opinions and justifications. Add another octagon so all three octagons are touching one another. "Are there any different opinions on whether I can cover this area?" Continue adding octagons so they cover the area with no gaps and no overlapping pieces. It is important to emphasize that the figures may extend past the edge of the square, and that is fine. The area of the square will be covered with no gaps and no overlaps.

Write "tessellate" on the board. "To tesselate means to cover an area completely." Write "tessellation" on the board. "The figure used to cover the area completely is a tessellation. Some figures tessellate and some do not. We can see that a regular (all sides and angles are equal) octagon will cover the area, or tessellate. We can also show that figures tessellate using a different method." Remove the octagons but keep the transparency on the overhead. Place one octagon in the middle of the square. Trace around the octagon, move the octagon to a position where it is touching the traced one along a side, and trace around the octagon. Move the octagon so that it is touching both traced octagons and trace it again. Continue moving and tracing until the area is covered. Again emphasize that any parts of figures that go beyond the area of the square are not drawn. Only draw the parts of the figure up to the edge of the overhead glass.

"Once again we see that a regular octagon will tessellate. An octagon is a tessellation. Now it is your turn to work with other figures to see if they will tessellate. Remember, the figure must cover the area with no gaps or overlaps." Distribute the Will It? activity sheet. The students may cut out the figures, or you may have the figures precut to save time and to keep the integrity of the figure. The students will determine which figures tessellate.

Answer Key: 1. yes; 2. yes; 3. no; 4. yes; 5. yes; 6. no, answers will vary

Related Activity: Provide each student with a 12-inch by 18-inch sheet of paper. Each student will choose a pentomino piece and predict if it will tessellate. The students will then verify their predictions by tracing the pentomino piece, moving it, tracing it, and moving it until the sheet of paper is covered or the piece will not tessellate.

■ 1-14. FLIP ROWS (Challenging Level)

Objective: To tessellate by flipping an irregular figure

Materials: 2-inch by 2-inch piece of index card
3-inch by 5-inch index cards
Scissors and tape
12-inch by 18-inch sheets of paper
Flip Rows activity sheet

Directions: "We have found that many figures will tessellate, or cover an area. Some have been regular figures like squares, equilateral triangles, and hexagons, and others have been irregular figures like the pentomino pieces. Now I want to test your prediction skills. I am going to create a figure and you will predict whether or not it will tessellate."

Take the 2-inch by 2-inch piece of index card. Start in the upper left corner and make a curved cut (1). Slide the piece directly to the bottom of the card and tape it into place (2). Go to the lower right corner, cut a triangle (3), slide it directly to the lower left corner, and tape it into place (4). Place the card on the overhead. "Will this figure tessellate?" Take several responses, asking students to justify their prediction. "Let me add one more idea and see if it will change your prediction. Will this figure tessellate if I sometimes flip the figure?" Flip the card horizontally on the overhead to emphasize the point. Again take several responses and the reasons for the predictions. "I am going to let you answer that question."

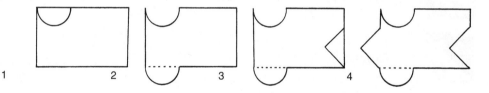

Distribute the 3-inch by 5-inch index cards, scissors, tape, paper, and the Flip Rows activity sheet. The students will make a figure and tessellate it over the 12-inch by 18-inch paper. After the students have traced a horizontal row across the paper, they will flip their figure horizontally and fit it into the row above what they have drawn. For each new row, the figure should be flipped horizontally. When the tessellation is completed, the students can give it a title and their artwork can be displayed throughout the school.

Answer Key: The figures will tessellate.

Related Activity: Obtain books or other resources about M. C. Escher (1898–1972). Introduce the students to Escher's works by looking for tessellations and exploring how Escher used them. The students can continue to make tessellations, exploring the use of turns and flips.

1-1. Turn, Flip, or Slide

Part One: For each figure below, decide if the second figure was moved by a turn, a flip, or a slide. Some could have been moved two ways. If so, identify all of the ways.

1. PF ꟻꟼ   Moved by a _____.

2. PF PF   Moved by a _____.

3. PF bꟼ   Moved by a _____.

4.  Moved by a _____ or a _____.

5.  Moved by a _____ or a _____.

6. 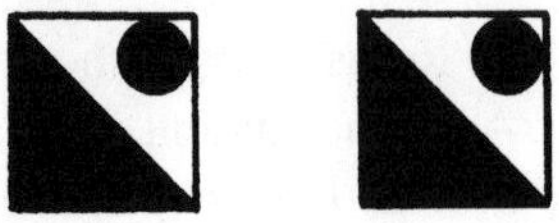 Moved by a _____.

Part Two: Draw each figure according to the directions. These figures may be helpful to you.

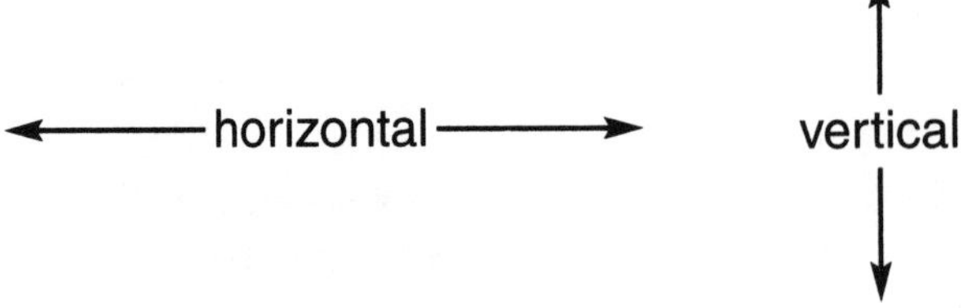

← ——— horizontal ——— →   ↕ vertical

The letter G flipped horizontally would look like this: ꟼ

The letter G flipped vertically would look like this: ꓷ

1-1. Turn, Flip, or Slide (continued)

7. B   Draw what this figure would look like if flipped horizontally: _____

8. R   Draw what this figure would look like if flipped vertically: _____

9. D   Draw what this figure would look like if turned halfway around: _____

10. X   Draw what this figure would look like if flipped horizontally: _____

Draw what this figure would look like if flipped vertically: _____

Draw what this figure would look like if turned halfway around: _____

Draw what this figure would look like if moved by a slide: _____

1-2. Draw the Ways

Trace the triangle below onto another piece of paper and cut it out. Place the cutout on top of this triangle. Are the two figures congruent? _____ If they are not, retrace and cut out the figure again.

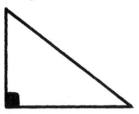

Use your cutout to follow the moves described below and draw the new position of the figure next to the original.

1. Move the figure ¼ turn and draw its new position.

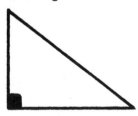

2. Flip the figure horizontally and draw its new position.

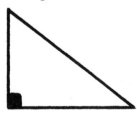

3. Move the figure ½ turn and draw its new position.

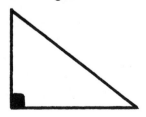

1-2. Draw the Ways *(continued)*

4. Flip the figure vertically, then flip it vertically again. Draw its new position.

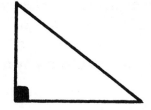

5. Flip the figure horizontally, then make a ¼ turn. Draw its new position.

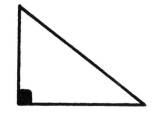

6. Slide the figure, flip it horizontally, flip it vertically, then flip it horizontally. Draw its new position.

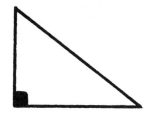

1-3. Turning and Turning

Rotational symmetry is the result of turning or rotating a motif (a design) around a point. The motif can be turned as much or as little as we want. If each of the turns is equal, then the pattern looks balanced, or symmetrical. Look at the figure below. The motif has been turned, or rotated, ¼ of the way around and then drawn, then rotated ¼ of the way and drawn, and finally repeated one more time.

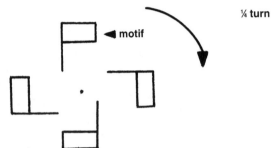

The resulting pattern is symmetrical due to turning. For each motif below, follow the directions and draw the motif in each of the positions.

1. Turn the motif halfway around and draw it as it would look in the new position.

B
•

2. Turn the motif ¼ way around (¼ turn) as many times as you can, drawing what the motif would look like each time.

F
•

1-3. Turning and Turning (continued)

3. Rotate the motif ¼ turn as many times as you can, drawing the motif each time.

A
·

4. Rotate the motif ½ turn as many times as you can, drawing the motif each time.

X
·

5. Describe the motif in each of its positions in question 3.

_____

_____

_____

6. Describe the motif in each of its positions in question 4.

_____

_____

Why did that happen? _____

_____

7. Define motif. _____

_____

1-4. Turn Around

Turn the pattern according to the directions to complete the design. Glue the cutouts on the vertical and horizontal lines so the pieces in one region touch the pieces in the next region.

- Start by gluing the cutouts onto the pattern in region I.

- Make a ¼ turn of the pattern into region IV and glue those cutouts.

- Make a ¼ turn of the pattern in region IV into region III and glue those cutouts.

- Make a ¼ turn of the pattern in region III into region II and glue those cutouts.

You have now completed a pattern block design by using turns.

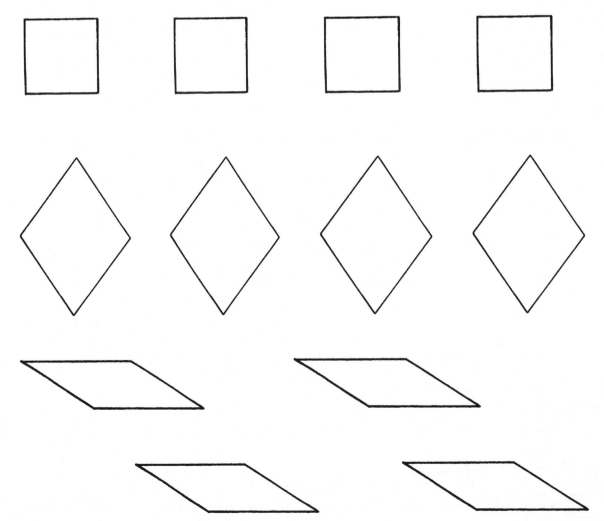

1-4. Turn Around *(continued)*

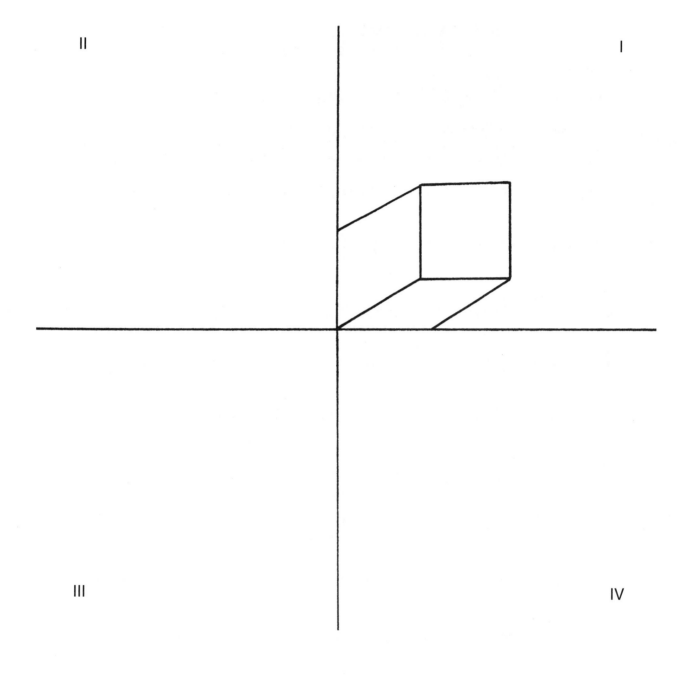

1-5. Flip Me Over

Flip the pattern according to the directions to complete the design. Glue the cutouts on the vertical and horizontal lines so the pieces in one region touch the pieces in the next region.

- Start by gluing the cutouts onto the pattern in region I.

- Flip the pattern vertically into region IV and glue those cutouts.

- Flip the pattern in region IV horizontally into region III and glue those cutouts.

- Flip the pattern in region III vertically into region II and glue those cutouts.

You have now completed a pattern block design by using flips.

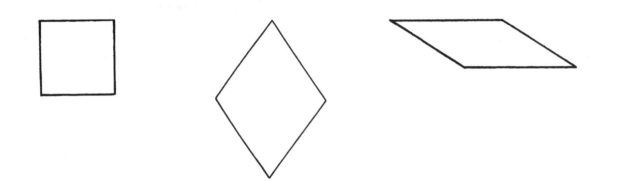

Name _____   Date _____

1-5. Flip Me Over (continued)

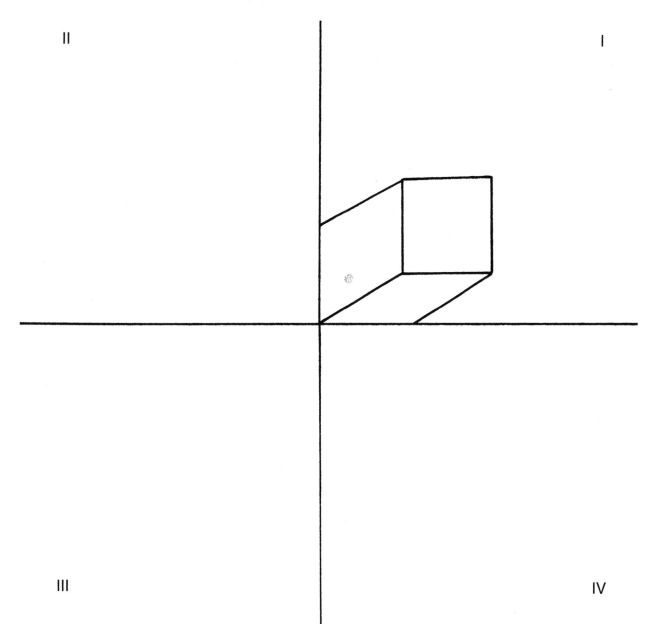

The motif was turned in the Turn Around activity and the motif was flipped in the Flip Me Over activity. Compare the design resulting from turning the motif to the design resulting from flipping the motif.

_____

_____

_____

1-6. Flip Me to Read Me

The words below have been flipped vertically. Use a mirror to read each question. Write your answer for number 1 flipped vertically. Write normally for the rest of the questions.

1. What is your name? _____

2. What is your favorite school subject? _____
   _____

3. There are three ways that a figure can be moved. In your own words, describe moving a figure using a turn.
   _____
   _____

4. In your own words, describe moving a figure using a flip. _____
   _____

5. In your own words, describe moving a figure using a slide. _____
   _____
   _____

1-7. Mirror Lines

Mirror (bilateral) symmetry is often shown by a line of symmetry within a figure. A line of symmetry divides a figure into two equal parts that are mirror images of each other. For each figure below, determine the number of different lines of symmetry each has. Then draw all of the lines of symmetry and complete the statement for each figure. You may draw each figure on another piece of paper, cut the figure out, and fold it in different ways to determine all of the lines of symmetry.

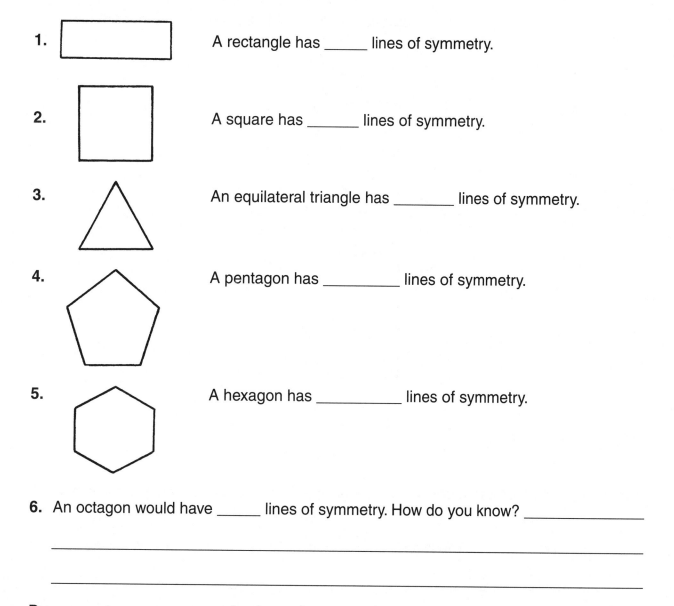

1. A rectangle has _____ lines of symmetry.

2. A square has _____ lines of symmetry.

3. An equilateral triangle has _____ lines of symmetry.

4. A pentagon has _____ lines of symmetry.

5. A hexagon has _____ lines of symmetry.

6. An octagon would have _____ lines of symmetry. How do you know? _____

_____

_____

Draw an octagon on a separate piece of paper and show all of its lines of symmetry.

1-8. Mirror, Mirror

Color this pattern by following the directions.
You may use a mirror to read the directions.

1. Color the regions marked with the number 1 red.

2. Color the regions marked with the number 2 green.

3. Color the regions marked with the number 3 orange.

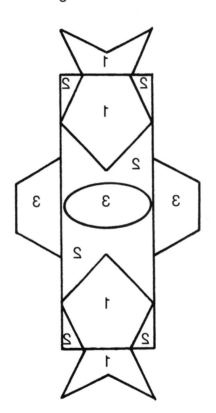

4. Add several figures to one side of the design. Then use the mirror to draw the figures on the other side so the design is still symmetrical.

5. Do you like writing backwards? Write your answer backwards. _____ Why?

_____

_____

Name _____   Date _____

1-9. Pentomino Search

Pentomino nets are made from 5 equal squares that are joined along their edges. The edges must join for the entire length and the pentomino nets cannot be joined at vertices. It is possible to make 12 different nets of 5 equal squares, but flips and turns of the nets are not allowed. A flipped or turned net is still the same net.

   Use your square cutouts to find the 12 different nets and shade each net on the grid. Remember, when joining the edges, this is okay: ⊞ . But this is not allowed: ⊡ . One net has been filled in for you.

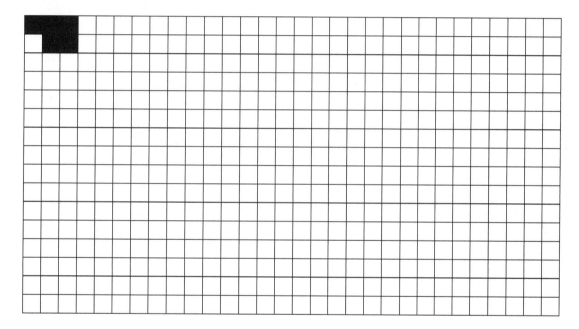

Six of the nets have bilateral symmetry. Draw them below and show the line of symmetry for each.

1-10. How Many Times?

Antonio and Christi were exploring pattern blocks. They found out that some of the blocks can be turned a number of times and still look the same. This is one type of rotational symmetry. Use pattern blocks or cutouts to trace and show how many times each figure can be turned and still look like the same position. Use the numbers to show each time the figure is turned.

1. An equilateral triangle can be turned ___ times and still look like its original position.

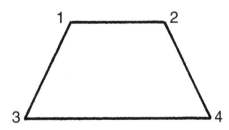

2. A square can be turned ___ times and still look like its original position.

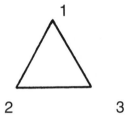

3. A trapezoid can be turned ___ times and still look like its original position.

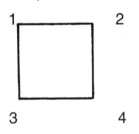

4. A hexagon can be turned _____ times and still look like its original position.

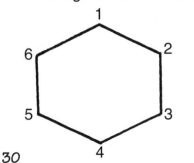

Name _____   Date _____

1-11. Rotate and Color

Color figure 1 according to the directions. The pattern has been moved using a ¼ turn to the right. Color figure 2 to show what the original figure 1 would look like if it had been moved ¼ turn. Then color figure 3 to show what figure 2 would look like if it had been moved ¼ turn. This would be the same as moving figure 1 ½ turn.

Finally, color figure 4 to show what figure 3 would look like after a ¼ turn. Be sure to picture the turned figures correctly before coloring.

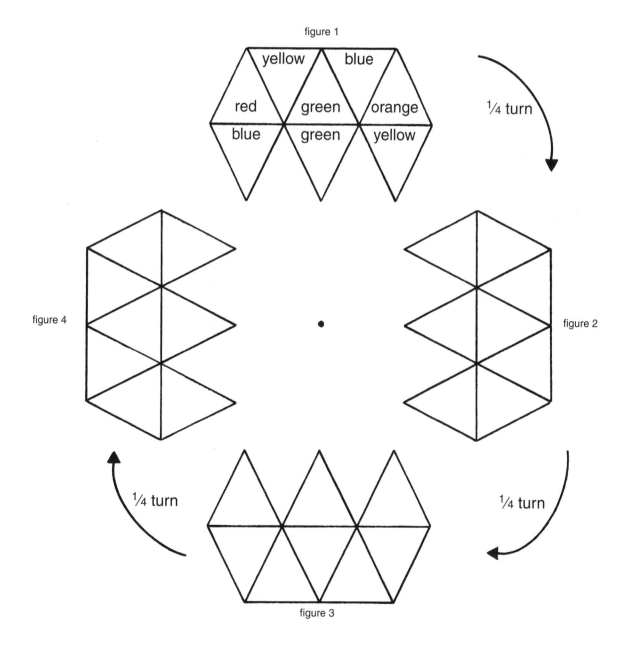

Name _____   Date _____

1-12. Alpha Time

A B C D E F G H I J K L M N
O P Q R S T U V W X Y Z

1. There are 17 letters that have one or more lines of symmetry. Write those letters below and draw the line, or lines, of symmetry for each.

_____   _____   _____

_____   _____   _____

_____   _____   _____

_____   _____   _____

_____   _____   _____

_____   _____   _____

_____   _____   _____

_____   _____   _____

2. There are 4 letters that have *both* rotational symmetry and one or more lines of symmetry. Which letters are they?

_____   _____   _____   _____

3. Some words have mirror or flip symmetry. One example is MOM. If you flip the word horizontally you get:

MOM | MOM

mirror

The word DAD does not work. When you flip the word horizontally you get:

mirror

Think of three words that have mirror or flip symmetry. Show the words and their mirror images.

_____|_____   _____|_____   _____|_____

    mirror   mirror   mirror

1-13. Will It?

To tessellate means to cover an area with no gaps or overlaps. You are going to determine if different figures tessellate. For each given figure, trace that figure in the space provided and then keep moving and tracing the figure, trying to cover the space. Then answer the question about each figure.

1. Will a square cover the area (tessellate)? _____

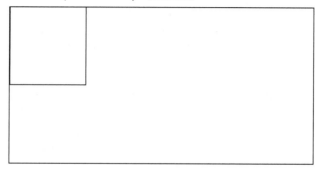

2. Will an equilateral triangle cover the area (tessellate)? _____

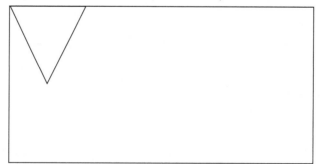

3. Will a pentagon tessellate? _____

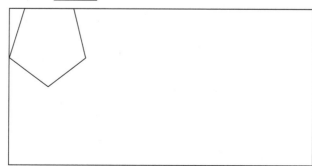

1-13. Will It? *(continued)*

4. Will a rhombus tessellate? _____

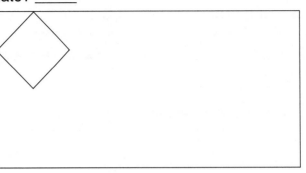

5. Will a hexagon tessellate? _____

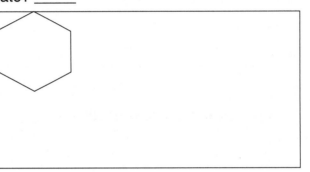

6. Did all of the figures tessellate? _____ Why do you think some figures will tessellate and some figures will not tessellate?

_____

_____

_____

Name _____ Date _____

1-14. Flip Rows

A tessellation is a motif that will cover an area with no gaps or overlaps. Many times, even an odd-shaped motif will tessellate. Take an index card, and start in any corner and make a cut.

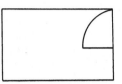

Slide the cut piece either from one side to the other, or from top to bottom, or from bottom to top. Be sure not to flip or turn the cut piece. Tape it into place.

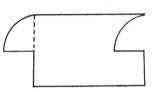

Move to another corner and make another cut. Once again, slide the piece across, up, or down, and tape it into place. If you desire, move to another corner and make a third cut. Move the cut piece across, up, or down, and tape it into place.

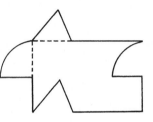

When you have finished, place the tessellation in the middle of a large piece of paper and trace around it. Then slide the tessellation to the right or left until it fits, and trace again. Keep sliding and tracing until you have completed one horizontal row across the paper.

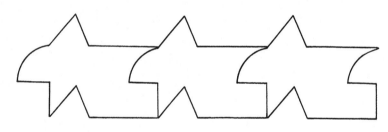

Then flip the tessellation horizontally and fit it in above the row. Keep moving and tracing until you have a second row that is opposite from your first row. Then flip the tessellation horizontally and add another row above the two rows. Once you have covered the top of the paper, work on the bottom of the paper. When finished, name your picture and share it with your classmates.

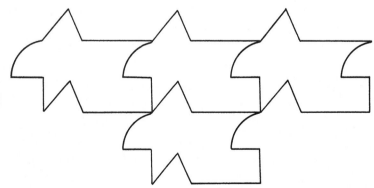

Section 2

GEOMETRY

Teacher Directions

■ **2-1. LINE UP (Learning Level)**

Objectives:　To match the definition to the correct term
　　　　　　　To identify lines, line segments, rays, points, intersecting lines, and parallel lines

Materials:　Line Up activity sheet

Directions:　This is an excellent reinforcement lesson for the vocabulary of geometry. The activity can be used several times either in copied form or as a discussion. The more the students use the correct vocabulary, the more precise their construction of the concepts will be.

"What do you think of when you hear the word *plane?*" Most probably the response will refer to airplanes. "What else?" (*flat land, a carpenter's tool, not fancy*) "What do you think of when you hear the word *point?*" (*the sharp tip of something, a piece of land, a position*) Take several responses. If the students' responses refer to a geometric plane or point, bring these back for discussion. A point is a specific location in space. The point itself is imaginary; it just indicates the location. Draw a small dot on the board. "This is the symbol for 'point,' but what I drew actually covers many points. It just indicates that we are referring to a specific point. What is a geometric plane?" (*three or more points that form a flat surface in all directions*) Use a tabletop and the cover of a book held at an angle as examples of planes. The tabletop and book cover only show the form of the plane. The plane extends beyond each item in all directions.

Draw ⟷ on the board. "What is this symbol? (*a line*) "What is the definition of a line?" (*points that make a straight path that goes on in two directions*) Point to the symbol. "What is the length of this line?" (*Cannot say. It goes on in both directions and does not stop.*) "That is correct, a line has no beginning and no end."

Draw •⟶ on the board. "What is this symbol?" (*a line segment*) "What is the definition of a line segment?" (*a specific part of a line*) Point to the symbol. "Can we determine the length of the line segment?" (*yes*) "How?" (*by measuring it*) "Yes, the line segment is a specific part of a line and it can be measured." Repeat this process for a ray, intersecting lines, and parallel lines. Locate parallel and intersecting lines in the room as examples.

Have a student come to the board and draw the symbol for a line segment. "How can we tell this line segment from other line segments?" (*Give it a name.*) "We can name the line segment by using two capital letters." Write "A" and "B" under the end points of the line segment. "This is line segment AB. We write it this way: $\overline{AB}$. When we see this (point to the symbol) we are referring to line segment AB." Repeat the process using a line and a ray. Then ask the students how to name a point. (*Use only one capital letter.*)

Review the definitions and symbols for point, line, line segment, ray, parallel lines, and intersecting lines. Have the students name objects in the room that represent the terms. Distribute the Line Up activity sheet and have the students complete the questions.

Answer Key:　1. D; 2. A; 3. F; 4. B; 5. G; 6. C; 7. E; 8. line; 9. line segment; 10. ray; 11. point; 12. intersecting lines; 13. parallel lines; 14. $\overline{ST}$; 15. $\overrightarrow{UV}$ or $\overrightarrow{VU}$; 16. $\overleftrightarrow{YZ}$

Related Activity:　Provide each student with a geoboard and a supply of geobands. Provide the following descriptions and allow the students to create the figures. The students will share their creations in small groups pointing out the required attributes. Then they will remove the geobands and create the next figure.

■ Create a five-sided figure with one pair of parallel sides.

■ Create a figure with one pair of parallel line segments and two line segments that intersect.

■ Create a seven-sided figure with two pairs of parallel line segments.

■ Create a six-sided figure with two parallel line segments and add a line segment that intersects the parallel line segments.

■ **2-2. ANGLES (Learning Level)**

Objective: To identify right, acute, and obtuse angles

Materials: Drinking straw for each student
Angles activity sheet

Directions: Write "angle" on the board and ask the students to define the word. (*An angle is made by two rays that have a common [same] point, the vertex.*) Take a straw and bend it in the middle to form an acute angle. Stress the idea that the size of the angle is determined by how far apart the rays are from each other, not how long the rays are. Slowly move the straw to form an obtuse angle and point out the size difference.

Give each student a straw and have them bend their straws in the middle. Form a right angle using the straw and write the term on the board. Have the students make right angles with their straws. "How many degrees are there in a right angle?" (*90 degrees*) Rotate your straw about ¼ of a turn. "What type of angle is this now?" (*still a right angle*) "How can it still be a right angle?" (*It was only rotated, not changed.*) "How large is it in degrees?" (*90 degrees*)

Pair the students, who will identify objects in the classroom that have right angles and will bend their straws against the objects to form right angles. Encourage the students to locate right angles in different positions to reinforce the concept that angles are the same even if turned.

Write "acute" and "obtuse" on the board and ask the students to define the terms. An acute angle is an angle that is less than a right angle, or less than 90 degrees, and an obtuse angle is an angle that is greater than a right angle, or greater than 90 degrees and less than 180 degrees. Have the students form acute angles with their straws and point out that even though they have made angles of various sizes, they are all acute angles since they are less than 90 degrees. Repeat the generalization, this time stressing that angles greater than 90 degrees but less than 180 degrees are obtuse angles. In pairs, the students can find acute and obtuse angles in the classroom and reproduce the angles. Distribute the Angles activity sheet, for which the students will identify right, acute, and obtuse angles.

Answer Key: 1. acute; 2. obtuse; 3. right; 4. obtuse; 5. acute; 6. right

Related Activity: Pair the students. One student will create a design using several geobands while keeping track of how many right angles, acute angles, and obtuse angles are created. When the design is completed, the other student will identify all of the right angles, the acute angles, and the obtuse angles. When the students agree on the number of each type of angle, they will switch roles and repeat the activity.

■ **2-3. MORE ANGLES (Learning Level)**

Objectives: To measure angles in degrees
To draw specific angles

Materials: Protractor and straight edge for each student
Overhead protractor or large protractor
Overhead transparency of Three Angles (see appendix)
Copy of Three Angles for each student
More Angles activity sheet

Directions: "We have used straws to find right, acute, and obtuse angles. Today we are going to explore measuring the specific sizes of angles with the protractor." Distribute the protractors to the students and place the protractor on the overhead. Point out the two sets of numbers on the protractor and ask if any students know why there are two sets of numbers. (*So you can measure the angle either way it opens.*) Display the Three Angles transparency and distribute a copy of Three Angles to each student. Point out that the angles are named using three capital letters. The first one is angle ABC. The middle letter is always the vertex. "Could we call this angle CBA?" (*yes*) "Why?" (*three letters with the vertex in the middle*) "How are angles ABC and CBA different?" (*They are not different. They are the same angle.*)

Have students name the second angle HIJ or JIH, and the third angle MNO or ONM. "How large is angle ABC? We need to measure to find out." Review how to position the protractor for measuring. Place the protractor on angle ABC and have the students do the same thing. Point out that since this is an acute angle, the measure must be less than 90 degrees. "Which scale should be used to measure the angle?" (*0 degrees through 90 degrees from the right side*) "Why?" (*It is an acute angle.*) "What is the measure of angle ABC?" (*30 degrees*)

Reposition the protractor onto angle HIJ and have the students move their protractors. Ask which scale should be read for this measure. (*The other scale. Even though either scale would be accurate, the angle opens from the left so we read from the left.*) The measure of angle HIJ is 90 degrees. Angle MNO is an obtuse angle that is measured from the left side. It measures 140 degrees. This time have the students watch as you measure the angle. However, measure the angle incorrectly and have the students identify the mistakes you make. Be sure to include the most common mistakes of reading the wrong scale and not lining up the protractor along one of the rays. After the students have identified your mistakes, challenge them to correctly read angle MNO.

You may wish to continue the rest of this lesson at another time. The students will need practice reading angles before they begin to draw specific angles. Pairs of students can find acute, right, and obtuse angles in the room and prove it by measuring the angles. Each student in the pair can measure the angle, and the students can verify each other.

Place a transparency on the overhead, draw a straight horizontal line, and label the left end "Y." Have the students copy this on a piece of paper. Present the problem of drawing a 60-degree angle. Allow them to give you directions and suggestions for drawing the angle. Each time they give a correct step, follow it and have them complete that step on their paper. (Place the protractor along the line with the center mark on Y. Find the correct scale. Mark the paper at 60 degrees. Remove the protractor. Draw a straight line from Y through the mark on the paper. Check the angle using the protractor. Label the rays "X" and "Z.")

Repeat the process with the students giving directions for drawing a 120-degree angle and following your demonstration. Then have them watch as you draw a 75-degree angle. Once again do it incorrectly and have the students identify your errors. Finally draw the angle correctly with the students following your steps.

Distribute the More Angles activity sheet. The students will measure angles and draw specific angles.

Answer Key: 2. $\angle STU = 60°$; 3. $\angle HIJ = 130°$; 4. $\angle ABC = 160°$; 5. $\angle EFG = 45°$; 6. $\angle LMN = 55°$

Related Activity: This activity could be used as a project to be completed at home with the findings presented in class. Each student will construct three different triangles of his or her choosing using a straightedge. The triangles should be drawn relatively large so their angles can be measured more easily. The students will measure all three angles of one of the triangles and calculate the total number of degrees in the triangle. Then they will do the same with the other two triangles. After calculating the number of degrees in each triangle, the students will answer the following questions. Allow class discussion and confirmation of the number of degrees the students found when measuring their triangles before answering question 1. The students will investigate questions 1 and 2 and present their findings in a written paragraph with drawings.

1. Do the three angles of a triangle always total 180 degrees? (*yes*) Why do you think so? (*same measure obtained by most if not all of the class*)

2. Lee felt that he could draw a triangle with two obtuse angles. Do you agree with Lee? (*no*) Why or why not? (*Two obtuse angles would each be more than 90 degrees and together would be more than 180 degrees without a third angle.*)

■ **2-4. THE ANGLE OF TIME (Challenging Level)**

Objective: To measure angles

Materials: Overhead transparency of Circles and Angles (see appendix)
Protractor for each student
Overhead transparency of a protractor
The Angle of Time activity sheet

Directions: Place the Circles and Angles transparency on the overhead. "This is a picture for a speed control device on a pretend spaceship. The handle for setting the speed is here at the top. If the handle is moved to the first position, the ship moves slowly. When it is moved to the second position, the ship moves faster. In the third position, it moves very fast, and when it comes all the way around . . ." Point to the word *Wow!* and let the students finish the sentence. "The space mechanics have been asked to make another speed control device and need exact plans to copy it. We can help by supplying the measurements for them. What we have to do is measure the angle from Start to each position so the mechanics know where to put the speeds on the next one."

Place the protractor on the transparency so the straightedge is along the vertical line in the center of the control and the center mark is on the vertices of the angles. "How many degrees would the handle move from Stop at the top to Slow?" (*60 degrees*) Have students explain how they chose the correct scale and read the protractor. "How many degrees would the handle move from Stop at the top to Faster?" (*180 degrees*) Again have students explain how they chose the correct scale and read the protractor. "Now we want to find the number of degrees from Stop at the top to Very Fast. How would we do that?" (*Rotate the protractor one-half turn, measure the angle, and add 180 degrees to it since the angle is larger than 180 degrees—225 degrees.*) Finally determine the angle from Stop at the top to Wow!" (*360 degrees*)

Distribute The Angle of Time activity sheets and protractors. Explain that the students will be asked to determine how many degrees the minute hand moves from 12 to each number on a clock, all the way back to 12.

Answer Key: 1. 60°; 2. 90°; 3. 120°; 4. 150°; 5. 180°; 6. 210°; the pattern increases by 30° each time; 7. 240°; 8. 270°; 9. 300°; 10. 330°; 11. 360°

Related Activity: The students will be given criteria for use in designing a new clock for a time system in another galaxy. The criteria are that the face must be round and there are now only nine hours on the clock. Present the problem and have a class discussion about solving the problem. Remind the students that there are 360 degrees in a circle and that the numbers from 1 to 9 should be equally spaced around the clock face. (There will be an angle of 40 degrees between each of the nine numbers.) Other than the two criteria, the students may design the remainder of the clock to their liking.

■   **2-5. TELL ALL ABOUT IT (Learning Level)**

Objective: To state the attributes of polygons

Materials: Tell All About It activity sheet

Directions: Write the word "attribute" on the board. "An attribute is a characteristic or feature that an object or a person has." Point to a table or chair in the room and describe its attributes. (*four legs, brown, made of wood, etc.*) Choose a student and describe attributes of him or her. (color of hair, color of eyes, number of arms, etc.) Draw an irregular pentagon on the board or overhead. "This is a polygon. What is the definition of a polygon? (*a simple closed curve made from three or more lines*) "What are some attributes of this polygon?" Write the responses on the board as they are given. (*five sides, five angles, closed figure, etc.*) "Of these attributes, which would you always find in a pentagon?" Mark these attributes as "always." (*five sides, five angles, closed figure*) "What attributes might you find in a pentagon?" Mark these as "might" and add any new attributes. (*size, shape*) "What attributes would you never find in a pentagon?" Mark these "never" and add any new attributes. (*more than five sides, less than five sides, more than five angles, less than five angles, an open figure*)

Have two or three students come up and draw other examples of pentagons. Then have two or three students come up and draw nonexamples of pentagons. They can refer to the "never" attributes to help generate nonexamples.

"Shapes, figures, objects, concepts, or people have attributes. When we determine the attributes they always have, might have, and never have, we know a lot more about them. Also, when we can see some examples and nonexamples of them, we know even more.

"We are now going to take a closer look at polygons." Distribute the Tell All About It activity sheet. Instruct the students to determine the attributes that the polygons always have, might have, and never have, and draw examples and nonexamples of each polygon.

Answer Key: 1. four sides, four angles, all sides equal, all angles equal; 2. large in size, small in size, rotated; 3. sides larger or smaller than other sides, angles larger or smaller than other angles, curved lines, open figure; □ ◇ ○ ⬡ 4. opposite sides parallel, opposite sides equal, four sides, four angles, closed figure; 5. size, might be thin, might be tilted; 6. opposite sides not equal, opposite sides not parallel, more or less than four sides, more or less than four angles; ▱ ▱ 7. six sides, six angles, closed figure; 8. size, shape; 9. more or less than six sides, more or less than six angles, open figure; ⬡ ➢

Related Activity: Provide each student with a set of tangram pieces. After some exploration of the materials, instruct the students to use only the square and the two small triangles to form a rectangle. Once they have done that, the same pieces should then be used to form a parallelogram, and then used to form a trapezoid. As a culminating activity, instruct the students to use all seven tangram pieces to form a square. If they happen to be familiar with making a square, then instruct them to form a rectangle from the seven pieces.

■   **2-6. SAME AND DIFFERENT WITH POLYGONS (Learning Level)**

Objective: To state how polygons are similar and different

Materials: Overhead transparency of Square and Rectangle (see appendix)
Polygons sheet (see appendix) for each student
Same and Different with Polygons activity sheet

Directions: Write the word "attribute" on the board and ask the students to define the word. (*An attribute is a characteristic or feature that an object or a person has.*) As a review, pick out some objects in the room and have the students describe the attributes. For the brave of heart, have the students describe attributes of you. Place the Square and Rectangle transparency on the overhead. Instruct the students to think about the attributes of each figure to themselves. "How are these two figures the same?" Have the student call out similarities and write the similarities on the board as they are given. (*four sides, four angles, right angles, closed figures, parallel sides, etc.*) "Now, how are these two figures different?" Write the differences on the board. (*sides on rectangle not all equal, rectangle is larger, position of rectangle is slanted*) Instruct the students to use the information and ideas that they just generated to make comparisons of other polygons. Distribute the Polygons sheet (for student reference) and the Same and Different with Polygons activity sheet to the students. Instruct the students to study the figures and state the similarities and differences on the activity sheet.

Answer Key: 1. number of sides, all right angles, closed figures, parallel sides; 2. sides on rectangle not all equal, size; 3. four sides, four angles, parallel sides, closed figures; 4. not all right angles in parallelogram, size; 5. closed figures, straight sides; 6. number of sides, number of angles, size; 7. closed figures, straight sides; 8. number of sides, number of angles, size

Related Activity: Supply scissors, construction paper, and glue. Each student will write a story that in some way includes the names of polygons. When they reach the name of a polygon in their story, they will not write the word but cut that figure out of paper and glue it in place of the word. Before they start writing, explore some ideas with the students and point out how some polygon words could be used as adjectives. For example: Hakeem walked around the ◯ walkway approaching the building that looked a lot like a ⬠ .

■ 2-7. CLASSIFYING POLYGONS (Learning Level)

Objectives: To classify polygons by their number of sides
To draw irregular polygons

Materials: Overhead transparency of Regular/Irregular (see appendix)
Classifying Polygons activity sheet

Directions: Write the words "regular" and "irregular" on the board. Ask the students to define the words in relation to polygons. If the definitions are not known, say, "When all of the sides of a polygon are equal in length and all of the angles of that polygon are equal, they are called regular polygons." Display the Regular/Irregular overhead and use the regular polygons as examples of the concept. "The rest of these polygons are not regular polygons. What do you think we call them?" (*irregular polygons*) "That is correct, they are irregular polygons. How do we define irregular polygons?" (*polygons whose sides and angles are not all equal*) Use the irregular polygons as examples of this concept.

"Another way we can classify polygons is by the number of sides of the polygon. Which of these polygons could go together because of the number of sides?" (*the four-sided polygons and the six-sided polygons*) "But some of these are regular polygons and some are irregular polygons. How can they be in the same group?" (*all have four sides or all have six sides*) "In review, we can look at polygons by their number of sides and whether they are regular or irregular." Distribute the Classifying Polygons activity sheet. For each regular polygon given, the students will draw three irregular polygons.

Answer Key: Answers for these will vary but the polygons should be closed figures with the correct number of sides.

Related Activity: Write "triangle" on the board. Draw a triangle next to it. Ask the students to name objects from home or school that have triangle shapes. Have a student draw a picture of one of the objects next to the triangle. Write "square" under "triangle." Choose a student to draw a square next to the word. Write the names of several objects that have the shape of a square and have a student draw one of the objects. Continue the process for a pentagon, a hexagon, and an octagon.

■ 2-8. MATCH THE PREFIX (Challenging Level)

Objectives: To match the prefix to the polygon with the correct number of sides
To draw specific polygons

Materials: Dictionaries
Match the Prefix activity sheet

Directions: Write "polygon" on the board and ask for its meaning. (*many-sided closed figure*) Ask what part of the word has the meaning "many." (*poly*) Allow students to refer to the dictionaries if no one knows. Polygons get their names from the number of sides in the figure. Write "tri" on the board and ask how many the word refers to. (*three*) Have the students name some words with tri as a prefix. (*tricycle, three wheels; triathlon, three events; tripod, three legs; trident, three -pronged spear*) State that a polygon with three sides is known as a triangle. Draw several different triangles on the board, each time emphasizing the prefix "tri" as you say "triangle."

Write "quad" on the board and instruct the students to use the dictionaries to determine the meaning of the prefix. (*four*) List some quad words from the dictionary on the board and emphasize the meaning of four. State that all polygons with four sides are quadrilaterals. Squares, rectangles, parallelograms, trapezoids, and rhombi are all special kinds of quadrilaterals.

"Triangles and quadrilaterals name polygons of three and four sides. Starting with five-sided figures up to twelve-sided figures, the names use a prefix and the ending 'gon.' Hexagon, heptagon, and dodecagon are polygons with different numbers of sides." Distribute the Match the Prefix activity sheet. Instruct the students to use the dictionaries to determine the prefix that is used to name the polygon with a specific number of sides and fill in the table. The students will then draw specific polygons.

Answer Key: The table: 5, penta; 6, hexa; 7, hepta; 8, octa; 9, nona; 10, deca; 11, undeca; 12, dodeca. 1. answer should show a 12-sided figure; 2. answer should show a 10-sided figure; 3. answers will vary

Related Activity: Pair the students and provide each with a geoboard and geobands. The pairs will sit back to back. One student will use a geoband to construct a polygon on the geoboard. That student will then give verbal directions as the other student attempts to copy the polygon, without looking. The directions could be as follows: "The figure is a hexagon. Start at the pin in the upper left corner of the geoboard. The first side goes to the right three pins. The second side goes straight down two pins. The third side goes diagonally right and down one pin." The student attempting to copy the polygon may ask questions, but neither student may look at the other's geoboard until they both declare they are finished. The students can then switch roles and play again.

■ 2-9. SAME AND DIFFERENT WITH POLYHEDRA (Learning Level)

Objective: To state the similarities and differences of polyhedra

Materials: Variety of three-dimensional shapes (tissue boxes may be substituted for rectangular prisms, soda cans for cylinders, tennis balls for spheres, dice for cubes)
Same and Different with Polyhedra activity sheet

Directions: Divide the students into small groups. Write "polyhedron" and "polyhedra" on the board. "We have been working with polygons, which are closed figures with three or more sides. What is a polyhedron?" (*a three-dimensional shape*) "What are polyhedra?" (*three-dimensional shapes*) "What is the difference between a figure and a shape?" (*A shape is an object that you can hold. A figure is something that is drawn.*) Provide each group with a cube or cubes. Instruct the students to examine the cube and determine its attributes. Write several of the attributes on the board. (*6 faces, 12 edges, 8 vertices, all faces equal*) Provide each group with a rectangular prism. If not enough rectangular prisms are available, then display a rectangular prism. "How are these polyhedra, the cube, and the rectangular prism the same?" (*6 faces, 12 edges, 8 vertices*) "How are these polyhedra, the cube, and the rectangular prism different?" (*faces on the prism not all equal, square faces and rectangular faces*)

"Polyhedra have attributes that we can compare to other polyhedra." Distribute the Same and Different with Polyhedra activity sheet. The students will work in groups to determine as many similarities and differences between specific polyhedra as possible, and record their findings on the activity sheet.

Answer Key: 1. 6 faces, 12 edges, 8 vertices; 2. faces on the rectangular prism not all equal, square faces, rectangular faces; 3. they have length, they can stand; 4. cylinder is round, prism has a point, round faces, triangular faces; 5. have points, have a base, triangular faces; 6. number of faces, square pyramid has a square face or base; 7. round, can roll; 8. cylinder has two circular faces

Related Activity: Prepare several copies of Nets 1, 2, 3, 4, and 5 (see appendix). Display a copy of Net 2 for all to see. State that this is really a three-dimensional shape but it is unfolded and is flat. When a three-dimensional shape is unfolded and flat, it is called a net. Have the students predict the shape that can be made from Net 2. (*rectangular prism*) Cut out the net, fold it, secure it with some tape, and show that it is a rectangular prism. Have the students predict the shape for Net 1 (*square pyramid*), Net 3 (*cylinder*), Net 4 (*cube*), and Net 5 (*cone*). Allow the students to choose some of the nets and make the three-dimensional shapes. The completed shapes can be displayed next to the nets confirming or denying the predictions.

■ 2-10. GORS (Challenging Level)

Objective: To use examples and nonexamples to determine the attributes of an unknown

Materials: Overhead transparency of Rogs (see appendix)
Gors activity sheet

Directions: Use a piece of paper to cover the "These are not Rogs" section of the Rogs sheet. "You want to know if we are going to go on a field trip today. You ask the question and I answer 'No!' Have you learned anything?" (*yes*) "What have you learned?" (*no field trip today*) "In the game 'Twenty Questions,' how does a 'no' answer help you?" Take several responses that demonstrate that information can be learned from a "no" answer.

Write "Rog" on the board. "This is a made-up word. It can be anything. I am going to need your help to define a Rog." Place the Rogs transparency on the overhead. "Here are some pictures of Rogs. Study the examples of Rogs and then look at the bottom of the sheet. Which of these are Rogs?" (*The typical answers will be b, c, and d.*) "How do you know these are Rogs?" (*triangles*) "What are the attributes of Rogs?" (*three sides, three angles*) "Now I have some additional information for you. Here are some things that are not Rogs. These would be like the 'no' answers we were just talking about." Uncover the "These are not Rogs" section. "Study what Rogs are and what they are not. Talk softly with a person near you and see if you want to change your answer of which are Rogs."

Allow the students to discuss the attributes and try to determine which are Rogs. (*b and d*) As students answer, have them justify their answers by describing the attributes. (*triangles with a right angle*) "Sometimes the negative, a 'no' answer or what something is not, gives us information and allows us to have a better understanding." Distribute the Gors activity sheet. The students will determine the Gors and describe their attributes.

Answer Key: 1. b and c; 2. three-dimensional shapes with six sides

Related Activity: Have the students make up their own activity sheet using the format ("These are _____ ; These are not ———; Circle the ———; Define ———") from the Gors activity sheet. They will choose a name for their shape and use something other than a six-sided three-dimensional shape. When finished, the students can trade activity sheets and complete the new activity sheet.

■ 2-11. ALL THAT GOLD (Learning Level)

Objective: To determine the surface area of an object

Materials: Base-10 blocks, 2 ones and 1 ten per student
Cuisenaire rods
All That Gold activity sheet

Directions: "What are some metals that are expensive to buy?" (*silver, platinum, gold*) "Let's think about gold. It is expensive but it is still used for making jewelry. Another way of using gold is gold leaf. Gold leaf is very thin gold, almost like a thin fabric. It is used to cover items to have the look of gold. It is expensive but not as expensive as an item that is all gold inside and out."

Have the students take a base-10 one block. "What is the size of this block?" (*1 cm on all sides*) "What is the area of one of the faces?" (*1 sq cm*) "Are all of the faces the same size?" (*yes*) "Let's say that we have gold leaf and it is just the size of one of the faces. What is that size again?" (*1 sq cm*) "We want to make this block look very elegant, but we also do not want to spend a lot of money. How many pieces of the gold leaf would it take to cover this block all the way around?" (*6*) "What is the size of one piece of gold leaf?" (*1 sq cm*) "How much gold leaf would it take to completely cover the block?" (*6 sq cm*)

Instruct the students to put two base-10 one blocks together and hold them. "Now we want to cover two blocks with gold leaf. However, where the blocks are touching we will not put the gold leaf since it cannot be seen there. Remember, we do not want to waste the gold leaf. How much gold leaf would it take to completely cover these blocks?" (*10 sq cm*) "Someone explain how you got your answer." Allow several students to explain their solutions. "What we are doing is finding the surface area. This is the area of all of the surfaces that are seen or exposed."

Continue, "Now put those blocks down and look at the tens block. How long is the block?" (*10 cm*) "How much gold leaf would it take to completely cover this block?" (*42 sq cm*) Once again, allow students to describe their solutions. Distribute Cuisenaire rods and the All That Gold activity sheet. The students will determine the surface area of each of the Cuisenaire rods. Save the completed activity sheets for the Related Activity.

Answer Key: First paragraph: 6, 6; 1. 2, 10; 2. 3, 14; 3. 4, 18; 4. 5, 22; 5. 6, 26; 6. 7, 30; 7. 8, 34; 8. 9, 38; 9. 10, 42

Related Activity: Return the completed All That Gold activity sheets to the students and display an overhead transparency of the All That Gold Table (see appendix). Point out the color of the rod and the length of the rod in the table. Have the students give the correct surface area of each rod as you record it on the table. After purple (4), pause and ask if anyone sees something happening in the surface areas. (*They increase by 4 sq cm from the previous rod.*) Without the students looking at their papers, have them state the remaining surface areas as you record them. Ask the students to explain why this happens. (*As the rod increases by 1 cm length, it adds 4 sq cm to the surface because of the four sides of the rod.*)

"The surface area for the Cuisenaire rods increased in a pattern. We should be able to determine the surface area of any rod, even a very long rod. Let's think about the white rod. How did you find the surface area of the white rod?" (*counted the faces.*) "What is the length of the white rod?" (*1 cm*) "The shape of a rod has four faces that show length and two end faces. Its surface area was 6 sq cm. I am thinking $1 + 1 + 1 + 1 + 2 = 6$." (Write this on the board.) "What is the length of the red rod?" (*2 cm*) "I see four faces that are 2 cm in length and two end faces. The surface area of the red rod was 10 sq cm. I am thinking $2 + 2 + 2 + 2 + 2 = 10$." (Also write this on the board.) Repeat with the green rod. ($3 + 3 + 3 + 3 + 2 = 14$)

"Who can explain my thinking?" (*The length of the rod four times plus two more for the ends equals the surface area of the rod.*) Provide additional examples until the students are able to explain the formula $l + l + l + l + 2$ = surface area. Check student comprehension by providing problems such as: "What is the surface area of a rod that is 12 cm in length?" (*$12 + 12 + 12 + 12 + 2 = 50$ sq cm*) "What is the surface area of a rod that is 30 cm in length?" (*$30 + 30 + 30 + 30 + 2 = 122$ sq cm*) "What is the surface area of a rod that is 45 cm in length?" (*$45 + 45 + 45 + 45 + 2 = 182$ sq cm*)

■ 2-12. COVER ME UP (Challenging Level)

Objective: To determine the surface area of several objects joined as one

Materials: Cuisenaire rods
Cover Me Up activity sheet

Directions: This activity deals with surface area and assumes that the students know how to find the area of a rectangle. If they do not, that instruction should take place before this activity.

"What is surface area?" (*The area of one or many surfaces.*) "Your desk is a surface. If we were going to paint your desk, we would want to know how large the surface is so we can buy the correct amount of paint. This wall is a surface. If we were going to paint the wall, we would again want to know the surface area of the wall. But sometimes the surface is not as easy to figure as a wall or a desktop."

Distribute Cuisenaire rods to the students. Have the students stand two green rods on their desks and place a red rod standing between them, all touching.

"If we were to paint this structure, we would paint all of the surfaces that are exposed, those that can be seen. We would also include the bottom, since it could be seen when we pick it up. The surfaces where the rods are touching would not be counted. They are not exposed, they cannot be seen." Have the students determine the surface area of the structure. (*30 sq cm*) Allow several students to explain and justify their solutions. (One method would be to calculate the area of all of the surfaces and then total them. Another would be to count the total number of square centimeters. The face of a white rod is 1 sq cm. A green rod is 3 cm in length, so one face of the green rod would equal 3 sq cm of surface area.)

Create a second structure like the one below and have the students determine its surface area.

(34 sq cm)

Distribute the Cover Me Up activity sheet. The students will build structures with the Cuisenaire rods and determine the surface area of each structure.

Answer Key: 1. 28; 2. 40; 3. 38; 4. 40

Related Activity: Provide the students with Cuisenaire rods and instruct each student to build a structure with 25 sq cm of surface area. The surfaces that are considered the bottom (the surfaces that touch the desk or table) should be counted, but surfaces where rods touch other rods are not counted. When they have finished, have the students confirm the surface area of one another's structures and then allow the students to move around and see the different ways that structures can be formed and still be 25 sq cm of surface area. Repeat the activity using a surface area chosen by the students.

■ 2-13. A SLICE OF PI (Beginning Level)

Objectives: To measure the diameter of a circle
To measure the circumference of a circle

Materials: Plastic snap-on lids or cylinders, one for each pair of students
Rulers, yardsticks, yarn or string, markers
Calculators
A Slice of Pi activity sheet

Directions: Draw a circle on the board. Inform the students that this is a path. Draw another path, a straight line from one edge of the circle to the opposite edge, passing through the center of the circle. "Two ants are walking along the paths. One ant walks all the way around the circle. The other ant walks along the straight path. Which path is the longer distance?" (*the circular path*) "How do you know?" (*It looks longer.*) "Which path is the shorter distance?" (*the straight path*) "How do you know?" (*It looks shorter.*) "The straight path looks shorter, but can we prove it? How can we show that the straight path is shorter in length?" (*Measure it.*) "How could we measure the straight path?" (*Use a ruler.*) "How could we measure the circular path?" (*measure around with string and then measure the string; roll the circle along a ruler; possibly others*)

"What do we call the measure around the circle?" (*circumference*) "The straight path has a name. What do we call it?" (*diameter*) Draw another straight line across the circle, but this time not through the center. "Is this also a diameter?" (*no*) "Why not?" (*The diameter must pass through the center of the circle.*) Distribute a lid or cylinder to each pair of students. If using cylinders, the students will measure the circular face of the cylinder. Instruct the students to determine the circumference and diameter of the lid or cylinder using a method that they choose.

"What do you think of when you hear the word *pi*?" (*a piece of pie*) "This word is different. It is spelled like this." (Write "pi.") "There is a symbol for pi. It looks like this." (π) "As you work through this activity sheet you will be learning about pi." Distribute the A Slice of Pi activity sheet. Allow the students to work in pairs to measure the circumference and diameter of the circles. They should be allowed to use calculators to perform the division. This activity is a good introduction to pi. However, questions 6 and 7 are more challenging. The students can be told to work through question 5, and then those who understand the concept can be allowed to work on questions 6 and 7. The rest of the students can come back to those questions at a later time.

Answer Key: 1. 1, 3, 3; 2. 2, 6, 3; 3. 3, 9, 3; 4. 3 or 3.14; 5. 3 or 3.14; 6. 15; 7. 30

Related Activity: The students now know pi as approximately 3. However, we normally think of pi as approximately 3.14. Present the following problem for the students to solve. Advise them to use 3.14 instead of 3 when doing their calculations. Have several students share how they solved the problem and discuss each method.

Mr. Johnson planted a tree in his front yard and wants to put a circular border around it. The diameter of the planted area is 4 feet. The border can be bought in one foot sections. Approximately how much border should Mr. Johnson buy to complete the job? (*13 feet*)

■ 2-14. PI AND THE CIRCLE (Learning Level)

Objective: To determine the area of a circle

Materials: Cylinder with a diameter of at least 6 inches (a large empty can will also do)
Straight pin or thumbtack and a piece of string or yarn
Calculators
Pi and the Circle activity sheet

Directions: Measure the diameter of the cylinder. Divide that measure by 2 to get the radius. Display the circular base of the cylinder. "We have talked about finding the diameter and the circumference of circles. We have also talked about the relationship of the diameter of the circle to the circumference of that circle. What is that relationship called?" (*pi*) "When we divide the circumference by the diameter, we get a value. What is that value?" (*It is called pi and it is approximately 3.14.*) "Today we want to explore another measure, the area. What is the area?" (*the number of square units needed to cover a figure*)

"What is the radius of a circle?" (*a straight line from the edge of the circle to the center of the circle*) Demonstrate the radius by moving your finger to show a radius on the cylinder. Also draw a circle and radius on the board. "If I wanted to cover this end of the cylinder, I would need to know how large it is, or its area. To find the area, we use pi and the radius of the circle. The formula for finding the area of the circle looks like this: $A = \pi r \times r$. The A stands for area. The symbol π is pi and the $r \times r$ means that we multiply the radius times itself. What is the difference between the radius and the diameter?" (*The radius is one-half the length of the diameter.*)

Push the pin into the cylinder at the center of the circular face. Place the string across the face to show the diameter. Then move the string to demonstrate the radius. Do this several times to show that the radius can be in many positions, not always horizontal. Measure the string to determine the radius. Substitute 3.14 for pi and the radius of your circle for *r*. Have the students use calculators to determine the area of the circle. Be sure to show the answer in square units (inches or centimeters). For practice, have the students find the area of a circle with a radius of 4 cm (*50.24 sq cm*) and a circle with a radius of 16 inches (*803.84 sq in*). Distribute the Pi and the Circle activity sheet. The students will calculate the area and circumference of circles.

Answer Key: 1. 1,256 sq ft; 2. 314 sq m; 3. 113.04 sq in; 4. 6,358.5 sq m; 5. 11,304 sq mi

Related Activity: A new garden is being designed for the city park. The garden will be in the shape of a semicircle (½ of a circle). The diameter of the semicircle will measure 24 feet. What will be the area of the garden? (A = 3.14 × 12 × 12 divided by 2 = 226.08 sq ft)

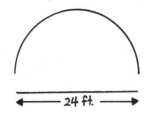

■ **2-15. BURRITOS (Learning Level)**

Objectives: To measure the angles of a circle graph
To draw the regions of a circle graph

Materials: Overhead transparency of Regions of a Circle (see appendix)
Overhead protractor
A copy of Regions of a Circle for each student
Protractors for the students
Burritos activity sheet

Directions: Display the Regions of a Circle transparency. "Children were surveyed to determine their favorite cookie. The data show the number of degrees in the region for each cookie. What we are going to do is use the data to make a circle graph. Which kind of cookie was the most popular?" (*chocolate chip*) "How do you know?" (*It has the largest region.*) "Why does that make it the most popular?" (*the more votes, the larger the region*) "Which cookie was the least popular?" (*oatmeal*) "How do you know?" (*The smallest region means the smallest number of votes.*) "Do we know how many votes each cookie received?" (*no*) "No, the number of votes is not given, just the size of the region."

Distribute a copy of Regions of a Circle and a protractor to each student. Use the radius of the circle as one ray of the angle. Use your protractor and describe the steps as you draw an angle of 140 degrees and have the students draw the angle on their paper. Label the region "chocolate chip and 140 degrees." Choose one ray of that angle and describe how to draw the angle for sugar cookies. Label it with the name and number of degrees as the students draw theirs. Continue with the last two regions. Review the data from the table and the data on the graph. It should be the same.

Distribute the Burritos activity sheet. The students will measure the degrees of regions of a circle graph and then construct a circle graph.

Answer Key: *Part One:* 1. bean and cheese, 150°; 2. chicken, 100°; 3. bean, 70°; 4. beef, 40°; 5. bean, beef; 6. bean and cheese, chicken. *Part Two:* The circle graph should show regions with the correct angles.

Related Activity: Provide each student with a copy of Create a Graph (see appendix). Instruct the students to create a set of data that shows the degrees for five regions on the circle graph. The data can be the results from a pretend survey of the students' choosing. Three of the regions should form acute angles and two should form obtuse angles. The students should fill in the key describing their data and the degrees of each region. The angles of the five regions must total 360 degrees.

■ **2-16. SPORTS TIME (Challenging Level)**

Objective: To calculate the area of figures

Materials: Calculators
Sports Time activity sheet

Directions: Review the formulas for finding the area of a rectangle and a circle. ($A = l \times w$; $A = \pi r^2$.) Draw two concentric circles on the board with a line that acts as the diameter for each circle.

State that the diameter of the smaller circle is 6 inches and the diameter of the large circle is 20 inches. Review that the radius is equal to ½ of the diameter. Tell the students that the small circle is going to be painted green and that the large circle is going to be painted yellow. What is the area that will be painted green? What is the area that will be painted yellow? Distribute the calculators and allow the students to solve the problems, conferring with other students as necessary.

The area of the yellow circle is 314 sq in. The area of the green circle is 28.26 sq in. However, part of the yellow circle will be painted green. The area of the yellow circle minus the area of the green circle is the area that will be painted yellow. ($341 - 28.26 = 285.74$ sq in)

Distribute the Sports Time activity sheet. You may wish to pair the students so they may discuss strategies. The students will calculate the areas of the figures.

Answer Key: *Part One:* 1. 342.76 sq ft. 2; 226.08 sq ft. *Part Two:* 1. The area of the ball field is ¼ the area of a circle; 2. 31,400 sq ft

Related Activity: A new ice skating rink is going to be built at the mall. Use the diagram below to determine the total area of the ice. (*6,056 sq ft*)

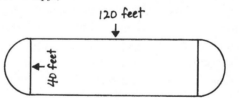

120 feet

40 feet

■ **2-17. AN EXACT COPY (Beginning Level)**

Objective: To match congruent figures

Materials: Overhead transparency of a page from this book
Overhead pattern blocks and regular pattern blocks
Piece of paper cut just slightly larger than a hexagon pattern block
Rulers and protractors
An Exact Copy activity sheet

Directions: "Who has used a photocopy machine? What did you use it for? Was the copy different from the original?" (If "yes" responses from enlargement or reduction, state that the class will be discussing those topics in the near future. At this time, concentrate on exact copies.) "The copy machine produces an exact copy of the original." Show a page from this book and then place the transparency over the page so it matches. Place two overhead hexagon pattern blocks on the overhead. "Are these two blocks exactly the same?" (*yes*) "How could you show that they are exactly the same?" (*Place one on top of the other.*) "When we are referring to shapes or figures that are the same shape and equal size, we use the word *congruent.*" Write "congruent" on the board. "We use this symbol to mean 'is congruent to.'" Write " ≅ " next to "congruent." State that one of the hexagons will be hexagon A and the other will be hexagon B. Write on the board "hexagon A ≅ hexagon B." Have the students read it as "hexagon A is congruent to hexagon B." Rotate one of the hexagons so they have a different look. "Are the hexagons still congruent?" (*yes*) "How can that be?" (*One was just turned. That did not change the size of the hexagons.*)

Remove one of the hexagons and place a regular hexagon pattern block on the overhead so the two blocks are away from each other. "Are these blocks congruent?" (Hopefully so. However, if they are different sizes, then use this opportunity to show that they are not congruent.) "How can we show that they are congruent?" (*Place one block on top of the other*.) Place the paper hexagon onto the overhead. "Are all three of these blocks congruent?" (Since they look the same, the responses should be yes. Place the blocks upon one another and show that one is actually larger. It is not congruent to the others.) "Sometimes what we see is not actually true. If I could *not* place the hexagons on top of one another, how could I find out if they are congruent?" (*Measure them.*) "What would I measure?" (*the length of the sides and the size of the angles*) "Congruent means that all of the matching sides are equal for both figures and that all of the matching angles are equal." Use a ruler to demonstrate that the sides of the paper hexagon are actually larger than the sides of the hexagon block. Use a protractor to demonstrate that in this case the angles of both are the same, but since the sides are not equal, they are not congruent. Review the definition of *congruent* and the meaning of the symbol.

Distribute the An Exact Copy activity sheet, a ruler, and a protractor to each student. The students will measure the sides and angles of the figures to find and match congruent figures.

Answer Key: 1. L; 2. J; 3. H; 4. G; 5. K; 6. I

Related Activity: Provide each student with two copies of Centimeter Grid (see appendix), a straightedge, and a marker. On one of the grids, the students will use the straightedge and marker to draw a design that incorporates several different polygons. The design should follow the lines on the grid as much as possible. When completed, two students will trade their grids and copy the other student design onto their blank grid. They should do this by counting grid lines to measure and copy the design exactly. When finished, the students can see if they have made an exact copy by placing one paper on top of the other and holding both papers up to the light.

■   **2-18. DRAW THE FIGURE (Learning Level)**

Objective: To draw congruent figures

Materials: Overhead transparency of Centimeter Grid (see appendix)
Blank transparency
Rulers, protractors, compasses, and markers
Draw the Figure activity sheet

Directions: Review the meaning of *congruent*. (*figures that have the same shape and the same size*) If the figures cannot be placed upon one another to see if they are congruent, then they can be measured. Place the transparency on the overhead. Use the grid and a ruler to carefully draw a rectangle that is 4 by 6 centimeters. Invite a student to draw a rectangle on the grid that is congruent. Ask the student why he or she is sure it is congruent. (*The student measured either by counting the grid lines or measuring with the* *ruler. Point out both methods.*) Draw a 6-by-6 centimeter square and invite another student to draw a square that is congruent and justify why it is congruent.

Replace the transparency with a blank. Use a ruler and a protractor to draw a rectangle. Describe the procedure for drawing the rectangle as you proceed emphasizing the use of the ruler for measurements and the protractor for right angles. Invite a student to draw a congruent figure. Assist the students verbally and ask questions such as "What will you do next?" and "How do you draw a right angle?"

Distribute the Draw the Figure activity sheet along with rulers, protractors, compasses, and markers. The students will draw congruent figures using the grid and the other tools.

Answer Key: Check for congruent figures.

Related Activity: Divide the students into groups of three or four. Provide each student with some sheets of paper, rulers, and scissors. Each member of the group will choose a different polygon and draw that polygon (irregular or regular) on one sheet of paper. The students will then place a second sheet of paper behind the original and cut out the polygon to make congruent figures. When each member of the group has completed the congruent figures, the group will explore the effects that a flip, a slide, and a turn have on congruent figures. Each group will answer the following sentence. What effect does a flip, a slide, or a turn have on two congruent figures? (*No effect. Their size and shape are still the same.*)

■ 2-19. IT'S THE SAME TO ME (Challenging Level)

Objective: To divide a figure into congruent regions

Materials: geoboards and geobands
It's the Same to Me activity sheet

Directions: Distribute the geoboards and geobands and allow the students to explore the materials for a short while. Instruct the students to make a 3-by-5 rectangle on the geoboard. Ask what it would mean to separate the figure into two congruent parts. (*Each part would be the same size and same shape.*) Have the students use another geoband to separate the rectangle into two congruent parts. When completed, have the students show their boards to one another to verify that there are two congruent parts and see if anyone did it differently. There should be three solutions: horizontally, vertically, and diagonally. Discuss why all three would be correct.

Remove the geobands and instruct the students to make the largest right triangle (a triangle with one right angle) on their geoboard. Again have them separate the figure into two congruent regions. Once again have the students verify each other's work and check for different solutions. This time there will be only one solution, a band from the right angle to the opposite side. Explain that some figures will have single solutions and other figures will have multiple solutions. Distribute the It's the Same to Me activity sheet. The students will use their geoboards to find three ways to form two congruent parts for each figure. The solutions will be drawn on the activity sheet.

Answer Key: 1. ⊟ ⊞ ⊠ ◺ ; 2. ⬡ ⬭ ⬯ ; 3. ▷ ▷ ▷

Related Activity: Provide each student with a copy of the Congruent Regions of a Polygon sheet (see appendix), a protractor, and a ruler. Starting with the hexagon, the students will draw a line from the vertex of each angle to the vertex of the opposite angle. Is each region of the hexagon congruent? (*yes*) Each angle at the center of the hexagon is _____. (*72 degrees*) They will then continue with the octagon (*yes, 45 degrees*), the square (*yes, 90 degrees*), and the dodecagon (*yes, 30 degrees*).

■ **2-20. THERE IS A SIMILARITY (Beginning Level)**

Objectives: To identify similar figures
                    To describe why figures are similar

Materials: Picture or page from this book and a reduced copy of the picture or page
                    Picture or page from this book and an enlarged copy of the picture or page
                    Overhead transparency of Similar Figures I (see appendix)
                    Rulers and protractors
                    There Is a Similarity activity sheet

Directions: "When we used the word *congruent,* we were referring to figures that had the same shape and size. The word *similar* is also used, but it has a different meaning." Display the picture and the reduced copy of the picture. "What do you see when you look at the picture and the copy?" (*same picture but smaller*) Point out details of the picture that are in the same location. "Everything is the same except smaller." Display the picture and the enlargement. Note that all of the details are the same except that they are larger.

"The same ideas occur when we examine figures. When two figures have the same shape, but their size is different, we say that they are similar figures." Display the top section of Similar Figures I that has two circles. "What is the same about these two figures?" (*They are circles.*) "What is different about the two figures?" (*their size*) "These two figures are similar. Why?" (*They have the same shape but are different sizes.*) Display the top two sections. Ask about the relationship between one of the new circles and the previous two circles. (*They are similar.*) Repeat for each new circle. Ask about the relationship of any of the circles to all of the others. (*They are all similar.*) "How can that be? (*All have the same shape but are different sizes.*) "Describe a circle that would *not* be similar to these circles." (*There are no circles that are not similar to other circles.*) "Do you mean that all circles are similar to other circles?" (*yes*) "We use the symbol ~ to mean 'is similar to.' " Write "circle G ~ circle H" on the board. Have several students read it as "circle G is similar to circle H."

Display the third section that has two squares. Repeat the same line of questioning that leads to the idea that all squares are similar to all other squares. The fact that all four sides of a square are always equal is what makes squares similar. They always have the same shape.

"To sum it up, all circles are similar to other circles and all squares are similar to other squares."

As a review, have the class discuss the difference between congruent and similar. Distribute the There Is a Similarity activity sheets, rulers, and protractors. The students will identify similar figures using rulers and protractors when necessary.

Answer Key: 1. yes; 2. same shape but different size; 3. circle A ~ circle B; 4. yes; 5. same shape but different size; 6. square A ~ square B; 7. no; 8. not the same shape; 9. congruent; 10. same shape and same size; 11. neither; 12. neither same shape nor same size

Related Activity: Provide each student with a geoboard and geobands. Instruct each student to make the smallest square possible near the center of the geoboard. Then make a slightly larger one with a second geoband. Then a slightly larger square with a third geoband. "Are the squares similar?" (*yes*) "Why?" (*same shape but different size*) "How do we know they are the same shape?" (*All squares are the same shape because their four sides are always equal to each other.*) "Turn your geoboards. Are the squares still similar?" (*yes*) "Why are they still similar?" (*They are still the same shape but different sizes.*)

Pair the students. Instruct one student to make the largest hexagon on the geoboard. The second student will make a similar hexagon (*same shape but smaller*) on the other geoboard. One student will turn the geoboard so the hexagons no longer have the same position. "Are the two hexagons still similar?" (*yes*) "Why are they still similar?" (*They are still the same shape but different sizes.*) "How do turns, flips, or slides effect two similar figures?" (*They have no effect.*)

■ 2-21. TRIANGLE, TRIANGLE (Learning Level)

Objective: To match similar triangles

Materials: Overhead transparency of Similar Figures II (see appendix)
Cutout of triangle DEF from the bottom of Similar Figures II
Rulers and protractors
Triangle, Triangle activity sheet

Directions: "In our discussion about similar figures, what conclusion did we draw about circles?" (*All circles are similar to other circles.*) "Why?" (*They all have the same shape even if they are different sizes.*) "And what conclusion did we draw about squares?" (*All squares are similar to other squares.*) "Why?" (*They all have the same shape, which is four equal sides, even if they are different sizes.*) Display the top section of the Similar Figures II overhead. "Which of these triangles are similar to each other?" Take several responses. "No, none of these triangles is similar to any other. They may be similar to other triangles, but not to one another. When we look at triangles, we have to think a little bit differently when we refer to similar. Two triangles are similar to each other when their corresponding angles are equal. Corresponding angles would be in the same position on both triangles." Display the next section of the transparency. "These two triangles have corresponding angles. Angle A of this triangle and angle D of this triangle are corresponding. They are in the same position. What other two angles are corresponding angles?" (*angles B and D; angles C and F*) "Sometimes the triangles are not in the same position, so you have to think about where the corresponding angles are." Display the second and third sections of the transparency. "Triangle DEF has been turned." Place the cutout of triangle DEF on the transparency. Then turn it so it is in the same orientation as triangle ABC. "If we turn it back again, we see that the corresponding angles are still A and D, B and E, C and F."

Use a protractor to measure the corresponding angles of either set of triangles. Each corresponding pair should be equal. "Are the corresponding sides equal?" (*no*) "Which two sides are corresponding sides?" (*AC and DF; AB and DE; BC and EF*) "So we can draw a conclusion that when the corresponding angles of two triangles are equal, and when the corresponding sides are unequal, the two triangles are similar to each other."

Distribute the Triangle, Triangle activity sheet. The students will match similar triangles.

Answer Key: *Part One:* 1. A and E, B and F, C and G; 2. AC and EG, AB and EF, BC and FG; 3. The corresponding angles are equal measurements; 4. The corresponding sides are not equal; 5. Yes, their corresponding angles are equal, but their corresponding sides are not equal. *Part Two:* 1. 6; 2. 7; 3. 4; 4. 3; 5. 8; 6. 1; 7. 2; 8. 5; 9. Their corresponding angles are equal but their corresponding sides are not equal.

Related Activity: Say, "The distance between each base of a baseball diamond is 90 feet. The distance between each base of a softball diamond is 60 feet. Draw a diagram and explain if the two ball diamonds would be similar, congruent, or neither."

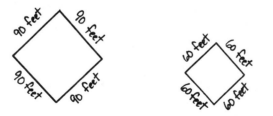

(*The two ball diamonds are similar because their corresponding angles are equal but the sides are not equal. The ball diamonds are also squares and all squares are similar to one another.*)

2-1. Line Up

Match the correct definition with its term.

_____ **1.** Line segment

_____ **2.** Point

_____ **3.** Intersecting lines

_____ **4.** Plane

_____ **5.** Parallel lines

_____ **6.** Line

_____ **7.** Ray

A. A specific location in space

B. Points that form a flat surface in all directions

C. Points that make up a straight path that goes on in two directions

D. A specific part of a line

E. A part of a line that goes in one direction and never stops

F. Lines that cross at one point

G. Lines that never intersect

Name the symbol.

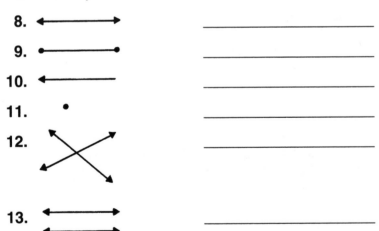

8. _____

9. _____

10. _____

11. _____

12. _____

13. _____

Draw the following figures.

14. line segment ST

15. ray UV

16. line YZ

Name _____   Date _____

2-2. Angles

Angles are formed by two rays that have a common point. The common point is called the vertex. Angles can be classified by the measurement between the sides, not the length of the sides.

Right angles are 90 degrees.

Acute angles are less than 90 degrees.

Obtuse angles are greater than 90 degrees.

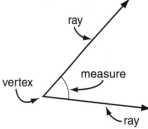

Identify each as being a right, acute, or obtuse angle.

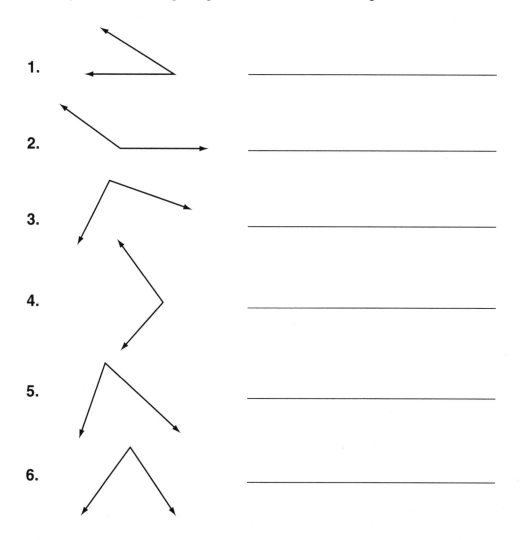

1. _____

2. _____

3. _____

4. _____

5. _____

6. _____

2-3. More Angles

Name the angles, then use a protractor to find the measure of the angles in degrees. When reading the protractor, remember that acute angles will be less than 90 degrees and obtuse angles will be greater than 90 degrees. The first one is done for you.

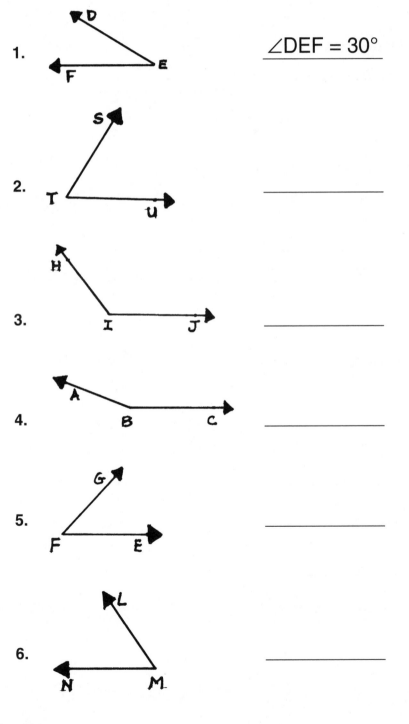

1. $\angle DEF = 30°$

2. _____

3. _____

4. _____

5. _____

6. _____

Name _____   Date _____

2-4. The Angle of Time

The numbers on a clock are spaced an equal distance apart. As the minute hand moves, it passes a different number every five minutes. A line has been drawn on the clock extending from the 12 and the 6. Use a straightedge to draw a line from the center of the clock through the number 1.

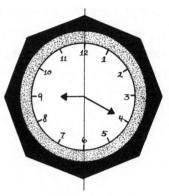

What is the size of the angle the minute hand makes moving from 12 to 1? _____
(Did you get the answer of 30 degrees?)

1. What is the size of the angle the minute hand makes moving from 12 to 2? _____

2. What is the size of the angle the minute hand makes moving from 12 to 3? _____

3. What is the size of the angle the minute hand makes moving from 12 to 4? _____

4. What is the size of the angle the minute hand makes moving from 12 to 5? _____

5. What is the size of the angle the minute hand makes moving from 12 to 6? _____

6. What is the size of the angle the minute hand makes moving from 12 to 7? _____

Describe the pattern that is occurring in the answers. _____

_____

Now use the pattern to answer questions 7 through 11.

7. What is the size of the angle the minute hand makes moving from 12 to 8? _____

8. What is the size of the angle the minute hand makes moving from 12 to 9? _____

9. What is the size of the angle the minute hand makes moving from 12 to 10? _____

10. What is the size of the angle the minute hand makes moving from 12 to 11? _____

11. How many degrees does the minute hand move going from 12 back to 12? _____

2-5. Tell All About It

For each figure, tell three attributes that you will *always* find in that polygon, two attributes that you *might* find in that polygon, and two attributes you will *never* find in that polygon. Then draw two examples of that polygon and two nonexamples of that polygon. The first one has been started for you. Finish it and go on to the others.

SQUARE

1. Three attributes you will always find in a square.

always four sides _____

2. Two attributes you might find in a square.

large in size _____

3. Two attributes you will never find in a square.

one side bigger than the other sides _____

PARALLELOGRAM

4. Three attributes you will always find in a parallelogram.

_____

5. Two attributes you might find in a parallelogram.

_____

6. Two attributes you will never find in a parallelogram.

_____

HEXAGON

7. Three attributes you will always find in a hexagon.

_____

8. Two attributes you might find in a hexagon.

_____

9. Two attributes you will never find in a hexagon.

_____

2-6. Same and Different with Polygons

You will be comparing some polygons to other polygons and looking for how they are the same and how they are different. For the following pairs of shapes, write three ways they are the same and two ways they are different.

Examine the rectangle and the square.

1. How are they the same?

_____

_____

_____

2. How are they different?

_____

_____

_____

Examine the square and the parallelogram.

3. How are they the same?

_____

_____

_____

4. How are they different?

_____

_____

_____

For the following pairs of shapes, write two ways they are the same and three ways they are different.

Examine the triangle and the square.

5. How are they the same?

_____

_____

_____

6. How are they different?

_____

_____

_____

Examine the rectangle and the hexagon.

7. How are they the same?

_____

_____

_____

8. How are they different?

_____

_____

_____

2-7. Classifying Polygons

Polygons are many-sided closed figures that can be classified in a few different categories.

- One category is the number of sides of the polygon.

- Another category is regular polygons. When all of the sides are equal in length and all of the angles are equal, they are called regular polygons.

- A third category is irregular polygons. Irregular polygons can be looked at in three different ways. Sometimes all of their sides are equal but their angles are not all equal. Sometimes their angles are all equal but their sides are not all equal.

Finally, sometimes their sides are not equal and their angles are not equal.

Complete the table below by drawing an example of a figure with the stated number of sides, a regular figure with that many sides, and then an irregular figure with that many sides.

Number of Sides	Example	Regular	Irregular
3			
4			
5			
6			
8			

2-8. Match the Prefix

Polygons are simple closed curves composed of three or more lines. Polygons get their names from the number of their sides. Use a dictionary to match the prefix to the correct polygon, and then fill in the name of the polygon. The first two have been done for you.

penta	deca	octa
nona	poly	hexa
dodeca	hepta	undeca

Number of Sides	Prefix	Name
3	tri	triangle
4	quad	quadrilateral
5		
6		
7		
8		
9		
10		
11		
12		
many		

1. Draw a dodecagon on the back of this sheet.

2. Draw a decagon on the back of this sheet.

3. Draw a figure of your choosing on a separate sheet of paper. Trade papers with a classmate and identify each other's figure.

2-9. Same and Different with Polyhedra

You will be comparing some polyhedra to other polyhedra, looking for how they are the same and how they are different. For each pair of shapes, write how they are the same and how they are different.

Examine a cube and a rectangular prism.

1. How are they the same?

_____

_____

_____

2. How are they different?

_____

_____

_____

Examine a cylinder and a triangular prism.

3. How are they the same?

_____

_____

_____

4. How are they different?

_____

_____

_____

Examine a triangular pyramid and a square pyramid.

5. How are they the same?

_____

_____

_____

6. How are they different?

_____

_____

_____

Examine a sphere and a cylinder.

7. How are they the same?

_____

_____

_____

8. How are they different?

_____

_____

_____

Name _____   Date _____

2-10. Gors

Below are some pictures of Gors. You don't know what Gors are? Study the attributes to tell what Gors are, and what they are not. Circle which are Gors and then describe their attributes.

These are Gors.

These are not Gors.

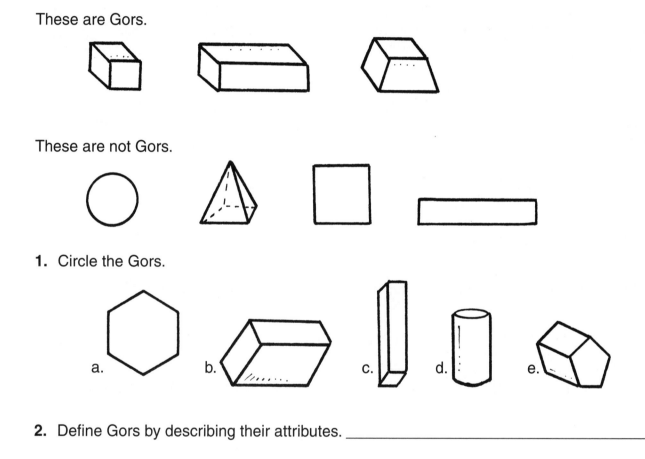

1. Circle the Gors.

    a.   b.   c.   d.   e.

2. Define Gors by describing their attributes. _____

_____

_____

_____

2-11. All That Gold

Examine a white Cuisenaire rod. The length of each edge is 1 centimeter. The area of each face is 1 square centimeter. Gold leaf is a thin sheet of gold. If you cut the gold leaf into squares that were 1 centimeter on each side, the area of each piece of gold leaf would be 1 square centimeter. How many pieces of gold leaf would it take to cover a white rod completely? Gold is very expensive, so do not waste any. It would take ___ pieces of gold leaf to cover the surface of the white rod. So, the surface area of the white rod is ___ square centimeters.

Use your rods to find the length and surface area, and fill in the blanks below. The surface area is the number of 1-square-centimeter pieces of gold leaf it would take to cover the rod completely.

1. The length of a red rod is ___ cm and the surface area of a red rod is ___ sq cm

2. The length of a green rod is ___ cm and the surface area of a green rod is ___ sq cm

3. The length of a purple rod is ___ cm and the surface area of a purple rod is ___ sq cm

4. The length of a yellow rod is ___ cm and the surface area of a yellow rod is ___ sq cm

5. The length of a dark green rod is ___ cm and the surface area of a dark green rod
   is ___ sq cm

6. The length of a black rod is ___ cm and the surface area of a black rod is ___ sq cm

7. The length of a brown rod is ___ cm and the surface area of a brown rod is ___ sq cm

8. The length of a blue rod is ___ cm and the surface area of a blue rod is ___ sq cm

9. The length of an orange rod is ___ cm and the surface area of an orange rod
   is ___ sq cm

2-12. Cover Me Up

Use your Cuisenaire rods to build a design to match the picture. Pretend that each figure will be spray-painted to make it more attractive. Determine the surface area that will need to be covered for each figure. Be sure to include the bottom, but not any surfaces that touch each other or are hidden.

1. The surface area of this figure is _____ sq cm

2. The surface area of this figure is _____.

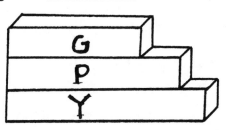

3. The surface area of this figure is _____.

4. The surface area of this figure is _____.

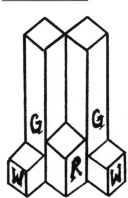

_____   Date _____

2-13. A Slice of Pi

The circle below has a line segment that passes through the center of the circle. The length of this line segment is called the diameter of the circle. Another measure is the distance around the circle. This distance is called the circumference.

For each circle below, measure the diameter and the circumference. Then use a calculator to divide the circumference by the diameter.

1. The diameter of the circle is _____ inches.

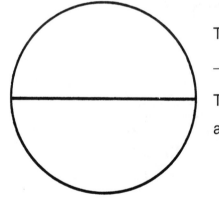

    The circumference of the circle is approximately _____ inches.

    The circumference divided by the diameter is approximately _____.

2. The diameter of the circle is _____ inches.

    The circumference of the circle is approximately

    _____ inches.

    The circumference divided by the diameter is

    approximately _____.

Name _____ Date _____

2-13. A Slice of Pi *(continued)*

3. The diameter of the circle is _____ inches.

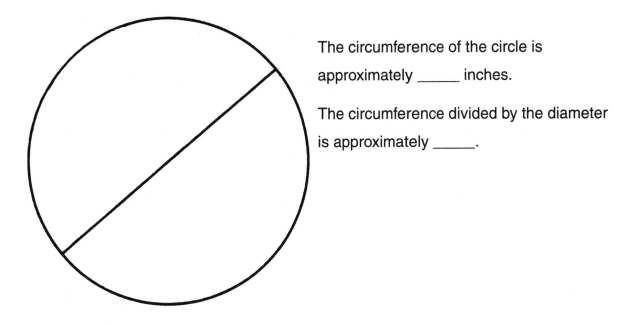

The circumference of the circle is approximately _____ inches.

The circumference divided by the diameter is approximately _____.

Each time you divided the circumference by the diameter, you should have gotten approximately 3. Dividing the circumference of any circle by its diameter will always give the same value. We call this value *pi*. The symbol for pi is π. The value of pi is approximately 3.14. This means that the circumference of any circle is about three times its diameter.

4. A circle has a diameter of 6 inches. What is the approximate value of the circumference divided by the diameter? _____

5. A circle has a diameter of 70 inches. What is the approximate value of the circumference divided by the diameter? _____

6. A circle has a diameter of 5 inches. The circumference of this circle is approximately _____ inches.

7. A circle has a diameter of 10 inches. The circumference of this circle is approximately _____ inches.

2-14. Pi and the Circle

Pi is the relationship of the circumference of a circle divided by the diameter of the circle. The symbol for pi is π and its value is approximately 3.14. Pi is used to find the area of circles. The area is equal to pi times the square of the radius of the circle. The formula looks like this; $A = \pi r^2$. (This is the same as $\pi r \times r$.) Now try to work out the following problems.

1. Hakeem is in charge of watering the lawn at his house. He uses a sprinkler that rotates in a circular path. If he adjusts the sprinkler to a radius of 20 feet, what is the area of lawn that is being watered by the sprinkler?

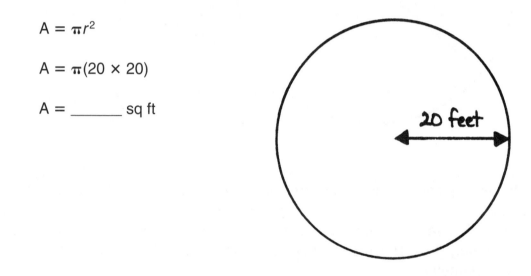

$A = \pi r^2$

$A = \pi(20 \times 20)$

$A = $ _____ sq ft

20 feet

2. A new circular space is going to be built on the playground. There is room to make it with a radius of 10 meters. What will be the area of the new space on the playground?
_____

3. Kanesha and Julie drew a circle graph with a diameter of 12 inches. What is the area of their circle graph? _____

4. A new fountain was built in the park that included a circular sidewalk around the fountain. The diameter of the sidewalk is 45 meters. How large is the area taken up by the fountain and sidewalk? _____

5. Radio station WMATH broadcasts 120 miles in all directions. How large is the area that you can listen to radio station WMATH? _____

Name _____   Date _____

2-15. Burritos

Part One: The students at Winter Lane Elementary School were surveyed to determine their favorite type of burrito. The data were used to construct a circle graph, which is seen below. Measure the angles of each region of the circle graph and fill in the chart.

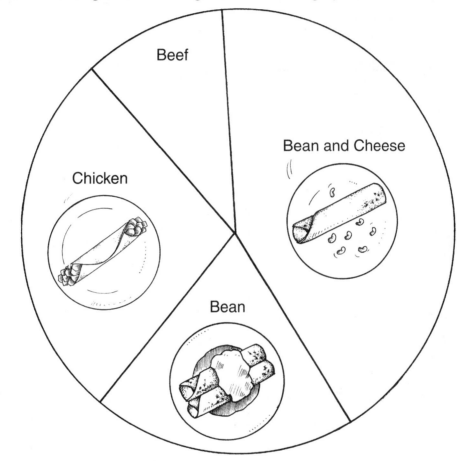

	Kind of Burrito	**Degrees of Angle**
1. Most popular burrito		
2. Second most popular		
3. Third most popular		
4. Least popular		

5. Which choices are represented by acute angles? _____

6. Which choices are represented by obtuse angles? _____

2-15. Burritos *(continued)*

Part Two: The students also voted for their favorite flavor of potato chip. The data show the number of degrees in the region for each flavor. Use the data to construct a circle graph. Label each region with the flavor it represents and the number of degrees in the angle.

Plain	160 degrees
Salt & Vinegar	120 degrees
Ranch	45 degrees
BBQ	35 degrees

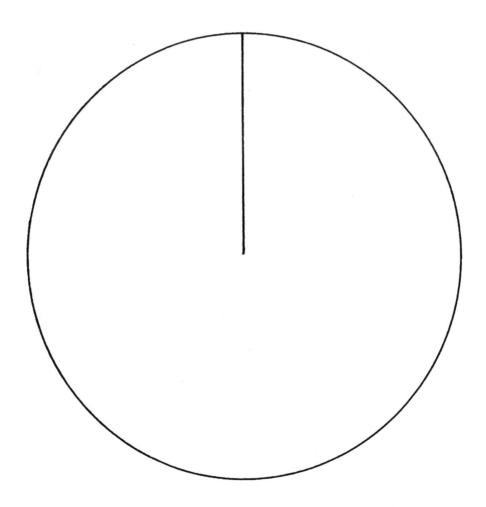

Name _____   Date _____

2-16. Sports Time

Part One: The basketball court at Winter Lane School is going to be painted using the school colors of red and blue. The lanes will be painted blue and the circles at the foul line will be painted red. The foul line is the diameter of the circle. Use the measurements in the diagram to determine the area that will be painted blue and the area that will be painted red.

- First find the size of one of the rectangles that is to be painted blue.

- Next find the area of one of the circles that is to be painted red.

- A part of the red circle is in the blue rectangle. That part is a common fraction.

- Find the area of the circle that is in the blue rectangle. Subtract that area from the area of the rectangle.

- Now determine the total area to be painted blue and the total area to be painted red.

1. The total area that will be painted blue is _____ sq ft.

2. The total area that will be painted red is _____ sq ft.

2-16. Sports Time (continued)

Part Two: The baseball field at the school needs to be watered. The maintenance person places a sprinkler at home plate and adjusts it to spray only between the foul lines. The foul lines from home plate to the fences are 200 feet each. The fence is the shape of an arc of a circle with home plate as the center of the circle. The foul lines make a 90 degree angle at home plate. How large of an area is the sprinkler covering?

This figure is a clue:

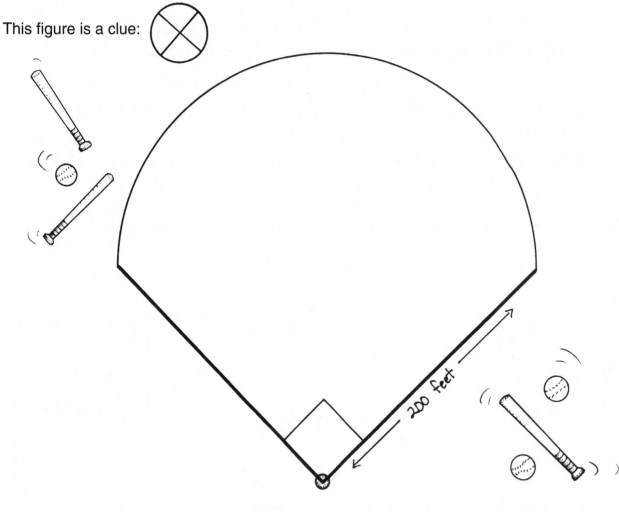

1. How does the clue help you solve the problem? _____

_____

_____

2. The sprinkler is covering _____ sq ft.

Name _____ Date _____

2-17. An Exact Copy

Photocopiers are machines that make exact copies of what we input. The copies are the same shape and the same size as the original. We could pick one up and place it right on top of the other. There would be no difference. Figures that have the same shape and the same size are called congruent figures. Each corresponding side would be the same size and each corresponding angle would be the same number of degrees. We use the symbol ≅ to mean "is congruent to."

Study the figures below, using a ruler and protractor to measure sides and angles. Find each pair of figures that are congruent.

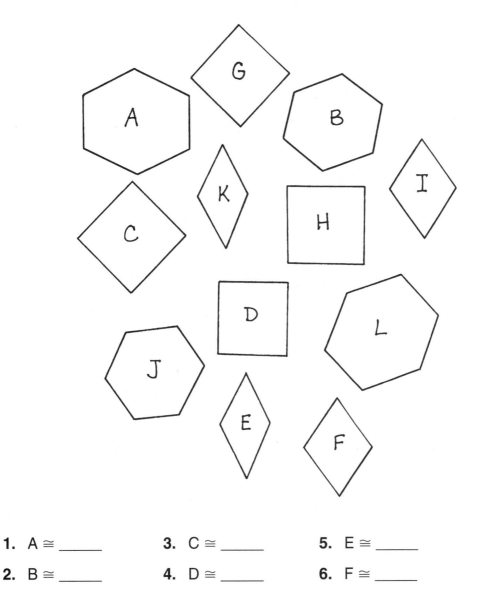

1. A ≅ _____   **3.** C ≅ _____   **5.** E ≅ _____

2. B ≅ _____   **4.** D ≅ _____   **6.** F ≅ _____

2-18. Draw the Figure

Use the grid, a ruler, a protractor, a compass, and a marker to draw congruent figures to match the ones below.

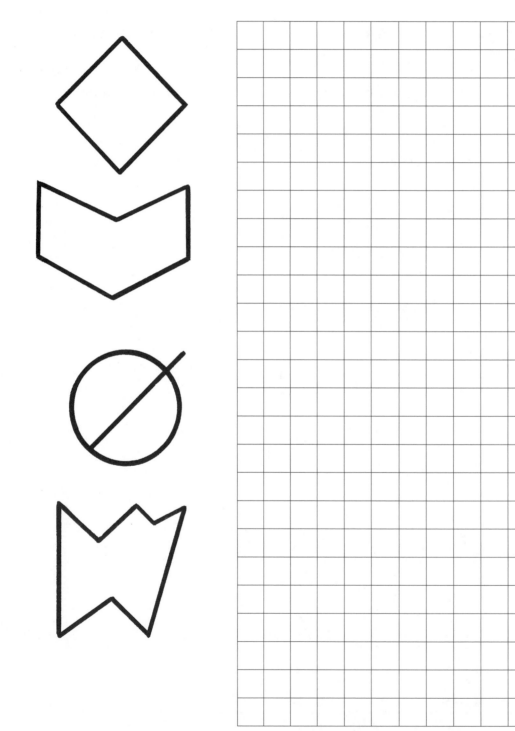

2-19. It's the Same to Me

Copy each figure onto a geoboard and use one geoband to separate the figure into two congruent parts. Draw the figure on the dots and show how you separated the figure into the congruent parts. Remove the geoband and separate the figure into two congruent parts a different way, then draw it. Find a third way and then draw it. Part of the first one has been done for you.

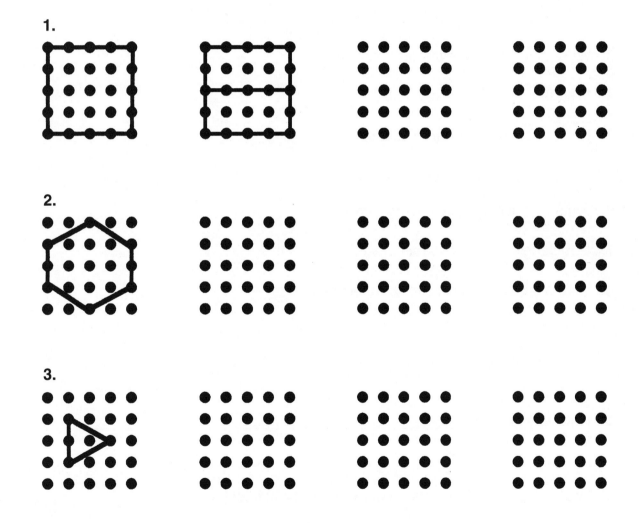

2-20. There Is a Similarity

Similar figures are those that have the same shape but not necessarily the same size. If we enlarge or reduce a figure on a photocopier, we make similar figures. They are either larger or smaller, but they keep the same shape. We use the symbol ~ to mean "is similar to."

1. Is circle A similar to circle B? _____

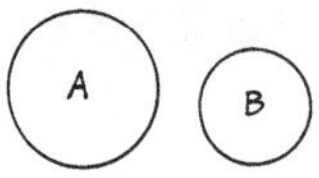

2. How is circle A similar to circle B? _____

   _____

3. Write that using the symbol for similar. _____

4. Is square A similar to square B? _____

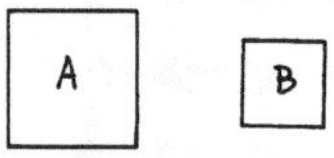

5. How is square A similar to square B? _____

   _____

6. Write that using the symbol for similar. _____

7. Is rectangle C similar to rectangle D? _____

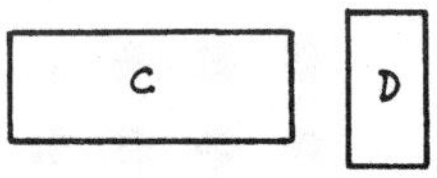

8. How is rectangle C not similar to rectangle D? _____

   _____

9. Is ∠ABC similar to or congruent to ∠DEF, or neither? _____

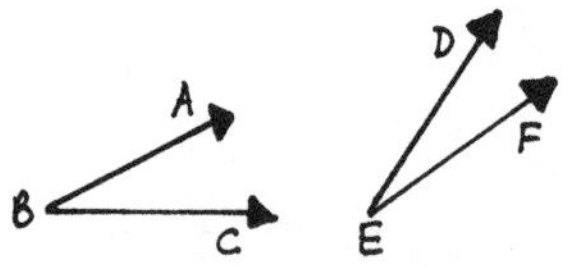

10. How do you know? _____

    _____

11. Is △MNO similar to or congruent to △PQR, or neither? _____

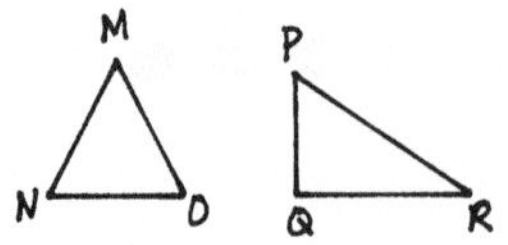

12. How do you know? _____

    _____

© 2004 by John Wiley & Sons, Inc.

Name _____   Date _____

2-2. Triangle, Triangle

Look at the title of this activity sheet. Something is strange. The second word is smaller. It looks the same, it has the same shape, but it is smaller. We can say the two words are similar. They have the same shape, but are not the same size.

Look at the two triangles below.

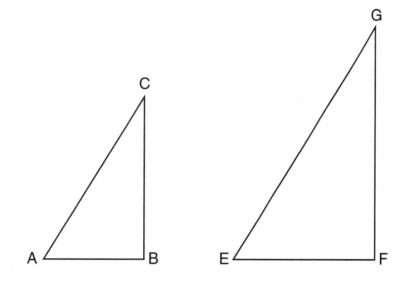

Part One:

1. Which are the corresponding angles? ___ and ___ , ___ and ___ , ___ and ___

2. Which are the corresponding sides? ___ and ___ , ___ and ___ , ___ and ___

3. Use your protractor to measure the angles of the triangles. What can you say about the sizes of the corresponding angles?

    _____

4. Use your ruler to measure the sides of the triangles. What can you say about the sizes of the corresponding sides?

    _____

5. Are the two triangles similar? _____ Why? _____

    _____

2-21. Triangle, Triangle *(continued)*

Part Two: Each triangle below has a similar partner. Use your protractor to find the two triangles that are similar.

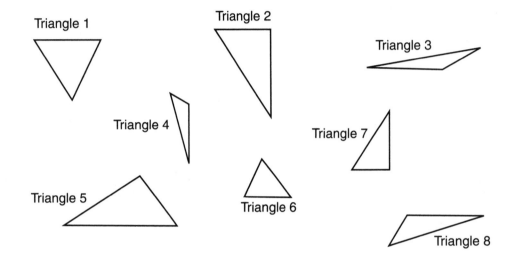

1. Triangle 1 is similar to triangle _____.

2. Triangle 2 is similar to triangle _____.

3. Triangle 3 is similar to triangle _____.

4. Triangle 4 is similar to triangle _____.

5. Triangle 5 is similar to triangle _____.

6. Triangle 6 is similar to triangle _____.

7. Triangle 7 is similar to triangle _____.

8. Triangle 8 is similar to triangle _____.

9. Complete the sentence. Two triangles are similar when _____

_____

Section 3

MEASUREMENT

Teacher Directions

■ **3-1. THE RIGHT UNIT** (Learning Level)

Objective: To choose the appropriate tool to measure a given object

Materials: Inch ruler and centimeter ruler
Yardstick and meter stick
The Right Unit activity sheet

Directions: Ask the students to use their fingers to show the size of an inch. Then have them show the size of a centimeter. (*It is smaller than an inch; approximately 2½ centimeters equals an inch.*) Show the inch ruler and the centimeter ruler as a comparison. Next, have the students use their arms to show the size of a yard. (*approximately the span from the nose to the tips of the fingers*) Hold the yardstick against your nose out to the tips of your fingers. Then show the size of a meter. (*approximately 3 inches longer than the yard*) Finally, have them use their arms to show a mile or a kilometer. (*cannot be done*) Write the words "inch," "centimeter," "yard," and "meter" on the board and ask the students to generate objects that are approximately each length.

"What is something that is a mile long?" (*a road*) "What is approximately one mile from school?" Provide some local landmarks to give the students the sense of a mile. "Where do people use kilometers?" (*most of the rest of the world*) "What would we measure using miles or kilometers?" (*distances from place to place*) "What are some of those places?" (Allow the students to generate some. For example: *from school to the beach; from New York to Washington;* etc.)

Briefly review the measures. Distribute the Right Unit activity sheet. The students will determine the correct tool for specific measurements.

Answer Key: 1. in, cm; 2. mi, km; 3. yd, m; 4. in, cm; 5. mi, km; 6. yd, m; 7. yd, m; 8. mi, km; 9. in, cm; 10. smaller objects; 11. objects larger than an inch or centimeter ruler, long distances

Related Activity: The students will list two things in their home that they believe would best be measured in inches or centimeters and two things that would best be measured in yards or meters. They will then think of two things they have done that they believe would be best presented in miles or kilometers, such as running in a race. When completed, the ideas could be displayed as three class bulletin boards.

■ **3-2. WHICH ONE?** (Learning Level)

Objectives: To choose the appropriate tool to measure a given object
To choose the appropriate measurement

Materials: Everyday containers with the capacities of an ounce, a cup, a quart, a liter, and a gallon
Which One? activity sheet

Directions: Display the containers. Ask the students to identify the capacity, that is, the largest amount each container can hold. As each is correctly identified, write the capacity on the board. (*cup, quart,* etc.) Review by having one student choose a container and another student state its capacity. (*That holds 1 quart.*) Have the students generate items that commonly come in each of the containers. (*1 gallon of milk or water, 1 quart of juice,* etc.)

"If you were going to measure the amount of gasoline in a car, which measurement (point to the capacities on the board) would you use?" (*gallons*) "Why?" (*Gasoline usually is sold in gallons. It is a larger amount of liquid so you would not use a small measure*.) "If you were going to measure the amount of ink in a pen, which measurement (point to the capacities on the board) would you use?" (*ounces*) "Why?" (*It is a small amount of liquid so you would not use a large measure*.) Repeat the process using items such as soda (quart or liter) and soup (cup). "In the metric system all capacities, the largest amount a container can hold, are measured using liters."

Review the names of the containers. Distribute the Which One? activity sheet. The students will choose the appropriate unit of measure.

Answer Key: *Part One:* 1. oz; 2. gal; 3. gal; 4. cups; 5. liters. *Part Two:* 1. 55 cm; 2. 2 mi; 3. 320 ft. *Part Three:* 1. 2 L; 2. 3 gal; 3. 4 oz

Related Activity: The average bathtub holds 28 gallons of water. Taking a shower with a restricted-flow shower head uses 2½ gallons of water each minute. Would you use more water taking a bath or a 10-minute shower? (*bath, 10-minute shower would use 25 gallons of water*)

If you reduced a 10-minute shower to a 5-minute shower, how much water would you save each day? (*12.5 gallons a day*) How many days would it take to save enough water to fill an 8,000-gallon swimming pool? (*8,000 ÷ 12.5 = 640 days or 1 year and 275 days*)

■ 3-3. SQUARES AND RECTANGLES (Learning Level)

Objective: To describe the pattern that occurs in the area and perimeter of squares and rectangles when their sizes increase

Materials: Overhead transparency of Growing Squares (see appendix)
Several orange, square overhead pattern blocks
Overhead pen
Squares and Rectangles activity sheet

Directions: Display the Growing Squares transparency and place one square pattern block between the table and the title of the transparency. "Today we are going to explore the relationship of the area and perimeter of a figure to the size of that figure. (Review the definitions of perimeter and area.) This square (point to the square pattern block) has an area of 1 square inch. What is the perimeter of the figure?" (*4 inches*) "How do you know?" (*Each side is 1 inch in length and you count the number of sides*.) Place a second square onto the overhead so the edges of the squares are touching. (▭) "We now have two squares that make up this figure. What is the area of the figure?" (*2 square inches*) Fill in "2" on the table for the area of two squares. "How do you know?" (*There are two squares each with an area of 1 square inch*.) "What is the perimeter of the figure?" (*6 inches*) "How do you know?" (*Each side is 1 inch in length and you count the number of sides*.) Add "6" to the table for the perimeter of two squares. Add a third square so one of its edges is completely touching an edge of one of the other squares. Continue the questions and fill in the table for the area and perimeter. (*area of 3 square inches and perimeter of 8 inches*) Then add the fourth square (*area of 4 square inches and perimeter of 10 inches*), and then the fifth square (*area of 5 square inches and perimeter of 12 inches*), questioning the students and completing the table each time.

Draw the students' attention to the column of the number of squares and the column for the area. Refer the students to the first question below the table. "As the number of squares increased, what happened to the area of the figure?" (*It also increased*.) "The figure increased one square each time. How did the area increase?" As the students respond, write, "The area increased one square inch at a time, or +1." Draw the students' attention to the column for the number of squares and the column for the perimeter. "As the number of squares increased, what happened to the perimeter of the figure?" (*It also increased*.) "The figure increased one square each time. How did the perimeter increase?" As the students respond, write, "The perimeter increased 2 inches at a time, or +2."

"The patterns that you have found will continue so long as the figure keeps increasing. If the figure increases by one square each time, then the area will always increase +1 and the perimeter will increase +2. Now you are going to explore the patterns that occur when squares and rectangles increase in size." Distribute the Squares and Rectangles activity sheet. The students will interpret the patterns and look for similarities and differences.

Answer Key: 1. +5, +7, +9, +11; 2. +4; 3. +2; 4. +4; 5. +3; 6. +2; 7. +8, +10, +12, +14; 8. +4; 9. Both area and perimeter increased. The perimeter in Tables A, B, and D was +4. The area in Tables B and C increased by the same amount each time. 10. The area in Tables A and D increased different amounts each time.

Related Activity: The Picture Shop sells 36-inch wooden strips for making frames. Can you frame a 3-inch by 5-inch picture with one strip of wood? (*yes*) Can you frame a 5-inch by 7-inch picture with one strip of wood? (*yes*) Can you frame a 4-inch by 6-inch picture with one strip of wood? (*yes*) What is the greatest area you can frame with one wooden strip? (*9 × 9, 81 sq in*) How do you know?

■ 3-4. TANGRAMS FOR TWO (Learning Level)

Objective: To use the area of a given figure to determine the area of other figures

Materials: 3 triangle, 1 rhombus, 1 trapezoid, and 1 hexagon pattern block for each student
Overhead pattern blocks
Set of tangrams for each student
Tangrams for Two activity sheet

Directions: Place a green triangle pattern block onto the overhead. "Place one triangle pattern block on your desk. The area of this block is 1 square unit." Place a rhombus pattern onto the overhead. "Knowing that the area of the triangle is 1 square unit, what is the area of the rhombus?" (*2 square units*) How do you know?" (*Two triangles equal the area of a rhombus.*) Have the students place two triangles on top of the rhombus to reinforce the area of 2 square units. "If the area of two triangles is 2 square units and two triangles cover the area of the rhombus, then the area of the rhombus must also be 2 square units."

Place the trapezoid onto the overhead. "Knowing that the area of the triangle is 1 square unit, what is the area of the trapezoid?" (*3 square units*) "How do you know?" (*Three triangles equal the area of a trapezoid.*) Have the students place three triangles on top of the rhombus to reinforce the area of 3 square units. "If the area of three triangles is 3 square units and three triangles cover the area of the trapezoid, then the area of the trapezoid must also be 3 square units. Is there another way to use the pattern blocks to show that the area of the trapezoid is 3 square units?" (*a rhombus and a triangle: 2 square units + 1 square unit = 3 square units*)

Place the hexagon block onto the overhead. Have the students determine the area of the hexagon and show it with their blocks. (*6 square units*) Point out the different ways that students show 6 square units. (*a trapezoid and three triangles; a trapezoid, a rhombus, and a triangle; some students may use six triangles*) "Now you are going to explore the area of other figures." Distribute the Tangrams for Two activity sheet and a set of tangrams for each student. You may pair the students if you feel it will be beneficial. The students will use the area of the square tangram to determine the areas of the other pieces.

Answer Key: 1. ½ unit, 1 unit; 2. 2 triangles = 1 square; 3. 1 unit; 4. 2 small triangles = 1 medium triangle; 5. 2 units, 4 units; 6. 4 small triangles = 1 large triangle; 7. 1 unit; 8. 2 small triangles = 1 parallelogram; 9. 8 units

Related Activity: Distribute centimeter grid paper to the students and present this problem. The Fancy Restaurant has an herb garden. The garden is 12 feet long and 9 feet wide. The chef wants it divided into equal sections for six kinds of herbs and spices. Draw three different ways that the garden can be divided into six equal sections. (*4' × 4½', 6' × 3', 2' × 9'*)

■ **3-5. PIZZA TIME (Challenging Level)**

Objective: To determine and justify comparable units

Materials: Overhead pattern blocks
Set of pattern blocks for each student
Pizza Time activity sheet

Directions: Place an orange square overhead pattern block onto the overhead. Distribute pattern block sets to the students and instruct them to place a square pattern block on their desks. "We are going to have to use our imagination for a while today. We will also need some critical thinking. Imagine that this square is a cookie. What are some ingredients that you like in cookies?" Take several responses and then use them in the description. "Here is our chocolate, sugar, peanut butter cookie, and it is delicious. We have calculated all of our expenses and we can sell this cookie for 10 cents. What a bargain!" Now add two more squares and form ▭▭▭. Have the students add the squares to their figure. "This is our larger cookie. Remember that our small cookie sold for 10 cents. What would be a fair price for the large cookie?" (*30 cents*) "Why?" (*The small cookie sells for 10 cents and has an area of 1 square unit. The large cookie has an area of 3 square units. It is three times as large and should cost three times as much.*)

Remove the squares and place a green triangle pattern block onto the overhead. Instruct the students to do the same at their desks. Now have them imagine that the triangle is a piece of candy. Build it up as the most delicious candy, much like what was done with the cookie. The ingredients for the candy cost more, so the candy will cost 25 cents. Add three more triangles and form △. Present this as the large piece of candy. Still as delicious, just larger. Ask the students to determine and justify the fair price of the large candy. (*$1.00*) The small candy sells for 25 cents and has an area of 1 square unit. The large candy has an area of 4 square units. It is four times as large and should cost four times as much.

Distribute the Pizza Time activity sheet. "Now you have a problem that involves pizza. Use your imagination and critical thinking to determine a fair price for the large pizza." You may allow the students to work together if you do not think they have the ability to determine the area of a circle proficiently.

Answer Key: 1. $16.00; 2. Using the pizzas' diameter to find their areas the small pizza is 28.26 sq in and the large pizza is 113.04 sq in; $113 \div 28 = 4.03$, or approximately 4 times as large. The $4.00 price times 4 equals a price of $16.00.

Related Activity: Pair the students, distribute centimeter grid paper, and present this problem. Mrs. Chang purchased 48 feet of fence to enclose a garden in her backyard. She wants the garden to be in the shape of either a square or a rectangle and she wants to use all 48 feet of fence. Draw the 12 different garden plans Mrs. Chang can choose from. Which one gives her the most area? Remember the commutative property (see the glossary) and do not duplicate garden plans. (*1 × 23, 2 × 22, 3 × 21, 4 × 20, 5 × 19, 6 × 18, 7 × 17, 8 × 16, 9 × 15, 10 × 14, 11 × 13, 12 × 12; 12 × 12 is the largest area, 144 square feet*)

■ **3-6. HOW MUCH TIME DOES IT TAKE? (Learning Level)**

Objectives: To determine which of two events has a longer duration
To determine the duration of an event

Materials: Calculators
How Much Time Does It Take? activity sheet

Directions: "Which do you think would take longer, counting from 1 to 10 at a normal pace or eating a hot dog?" Take several responses and ask the students to state why they believe their response would take longer. Most answers will probably be "It takes longer to . . ." but give some other ideas, such as "You take a bite of the hot dog and then you have to chew it, and then you take another bite." Try to get students to see the details within the events. "Which do you think would take longer, washing your hands or brushing your teeth?" Once again, have the students justify their answers with details of the event. You may wish to have two students pantomime the actions to determine which takes longer.

Distribute the calculators. Review the time equivalents of 60 seconds = 1 minute and 60 minutes = 1 hour. Have the students convert 120 seconds to minutes (*2 minutes*), 155 seconds to minutes and seconds (*2 minutes 35 seconds*), and 200 seconds to minutes and seconds (*3 minutes 20 seconds*). Each time have the students explain how they determined their answers. Repeat the process, converting 120 minutes to 2 hours, 245 minutes to 4 hours 5 minutes, and 190 minutes to 3 hours 10 minutes. Each time have the students explain how they determined their answers.

Distribute the How Much Time Does It Take? activity sheet. The students will state and justify the longer of two events, and convert time measures.

Answer Key: 1–4. Answers will vary; 5. 1 hr 17 min, 1 hr 58 min, 2 hrs 45 min, 3 hrs 23 min; 6. 2 hrs 45 min; 7. 8 min 35 sec

Related Activity: Christi's family was going on a trip and bought an automatic water dispenser for her pet cat. The dispenser holds 3 liters of water and releases 50 mL of water each hour. Christi's family will leave at 9:00 A.M. on Friday and return 7:00 P.M. on Sunday. Is the dispenser large enough to water the cat while the family is away, or should they buy a larger dispenser? Explain your answer. (*The dispenser releases 1,000 mL, or 1 L, in 20 hours. It can dispense 3 L of water over 60 hours. The trip will last two days, 48 hours, plus 10 more hours on Sunday, equaling 58 hours. The dispenser is large enough.*)

■ 3-7. HOW LONG WILL IT TAKE? (Learning Level)

Objective: To determine the duration of time for events

Materials: Overhead transparency of How Long Will It Take? Clocks (see appendix)
How Long Will It Take? activity sheet

Directions: Write "duration" on the board. Ask the students to define duration. (*the time it takes for an event to occur*) Use the students' time at art or music (or other special programs) as an example of duration. Have the students generate other examples. (*the time between getting on the bus and arriving at school, the time spent sleeping at night,* etc.) Display the top two clocks of the How Long Will It Take? Clocks overhead. "We can tell the duration of an event by knowing some information about the event. If we know when it started and when it ended, we can determine the duration. Look at these two clocks. The plane left one airport at this time (3:00 P.M.) and arrived at another airport at this time (6:00 P.M.). What was the event?" (*the plane flight*) "How long was the flight?" (*3 hours*) "Yes, the duration of the flight was 3 hours. How did you figure 3 hours?" Allow several students to describe different methods for solving the problem. (*counting hours, subtraction,* etc.)

Draw attention to the second set of clocks. "Mr. Johnson works part-time at the grocery store. He starts work at this time (7:00 A.M.) and stops working at this time (9:30 A.M.). What is the event?"

(*Mr. Johnson's working time*) "How long does Mr. Johnson work?" (*2 hours 30 minutes*) "That is correct. The duration of Mr. Johnson's working time is 2 hours 30 minutes." Once again allow several students to describe their different methods for solving the problem.

Have the students independently solve the problem involving Daniel's band practice. When they finish, have them whisper their answer to a neighbor and see if he or she agrees. Discuss any disagreements as a class, allowing students to correct themselves. "Sometimes we do not know the starting and ending times. If we know one of the times and the duration, we can determine the other time." Instruct the students to read the problem dealing with Hakeem's karate practice. "What is the event?" (*getting to karate class*) "What do we know from reading the problem?" (*the duration of the event and the ending time of the event*) "What are we asked to find out?" (*the beginning time of the event*) Allow the students to solve the problem and then discuss the different ways that they determined 6:35.

Distribute the How Long Will It Take? activity sheet. The students will determine the duration of different events.

Answer Key: 1. 3½ hrs; 2. 2 hrs 45 min; 3. 5½ hrs; 4. 50 min; 5. 3½ hrs; 6. 4 hrs 45 min; 7. 7:50 A.M.

Related Activity: This activity allows the students to explore the relationship between the length of a pendulum and the number of swings during a fixed duration. The class is optimally divided into groups of three. Tie a 24-inch string onto a 2- to 3-inch washer. Provide each group with a washer and a ruler. A clock with a second hand that all the groups can see is also necessary. The students will conduct three experiments and record the data.

One student will measure and hold the string 6 inches from the washer, forming a pendulum. This student will hold the pendulum in front of her or him with her or his arm straight and parallel to the floor. The second student will raise the pendulum to a horizontal position, release the pendulum, and time 15 seconds on the clock. The third student will count the number of times the pendulum crosses the midline of the pendulum holder in the 15 seconds. This is considered the number of swings. The data are recorded for the length of the pendulum and the number of swings.

The students will switch roles and repeat the experiment with a 12-inch and an 18-inch pendulum, recording the data each time. When the experiments are completed, a class line graph can be constructed showing the average number of swings for each pendulum length. A discussion can follow leading to the generalization that the shorter the pendulum, the greater the number of swings.

■ **3-8. CHALLENGE TIME (Challenging Level)**

Objective: To determine the duration for events

Materials: Large display clock with movable hands
Individual clock with movable hands for each student
Challenge Time activity sheet

Directions: Distribute the individual clocks and place the display clock where all can see. "Here is a situation that we can explore that involves time. I have a friend named Mrs. Garcia who is a teacher at another school. She wants to have individual math conferences with each of the twenty students in her class. The conference with each student will last for 3 minutes. It will take 1 minute for a student to leave the table after the conference and the next student to come to the table and be ready for the conference. With this plan for time, can Mrs. Garcia complete all of her conferences in one hour?" Give the students a short time to think and take several "yes" or "no" responses. "What is the event?" (*having a conference with twenty students*)

Move the hands of the display clock to 1:00 and have the students do the same. "One o' clock is a convenient time to begin our exploration. The first student comes to the table. How long will the conference last?" (3 minutes) "Yes, the duration of the conference will be 3 minutes." Move the minute hand 3 minutes and have the students do the same. "Now the first student is finished. How long does it take to change students?" (1 minute) Move the minute hand 1 minute and have the students do the same. Repeat the dialogue for the second student's conference and move the minute hand, then the time for changing, and move the minute hand. There should be 8 elapsed minutes at this point. Repeat again for the third student. After the change, the duration of the event should be 12 minutes. "Now that you know that the duration for conferring with three students is 12 minutes, would anyone like to change their answer for Mrs. Garcia completing all of the conferences in one hour?" Allow the students to respond and state the reasons for their change. At this point, instruct the students to solve the problem and write a statement whether Mrs. Garcia can complete all of the conferences in one hour. (Mrs. Garcia cannot complete all of the conferences in one hour. It will take 79 minutes to complete all of the conferences.) You may wish to end the lesson here and return to it the next day. Save the students' work.

Briefly review the math conference problem and have the students share the different ways that they solved it. "Sometimes the duration of an event can be off and on over several days, or longer. We still look at how long it takes to complete the event. When you turn in your homework, then I have to review it. Let's say I spend 1 hour 30 minutes reviewing homework on Tuesday and 1 hour 45 minutes reviewing homework on Wednesday. How much time did I spend reviewing homework?" As you are stating the problem, write it on the board:

$$1 \text{ hr } 30 \text{ min}$$
$$+ 1 \text{ hr } 45 \text{ min}$$

"How would I go about solving this problem?" Have the students give the directions as you perform the steps. Make common errors such as those below and let the students correct you.

Wrong:

	60 minutes
1 hr 30 min	1 hr 30 min
+ 1 hr 45 min	+ 1 hr 45 min
2 hr 75 min	62 hr 15 min

Here are the correct steps: 1. Add the minutes. You are allowed to have up to 59 minutes in that column. 2. If there are more than 59 minutes, subtract 60 minutes. 3. Subtract 60 minutes from 75 minutes and leave 15 minutes. 4. Regroup the 60 minutes to 1 hour in the hours column. 5. The result is 3 hours 15 minutes.

$$1 \text{ hr}$$
$$1 \text{ hr } 30 \text{ min}$$
$$+ 1 \text{ hr } 45 \text{ min}$$
$$3 \text{ hr } 15 \text{ min}$$

This is intended to be review work for adding time. If this is introductory, then show several more examples before moving on.

Distribute the Challenge Time activity sheet. The students will determine the duration for several events. Since this is a challenging activity, you may wish to allow the students to work together in pairs or small groups.

Answer Key: 1. yes; 2. 15 groups at 5 min = 75 min, 14 groups at 3 min = 42 min, 75 min + 42 min = 117 min, which is less than 120 min (2 hrs); 3. 6; 4. 1½-hr movie + 30 min = 2 hrs—11:00, 1:00, 3:00, 5:00, 7:00, 9:00; 5. 13 hrs; 6. 2 hrs + 4 hrs + 5 hrs = 11 hrs, 45 min + 30 min + 45 min = 120 min = 2 hrs, 11 hrs + 2 hrs = 13 hrs; 7. 6:15 A.M.; 8. 10:45 + 7 hrs = 5:45, + ½ hr = 6:15.

Related Activity: Pair the students. Provide each group with a pair of dice of different colors (for example, a red die and a white die), paper, and a pencil. The students will take turns rolling the dice. The die of one color represents hours (1–6) and the die of the other color represents the minutes (10, 20, 30, 40, 50, 60). Both players start at 12:00 P.M. As they roll the dice they add the hours and minutes to their time. For example, a roll of 2 and 5 would be 2 hours 50 minutes. When added to 12:00, the new time would be 2:50 P.M. The first to make it to or past 12:00 A.M. wins.

■ **3-9. AROUND THE CLOCK (Learning Level)**

Objective: To correctly interpret a 24-hour clock

Materials: Overhead transparency of 24-Hour Clock (see appendix)
Around the Clock activity sheet

Directions: Write "military time" on the board and ask the students what it is. If any know, have them describe military time as best as they can. If no one knows the meaning, give the clue of "24-hour clock." *Military time* is a name given to the 24-hour clock since this way of telling time is used in the military. Our regular '12-hour clock' way of expressing time can cause confusion. The 24-hour clock keeps confusion to a minimum. Let's say that you have a very important plane to catch tomorrow. I call you to tell you to be at the airport no later than twelve-fifteen. When do you go to the airport? Fifteen minutes after noon? Fifteen minutes after midnight? Which midnight, the midnight of today or the midnight of tomorrow morning? The 24-hour clock takes away that confusion."

Continue, "The 24-hour clock time is the same as the regular time that you are familiar with. From 1:00 A.M. until 1:00 P.M. there is only one minor change. The time on a 24-hour clock is always written with four digits. Eight o'clock in the morning is written this way." Write "0800" on the board. "Ten o'clock is written like this. (1000) "Do you see any difference?" (*no*) "How do you think seven-thirty is written?" (*0730*) State several more times and have the students write them on the board. (*0615; 1155; 1230; 0220*) "This is very similar to the way we tell time now. The only difference is the four digits in the 24-hour clock."

"The difference in the 24-hour clock begins at 1:00 P.M. The number that comes after 12 is 13. When using the 24-hour clock, one o'clock becomes thirteen hours. It is written like this." (*1300*) "There is no confusion with A.M. or P.M. It means one o'clock in the afternoon." Display the 24-Hour Clock transparency. "Two o'clock in the afternoon becomes 14 hours, three o'clock becomes 15 hours, and it continues right around the clock." Use your finger to trace around the clock face, starting at 1 through 12 and then moving to 13 through 24. "Each position on the clock has two numbers. What is the difference between the two numbers?" (*12*) "So for each time that we know as P.M. you add 12 and you get the 24-hour time." Give the following times and have the students write the correct 24-hour time on the board. (8:00 P.M.—2000; 10:00 P.M.—2200; 7:30 P.M.—1930; 11:57 P.M.—23:57) Then give the following 24-hour times and have the students write the correct 12-hour time. (1415—2:15 P.M.; 1923—7:23 P.M.; 1020—10:20 A.M.; 1645—4:45 P.M.)

"Now you have the chance to practice using the 24-hour clock." Distribute the Around the Clock activity sheet. The students will interpret 24-hour time. If you feel it would be helpful, display the 24-Hour Clock transparency for student reference.

Answer Key: 1. 6:00 P.M.; 2. 9:00 A.M.; 3. 9:00 P.M.; 4. 5:30 A.M.; 5. 5:45 P.M.; 6. 1:10 P.M.; 7. 0943; 8. 1837; 9. 2325; 10. 1030; 11. 1215; 12. 2410; 13. 1800; 14. 0800; 15. 1700; 16. 0700

Related Activity: Fold two sheets of 8½-inch by 11-inch paper in half to form booklets, one for each student. Staple the sheets in the middle if possible. The students can decorate the front of their "personal calendar" and title the individual pages Monday, Tuesday, Wednesday, Thursday, Friday, Saturday, Sunday. Relate to the students how personal calendars are used to structure people's days and help to remind them of appointments, etc. Give the students a few events to put into their calendar such as music, art, physical education, or any assemblies. Have the students enter the events using the 24-hour clock. Then have the students add nonschool and personal events such as soccer practice, ballet class, parties, or visiting friends, once again using the 24-hour clock. Ask the students to keep adding to the calendar during the week.

■ **3-10. CHECK MY TEMPERATURE I (Learning Level)**

Objective: To convert Fahrenheit to Celsius

Materials: Individual thermometers with both Fahrenheit and Celsius scales
Calculators
Check My Temperature I activity sheet

Directions: Distribute the thermometers. Review the two scales by name (Fahrenheit and Celsius) and attributes (freezing temperature, boiling temperature). Instruct the students to read the scales and determine the temperature in both scales. Record both temperatures on the board. Then have the students hold the bulb of the thermometer between two fingers and watch the temperature reading rise. After a few minutes determine the temperatures in both scales again and record on the board.

"The thermometer measures the same amount of heat. The two scales show the temperatures in different ways." Compare the Fahrenheit and Celsius measures of the two temperatures taken earlier. "Using a thermometer with two scales is one way to get an approximate temperature for both Fahrenheit and Celsius, but there is a more accurate way. If we know the Fahrenheit temperature, we can use a formula to determine the Celsius temperature. Why might we want to find a Celsius temperature if we know the Fahrenheit?" (*may need it in a science experiment; may want to explain temperature to a friend who only understands Celsius; may need to do it for homework,* etc.)

Write the formula on the board as you state it. "C = 5/9 (F − 32). F stands for Fahrenheit. If we know the Fahrenheit temperature, we can determine the C, the Celsius temperature. Let's say that the temperature in the room is 72°F. Put 72 into the formula in place of F. Since F − 32 is in parentheses, we calculate that first as 72 − 32 = 40. The 40 is then multiplied by 5/9. Many calculators will not do calculations of fractions, so we multiply 40 by 5 and then divide the product by 9. That will give us the same value." Distribute the calculators and guide the students through the calculations. "Your answer should be 21.111111. We can round that to 21.1°C. How does it feel sitting in a room that is 21 degrees? Remember, it is all about numbers. The temperature of the air is still the same."

Distribute the Check My Temperature I activity sheet. Read through the sample conversion of 50°F together and then work through the 90°F sample together (*32.2 degrees Celsius*). The students will then convert the remaining temperatures into Celsius.

Answer Key: 1. 15; 2. 5; 3. 37

Related Activity: Choose a daily class meteorologist to take the local Fahrenheit temperature and convert it to Celsius without the rest of the class seeing this. Announce the Celsius temperature and have the class estimate the Fahrenheit temperature. Then have the meteorologist show how the temperature was calculated. Display both temperatures for each day of the week so the students can develop a sense of Celsius temperatures.

■ **3-11. CHECK MY TEMPERATURE II (Learning Level)**

Objective: To convert Celsius to Fahrenheit

Materials: Calculators
Check My Temperature II activity sheet

Directions: Review how to convert Fahrenheit to Celsius. State that temperature can also be converted from Celsius to Fahrenheit. "Many countries in the world use Celsius temperatures. When we travel, we would want to bring appropriate clothing for the climate. If we were to visit a country and the temperature was predicted to be around 28°C, what kind of clothing would you bring?" Take several responses.

Write the formula on the board as you state "F = 9/5C + 32. The C stands for Celsius. The Celsius temperature is multiplied by 9/5. Once again, many calculators will not perform this calculation, so multiply C by 9, divide the product by 5, then add 32." Distribute the calculators and guide the students through the calculations. "Your answer should be 82.4 degrees Fahrenheit. Some of you will be dressed for the weather. Some of you may need to buy cooler clothing when you get there."

Distribute the Check My Temperature II activity sheet. Read through the sample conversion of 15°C together and then work through the 30°C sample together (*86°F*). The students will then convert the remaining temperatures into Fahrenheit.

Answer Key: 1. 77; 2. 68; 3. 41

Related Activity: Provide temperatures from major cities around the world either from the newspaper or the Internet (weather.com is just one site). If the temperatures are reported in Fahrenheit, as some U.S. newspapers do, have the students convert them to Celsius. Locate the cities on a globe. Use the temperatures to start a discussion as to the season of the year for that part of the world (north or south of the equator), and if the temperatures in these areas change during the year, or are stable through the year (near to or far from the equator).

Keep track of the temperatures of two or three cities, one city approximately the same latitude as your location, and others in different latitudes, for an extended period of time. Study the temperatures to determine similarities and differences with your local temperatures.

■ **3-12. SARANTONIO (Challenging Level)**

Objective: To approximate Celsius and Fahrenheit temperatures

Materials: Calculators
Sarantonio activity sheet

Directions: Ask the students to state the formula for converting temperatures from Fahrenheit to Celsius and from Celsius to Fahrenheit. (Even though they have worked with the formulas recently, most students will not be able to remember. There is a noticeable lack of retention when teaching by rote.) The formulas are important, but can always be looked up. What is important is knowing what to do with them once you have them. Offer assistance in reconstructing C = 5/9(F − 32) and F = 9/5C + 32. Inform the students that there may be an easy way to get a good approximation of the temperature.

Distribute the Sarantonio activity sheet and calculators to the students. You may wish to allow the students to work in pairs. Read the first two paragraphs of the activity sheet with the students. The students will then convert temperatures using the standard method and this alternate method, and compare the results.

Answer Key: 1. 1.6°C, 2.5°C; 2. 12.20°C, 12°C; 3. 24.40°C, 23°C; 4. 121.1°C, 115°C; 5. close for 1 and very close for 2 and 3; 6. yes, easier to calculate; 7. 33.8°F, 32°F; 8. 50°F, 50°F; 9. 80.6°F, 84°F; 10. 230°F, 250°F; 11. close for 7, 8, and 9; 12. yes, close for the lower temperatures, easier to calculate

Related Activity: Write the standard Fahrenheit and Celsius conversion formulas on the board with the respective Sarantonio formula underneath. Rewrite the Sarantonio Celsius formula as C = 1/2 (F − 30) and ask if there is a difference between "one-half times" and " divide by 2." (*no difference, it means the same thing*) Instruct the students to conference with another student and determine why the Sarantonio method gives an answer that is close to the actual temperature. Provide hints as necessary. (C = 5/9 (F −32) and C = 1/2 (F – 30); 5/9 is close to 5/10, which would equal 1/2. 30 is close to 32 but is easier to subtract. F = 9/5C + 32 and F = (2 × C) + 30; 9/5 is close to 10/5, which would equal 2. 30 is close to 32 but is easier to add.)

■ **3-13. FROM HERE TO THERE (Beginning Level)**

Objective: To determine distance on a map

Materials: Overhead transparency of Jogging Path (see appendix)
Overhead pen
Calculators
From Here to There activity sheet

Directions: Display the Jogging Path transparency. "This is a map of a jogging path. What is this in the center?" (*a lake*) "Yes, a lake for pleasant scenery while jogging. Where would one begin jogging on this path?" (*at start*) "What other locations do you see on the map?" (*turn 1, turn 2, turn 3, and turn 4*) "What else do you see?" (*arrows and distances*) "The arrows show the direction for jogging and we also can see how far it is from one location to another. How far is it from the start to turn 1?" (*400 feet*) Record the distance on the transparency. Have the students determine the rest of the distances as you record them.

"If I were to make one complete lap, from start back to start, how far have I gone?" (*1,700 feet*) "How did you know?" Allow several students to explain their method for calculating the distance. "If I jogged around one time, have I jogged a mile?" (*no*) "Why not?" (*a mile is 5,280 feet; the path is only 1,700 feet*) "How many times would I have to go around the path to jog a mile? Don't figure it yet. Tell me how you would do it." Have several students explain their strategy for determining a mile. One example would be 5,280 − 1,700 = 3,580 − 1,700 = 1,880 − 1,700 = 180. It would take three laps plus approximately half the distance from start to turn 1.

Distribute the From Here to There activity sheet and calculators. "We know that 5,280 feet equals one mile. How would I find out the number of yards that equal one mile?" (*divide 5,280 by 3*) "Why?" (*There are 3 feet in 1 yard.*) "Now you will have the opportunity to look at another map and answer some questions." The students will determine distances on the map.

Answer Key: 1. 980 yds; 2. past start to playground is 450 yds, which is less than the other route of 530 yds; 3. no, 1,760 yds = 1 mi, only walked 1,430 yds; 4. 3 times completely around plus around to ball field. 2 mi = 3,520 yds, 980 yds × 3 = 2,940 yds + 150 yds + 300 yds + 230 yds = 3,620 yds

Related Activity: Mark off 5 or 6 yards in one-yard increments on the floor or preferably outside. Have the students determine the distance of their pace by walking normally and counting their steps until they are close to a whole yard: for example, 4 steps = 3 yards. Each student will then draw a map of the playground or outside area of the school. They will pace off distances between two locations and then convert the steps to yardage. For example, from the slide to the tree, 24 steps; if 4 steps = 3 yards, then 24 steps = 18 yards. When completed, the students can compare similar locations and see how close their estimated distances are.

■ **3-14. GO THAT WAY! (Learning Level)**

Objectives: To correctly interpret direction and distance on a map
To plot coordinates on a map

Materials: Rulers
Go That Way! activity sheet

Directions: Distribute rulers and the Go That Way! activity sheet. State that there are many different kinds of maps. This map is constructed as a grid. Here the roads all intersect at right angles. Have the students locate Main Street (*lower left of the grid*) and the road names that intersect Main Street (*1st through 7th Avenues*). Then locate the roads parallel to Main Street (*1st through 6th Streets*). What do the arrows indicate? (*one-way streets*) Finally, locate the compass and review the directions in relation to the map.

When locating positions on the map, emphasize using the avenues first and then the streets. This corresponds to the *x*-axis and the *y*-axis of a coordinate grid. This lesson will eventually ask the students to use the map as a coordinate grid. "Where is the house located?" (*1st Avenue and 1st Street*) "Where is the airport located?" (*2nd Avenue and 5th Street*) "Where is the fire station located?" (*4th Avenue and 4th Street*) "Where is the store located?" (*5th Avenue and 2nd Street*) "And finally, where is the school located?" (*7th Avenue and 6th Street*)

"This activity sheet asks you to follow a route on the map and then find other routes. You may draw the routes on this map and use a ruler if you desire. There are some questions that use the map like a coordinate grid. You may write in the numbers for the grid if you wish." The students will interpret direction and distance on the map.

Answer Key: 1. 13 blocks; 2. Answers will vary; 3. Answers will vary; 4. (4,2); 5. (3,4); 6. (1,5); 7. straight line (0,1) to (6,6)

Related Activity: Pair the students and provide each with a Go for the Gold activity sheet (see appendix). Without their partners seeing, the students will write the letters G, O, L, D, S, I, L, V, E, R on a different coordinate. The students will take turns calling out a coordinate, for example (3,4). If a letter is on that coordinate, it is recorded at the bottom of the caller's activity sheet. The object of the activity is to find the gold and silver on the other student's sheet.

3-1. The Right Unit

To do a good job you need the right tool. Listed below are some units of measure and tools that we would use for measuring in standard and metric systems. For each task listed, choose the correct standard unit or tool and the correct metric unit or tool for the task.

Standard	Metric
an inch ruler	a centimeter ruler
a yardstick	a meter stick
miles	kilometers

1. The length of an earthworm: _____ _____

2. The distance from your house to school: _____ _____

3. The height of a large tree: _____ _____

4. The length of your thumb: _____ _____

5. The distance from San Francisco to Tokyo, Japan: _____ _____

6. The distance from your classroom to the school office: _____ _____

7. The length of all your classmates lying head-to-toe: _____ _____

8. The distance a police car goes in one day: _____ _____

9. The length of your foot: _____ _____

10. In general, when would you measure using inches or centimeters? _____

_____

11. In general, when would you measure using yards or meters? _____

_____

12. In general, when would you measure using miles or kilometers? _____

_____

Name _____   Date _____

3-2. Which One?

Part One: For each example, identify the most appropriate unit of measure from those listed below.

ounces	cups	liters	gallons

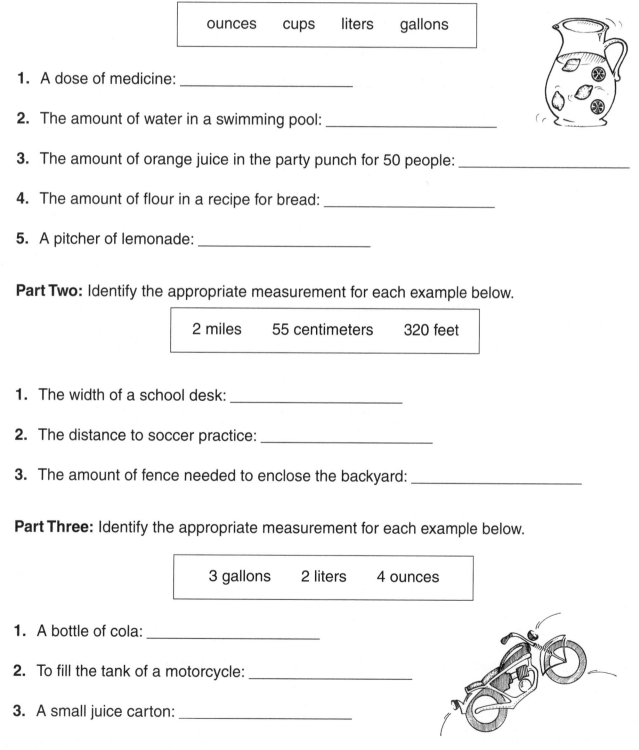

1. A dose of medicine: _____

2. The amount of water in a swimming pool: _____

3. The amount of orange juice in the party punch for 50 people: _____

4. The amount of flour in a recipe for bread: _____

5. A pitcher of lemonade: _____

Part Two: Identify the appropriate measurement for each example below.

2 miles	55 centimeters	320 feet

1. The width of a school desk: _____

2. The distance to soccer practice: _____

3. The amount of fence needed to enclose the backyard: _____

Part Three: Identify the appropriate measurement for each example below.

3 gallons	2 liters	4 ounces

1. A bottle of cola: _____

2. To fill the tank of a motorcycle: _____

3. A small juice carton: _____

95

3-3. Squares and Rectangles

Draw the different squares and rectangles on the centimeter grid paper. Fill in the area and perimeter on the tables and then describe the patterns you see.

Squares: Table A

Length	Width	Area	Perimeter
2	2	4	8
3	3		
4	4		
5	5		
6	6		

1. Describe the pattern for the area of a square as the sides increase in size.

_____

2. Describe the pattern for the perimeter of a square as the sides increase in size.

_____

Rectangles: Table B

Length	Width	Area	Perimeter
3	2	6	10
4	2		
5	2		
6	2		
7	2		

3. Describe the pattern for the area of a rectangle as the length increases in size.

_____

4. Describe the pattern for the perimeter of a rectangle as the length increases in size.

_____

3-3. Squares and Rectangles (continued)

Table C

Length	Width	Area	Perimeter
3	4	12	14
3	5		
3	6		
3	7		
3	8		

5. Describe the pattern for the area of a rectangle as the width increases in size.

_____

6. Describe the pattern for the perimeter of a rectangle as the width increases in size.

_____

Table D

Length	Width	Area	Perimeter
4	3	12	14
5	4		
6	5		
7	6		
8	7		

7. Describe the pattern for the area of a rectangle as the length and width increase in size.

_____

8. Describe the pattern for the perimeter of a rectangle as the length and width increase in size.

_____

9. What are some similarities in the patterns of Tables A, B, C, and D?

_____

10. What are some differences in the patterns of Tables A, B, C, and D?

_____

3-4. Tangrams for Two

There are seven pieces in a set of tangrams: two small triangles, a medium triangle, two large triangles, a square, and a parallelogram. The area of the square is 1 unit. Compare the other pieces to the square and determine the area of each piece. Then determine the area of all seven pieces together.

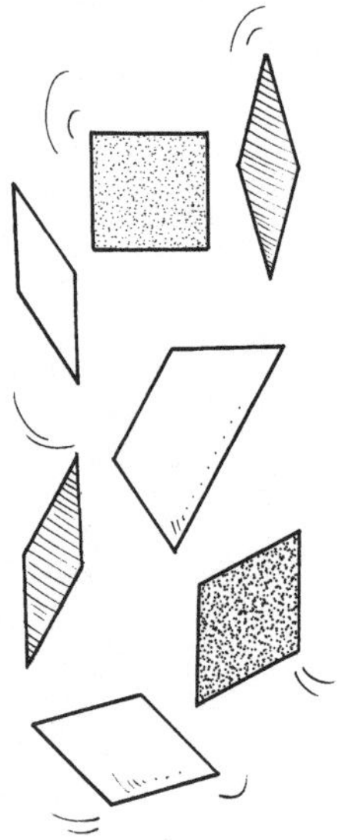

The area of the square is _____1 unit_____.

1. The area of one small triangle is _____.

   The area of the two small triangles together is _____.

2. How do you know? _____

   _____

3. The area of the medium triangle is _____.

4. How do you know? _____

   _____

5. The area of one large triangle is _____.

   The area of the two large triangles together is _____.

6. How do you know? _____

   _____

7. The area of the parallelogram is _____.

8. How do you know? _____

   _____

9. The area of all seven pieces together is _____.

3-5. Pizza Time

Mrs. Antonelli is opening a pizza store. She will be serving a 6-inch small cheese pizza and a 12-inch large cheese pizza. The small cheese pizza will sell for $4.00. Use this information to determine a fair price for the large cheese pizza.

6-inch pizza

12-inch pizza

The illustration shows that the 12-inch pizza is more than twice the size of the 6-inch pizza, so the answer would not be $8.00. One way to solve this problem is to determine the number of square inches in each pizza and then compare them.

1. What is a fair price for the large cheese pizza? _____

2. Justify your answer (tell why you think it is correct) by describing the steps you took to solve the problem.

3-6. How Much Time Does It Take?

Any event takes time to occur. Brushing your teeth takes an amount of time. Eating your breakfast takes an amount of time. Some events take more time than others, and some events take less time.

Think about each pair of events listed below. Draw a small clock over the event that you believe would take more time to complete. Each event would occur as it normally does. It is not completed as fast as possible.

© 2004 by John Wiley & Sons, Inc.

1. Walking around the outside of your school   Eating an ice cream cone

    Why do you think so? _____

2. Running around the outside of your school   Untying and tying your shoes 15 times

    Why do you think so? _____

3. Singing "The Star-Spangled Banner"   Singing "America the Beautiful"

    Why do you think so? _____

4. Eating lunch at school   Eating lunch at home

    Why do you think so? _____

5. Listed below are durations of four events. Rewrite the list in order from the event of shortest duration to the event of longest duration.

    3 hours 23 minutes   1 hour 17 minutes   2 hours 45 minutes   1 hour 58 minutes

    _____   _____   _____   _____

6. Hakeem spent 165 minutes doing his homework last week. How many hours and minutes is that? _____ hours _____ minutes

7. Julie took 515 seconds to eat her breakfast one morning. How many minutes and seconds is that? _____ minutes _____ seconds

3-7. How Long Will It Take?

Duration is the time during which an event occurs. It is how long an event takes. At some restaurants, dinner can take 20 minutes to finish. At fancy restaurants, it can sometimes take 2 hours to finish dinner. The event is the same, but the duration of time for the event is different. Determine the duration for each event below.

1. The football game started at ⬤ P.M. and ended at  ⬤ P.M.

   How long did it take to play the football game? _____

2. The school band concert started at ⬤ 3 P.M. and ended at  ⬤ P.M.

   How long was the school band concert? _____

3. Daniel's school day begins at ⬤ A.M. and ends at ⬤ 3 P.M.

   How long is Daniel's school day? _____

4. Mr. Gonzalez leaves home at 6:00 A.M. and arrives at school at 6:50 A.M. How long

   does it take Mr. Gonzalez to drive to school? _____

5. Michael's mother works part-time at the hospital. She begins work at 11:00 A.M. and

   finishes at 2:30 P.M. How long does her workday last? _____

6. Juan is flying to visit a friend in New York City. Juan's plane leaves Miami airport at
   10:15 A.M., stops one time in Washington, D.C., and arrives at the airport in New York
   at 3:00 P.M. How long was Juan's plane trip from Miami to New York?

   _____

7. Kanesha arrived at school at 8:45 A.M. It took her 20 minutes to walk to school,
   5 minutes to look in the window of the pet store along the way, and 30 minutes to
   eat breakfast and get ready to leave. What time did Kanesha sit down to eat breakfast?

   _____

Name _____   Date _____

3-8. Challenge Time

Solve each problem and justify your answer (tell why you think it is correct).

1. Mr. Johnson divides his class into 15 groups. Each group is to develop a 5-minute report. It takes 3 minutes between groups to move one group out and for the next group to set up. If each group takes its full five minutes, can all of the groups finish in less than 2 hours? _____

2. Explain why you think your answer is correct. _____

_____

3. The local movie theater is open from 11:00 A.M. until 11:00 P.M. A new movie is $1\frac{1}{2}$ hours long. It takes 30 minutes to empty and clean the theater between showings. What is the maximum number of times the theater can show the new movie?_____

4. Explain why you think your answer is correct. _____

_____

5. Sara works as a babysitter after school and on the weekends. On Thursday afternoon, she worked 2 hours 45 minutes. On Friday evening, she worked 4 hours 30 minutes. On Saturday night, she worked 5 hours 45 minutes. How many whole hours did Sara work those three days? _____

6. Explain why you think your answer is correct. _____

_____

_____

7. Mr. Brown drives a delivery truck for the bakery. He begins at 10:45 P.M. and works for $7\frac{1}{2}$ hours. What time is it when Mr. Brown stops working? _____

8. Explain why you think your answer is correct.

_____

_____

_____

Name _____   Date _____

3-9. Around the Clock

The time on a 24-hour clock is always written with four digits. The first two digits show the hour and the second two show the minutes. The symbols A.M. and P.M. are not necessary since there is no confusion over what time of the day one is referring to.

12-Hour Clock	24-Hour Clock	12-Hour Clock	24-Hour Clock
A.M. 1:00	0100	P.M. 1:00	1300
2:00	0200	2:00	1400
3:00	0300	3:00	1500
4:00	0400	4:00	1600
5:00	0500	5:00	1700
6:00	0600	6:00	1800
7:00	0700	7:00	1900
8:00	0800	8:00	2000
9:00	0900	9:00	2100
10:00	1000	10:00	2200
11:00	1100	11:00	2300
12:00	1200	12:00	2400
		also written as 0000	

Write the correct 12-hour time for each 24-hour time below. Use the A.M. or P.M. symbol.

1. 1800 _____

3. 2100 _____

5. 1745 _____

2. 0900 _____

4. 0530 _____

6. 1301 _____

Write the correct 24-hour time for each 12-hour time below.

7. 9:43 A.M. _____

9. 11:25 P.M. _____

11. 12:15 P.M. _____

8. 6:37 P.M. _____

10. 10:30 A.M. _____

12. 1:10 A.M. _____

When it is 12 noon (Eastern Standard Time) in New York, it is different times around the world. What time is it in the following cities in 24-hour time?

13. It is 6 hours later in Amsterdam. _____

14. It is 4 hours earlier in Anchorage. _____

15. It is 5 hours later in London. _____

16. It is 5 hours earlier in Honolulu. _____

3-10. Check My Temperature I

The first known thermometer was invented in 1593 by an Italian astronomer named Galileo. A German physicist named Gabriel Fahrenheit developed a more accurate thermometer using mercury in 1714. Anders Celsius presented his temperature scale in 1742.

If you know the Fahrenheit temperature, you can convert it to Celsius by using the following formula: $C = 5/9 (F - 32)$. Let's say that the temperature is 50°F.

Step 1. $(F - 32)$: $50 - 32 = 18$
Step 2. Multiply by 5: $18 \times 5 = 90$
Step 3. Divide by 9: $90 \div 9 = 10°C$, so 50°F = 10°C

Now it's your turn. Convert 90°F to Celsius.

Step 1. $(F - 32)$: _____

Step 2. Multiply by 5: _____

Step 3. Divide by 9: _____, so 90°F = _____°C

Convert the Fahrenheit temperatures to Celsius. Show your work.

1. One winter day in Atlanta, Georgia, the temperature was 59°F. What would be the Celsius temperature?

   Step 1. $(F - 32)$

   Step 2.

   Step 3.   59°F = _____°C

2. One winter day in Philadelphia, Pennsylvania, the temperature was 41°F. What would be the Celsius temperature?

   Step 1.

   Step 2.

   Step 3.   41°F = _____°C

3. The normal body temperature of a person is 98.6°F. What would be the Celsius temperature?

                                              98.6°F = _____°C

3-11. Check My Temperature II

Anders Celsius of Sweden presented his Celsius scale of temperatures in 1742. He based his temperature scale on his experiments with two fixed points: the temperature of thawing snow or ice, and the temperature of boiling water. Celsius temperatures are used in most of the countries in the world.

If you know the Celsius temperature, you can convert it to Fahrenheit by using the following formula: $F = 9/5C + 32$. Let's say that the temperature is 15°C.

Step 1. Multiply C by 9: $15 \times 9 = 135$

Step 2. Divide by 5: $135 \div 5 = 27$

Step 3. Add 32: $27 + 32 = 59$, so 15°C = 59°F

Now it's your turn. Convert 30°C to Fahrenheit.

Step 1. Multiply C by 9: _____

Step 2. Divide by 5: _____

Step 3. Add 32: _____, so 30°C = _____°F

Convert the Celsius temperatures to Fahrenheit. Show your work.

1. One winter day in Mexico City, the temperature was 25°C. What would be the Fahrenheit temperature?

   Step 1. Multiply C by 9:

   Step 2.

   Step 3.   25°C = _____°F

2. One winter day in Hong Kong, the temperature was 20°C. What would be the Fahrenheit temperature?

   Step 1.

   Step 2.

   Step 3.   20°C = _____°F

3. One winter day in London, the temperature was 5°C. What would be the Fahrenheit temperature?

                                             5°C = _____°F

3-12. Sarantonio

Sara and Antonio have been exploring the Fahrenheit and Celsius temperature scales. If you know the Celsius temperature, you can find the Fahrenheit temperature by using the formula F = 9/5C + 32. If you know the Fahrenheit temperature, you can find the Celsius temperature by using the formula C = 5/9 (F − 32).

Sara and Antonio want to present the Sarantonio method. They say it is easier to use. What we do not know is if it works. Let's take a look at the Sarantonio method.

- If you know the Fahrenheit temperature, you find the Celsius by using the formula:

    C = (F − 30) ÷ 2.

- If you know the Celsius temperature, you find the Fahrenheit by using the formula

    F = (2 × C) + 30.

Part One: For each given Fahrenheit temperature, use the standard formula and the Sarantonio formula to convert to Celsius. Round your answers to the nearest tenth of a degree.

Fahrenheit Temperature	Standard C = 5/9(F − 32)	Sarantonio C = (F − 30) ÷ 2
1. 35°F		
2. 54°F		
3. 76°F		
4. 250°F		

5. How close are the Celsius temperatures using the Sarantonio method to the standard Celsius temperatures? _____

_____

6. Do you think the Sarantonio method is a good way to estimate the actual Celsius temperature? _____ Why? _____

_____

Name _____   Date _____

3-12. Sarantonio (continued)

Part Two: For each given Celsius temperature, use the standard formula and the Sarantonio formula to convert to Fahrenheit. Round your answers to the nearest tenth of a degree.

Celsius Temperature	Standard $F = 9/5C + 32$	Sarantonio $F = (2 \times C) + 30$
7. 1°C		
8. 10°C		
9. 27°C		
10. 110°C		

11. How close are the Fahrenheit temperatures using the Sarantonio method to the standard Fahrenheit temperatures? _____

_____

12. Do you think that the Sarantonio method is a good way to estimate of the actual Fahrenheit temperature? _____ Why? _____

_____

3-13. From Here to There

The city park has a walking path that many adults and children use for exercise. The distances from one area of the park to another are marked so the walkers know how far they have traveled.

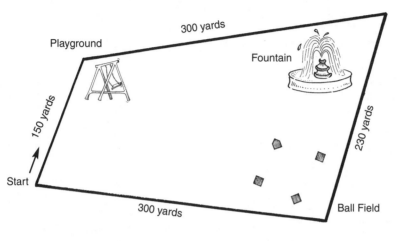

1. How far is it to walk around the path one time? _____

2. You are at the ball field and want to go to the playground. Using the path, which would be the shortest way? Explain how you determined your answer. _____

_____

3. Sara and Keisha walked around the course one time and then stopped when they got to the fountain the second time. Did the girls walk a mile? _____.

   How do you know? _____

   _____

4. In order to walk 2 miles, how many times would you have to walk completely around the path, and where would you stop after the last time around? _____

   Explain how you determined your answer. _____

   _____

   _____

Name _____   Date _____

3-14. Go That Way!

Ms. Rosa has a favorite route that she takes from her house to school each day. There are several one-way streets in town, so drivers must be careful. Trace Ms. Rosa's route on the street map.

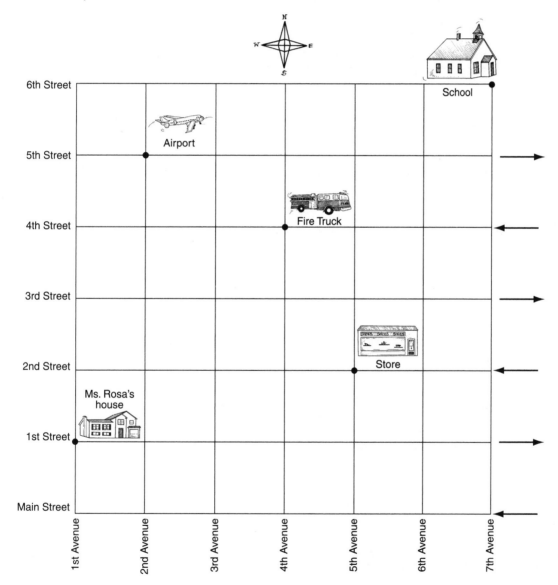

Each morning Ms. Rosa leaves her house and drives 2 blocks east on 1st Street. She then turns north on 3rd Avenue and drives 3 blocks. Ms. Rosa then turns west on 4th Street and then north on 2nd Avenue. She follows 2nd Avenue, turns east on 6th Street, and then drives 5 blocks to the school.

3-14. Go That Way! *(continued)*

1. How many blocks long is Ms. Rosa's route? _____

2. Determine a route from the house to school that is 11 blocks long and give Ms. Rosa the directions.

   _____

   _____

   _____

   _____

3. Determine the shortest route from school to Ms. Rosa's home and give her the directions.

   _____

   _____

   _____

The streets and avenues are designed like a coordinate grid. Main Street and 1st Avenue would be (0,0). The school would be (6,6).

4. Give the coordinates for the store. (____, ____)

5. Give the coordinates for the fire station. (____, ____)

6. Give the coordinates for the airport. (____, ____)

7. Ms. Rosa always thinks about a faster way to get to school. If Ms. Rosa had a helicopter, what would be the shortest distance from her home to school? Describe the route using coordinates.

   _____

   _____

   _____

Section 4

STATISTICS

Activity	Concept	Knowledge Level
4-1. Awards Assembly	Picture Graph	Learning
4-2. Play Ball!	Picture Graph	Challenging
4-3. Home-Run Leaders	Bar Graph	Learning
4-4. Sporting Goods Stores	Bar Graph	Learning
4-5. Run, Run, Run!	Bar Graph	Challenging
4-6. Average Rainfall in Florida	Line Graph	Learning
4-7. Student Absence	Line Graph	Learning
4-8. Terrific Tech Stock	Line Graph	Challenging
4-9. New Cars	Circle Graph	Beginning
4-10. School Lunches I	Circle Graph	Learning
4-11. School Lunches II	Circle Graph	Learning
4-12. Choose the Graph	Graphs	Challenging
4-13. Compact Discs	Mean	Beginning
4-14. Lunch Choices	Mean	Learning
4-15. Just Your Average Means	Mean	Challenging
4-16. Creating Data Sets	Central Tendencies	Challenging
4-17. Baseball	Stem-and-Leaf	Beginning
4-18. Canned Food Drive	Stem-and-Leaf	Learning
4-19. World Weather Watch	Stem-and-Leaf	Challenging

Teacher Directions

© 2004 by John Wiley & Sons, Inc.

■ **4-1. AWARDS ASSEMBLY (Learning Level)**

Objective: To interpret the data from a picture graph when each symbol is equal to more than one

Materials: Overhead transparency of the Bicycles Ridden to School picture graph (see appendix)
Awards Assembly activity sheet

Directions: Write a "/" on the board or overhead. "Let us say that I am counting ants at a picnic. Each slash is a symbol for, or represents, or is equal to 3 ants." Write a second "/" on the board. "How many ants does this represent?" (*6*) "Why six?" (*2 symbols each representing 3, 3 + 3 = 6*) Add two more slashes for a total of four. "How many ants does this represent?" (*12*) "Why?" (*4 symbols each representing 3, 4 × 3 = 12*)

Display the overhead of Bikes Ridden to School picture graph. "This is a picture graph, or pictograph. A picture graph uses pictures or representations to display data." Have the students interpret the data by determining how many bikes were ridden to school on Monday. (*35*) Ask why the answer is 35 and not 7. (*each symbol equals 5 bikes*) How do they know that each symbol is equal to 5 bikes? (*look at the key*) Continue with similar questions for the rest of the days. Stress that it is important to know the value of each symbol. Sometimes each is equal to only one, but often each symbol represents more than one.

Distribute the Awards Assembly activity sheet to the students. Have the students answer the questions by interpreting the data in the picture graph.

Answer Key: 1. 72; 2. 66; 3. 192; 4. 12; 5. 18; 6. 18; 7. 4

Related Activity: Provide pairs of students with a blank picture graph (see appendix). Relate the following story and record the data on the board at the same time. "Christi's class sold decorator candles for four weeks as part of their school's fundraising project. The class sold 8 candles the first week; they sold 16 candles the second week; 20 candles the third week; and 12 candles the fourth week. Use the data to construct a picture graph to show the candle sales for Christi's class with each symbol equal to 4 candles sold."

■ **4-2. PLAY BALL! (Challenging Level)**

Objective: To construct a picture graph with each symbol equal to more than one

Materials: Overhead transparency of a blank picture graph (see appendix)
Play Ball! activity sheet

Directions: Display this set of data on the board or where it can be seen by the students.

Animals at the veterinary hospital	
Cats	6
Dogs	9
Rabbits	3
Ferrets	2
Birds	5

Inform the students that the data are the inventory of animals that were in the veterinary hospital one night and that the data will be used to make a picture graph. Ask the students what would be a good title for the graph and write it on the blank graph once a title is decided on. Write the animals along the horizontal axis, one animal for each column. A symbol or picture is used to represent the data. Have the students decide on an easy-to-draw symbol (something simple, such as a red cross or an H for hospital) that will represent the animals.

Each symbol will represent two animals. Ask where that information will be displayed. (*the key*) Draw the symbol near the bottom of the overhead and follow with "= 2 animals." Draw a rectangle around it and label it "The Key." "Since there are 6 cats in the hospital and each symbol equals 2 cats, how many symbols would represent 6 cats?" (*3*) Starting with the bottom cell in the column labeled "Cats," draw the symbol to represent 2 cats, one more above that to represent 4 cats, and one more above that to represent 6 cats. "There are 9 dogs in the hospital. How many symbols would represent 9 dogs?" (*4 ½*) Starting with the bottom cell in the column labeled "Dogs," draw the symbol to represent 2 dogs, one more above that to represent 4 dogs, one more above that to represent 6 dogs, and one more above that to represent 8 dogs. "If I draw another symbol, that would represent 10 dogs. If I do not draw another symbol, that would represent 8 dogs. What do I do now?" (*draw ½ of a symbol*) "Why would we draw one-half of a symbol?" (*½ of 2 would be 1 and 8 + 1 = 9*)

Discuss ways that ½ of the symbol could be drawn and use the one that makes the most sense to the students. Continue with the data for the rabbits, ferrets, and birds. Have the students describe how to enter the data on the graph, and you draw, or allow students to draw, the symbols on the graph as they describe the process. Compare the data from the table and the completed picture graph. Stress that the data are the same, they just are in different forms.

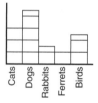

Distribute the Play Ball! activity sheet. Review the data in the table with the students and instruct them to construct a picture graph using those data. The students will create their own symbols. Have the students generate a couple of ideas for each sport so individuals can spend their time on the graph, not trying to think of symbols. Each symbol will equal two players.

Answer Key: *Part One:* baseball, 4½ symbols; basketball, 2½ symbols; football, 5½ symbols; field hockey, 5½ symbols; ice hockey, 3 symbols; volleyball, 3 symbols; water polo, 3½ symbols. *Part Two:* Answers will vary according to the students' questions.

Related Activity: Review the Bikes Ridden to School picture graph from Activity 4-1. Provide the students (they may be placed in pairs) with a blank picture graph. State that the data are changing and record the following data for all students to see: Monday, 65 bikes; Tuesday, 50 bikes; Wednesday, 55 bikes; Thursday, 40 bikes; and Friday, 25 bikes. Instruct the students to create a picture graph to show the new data, although this time each symbol is equal to 10 bikes.

■ **4-3. HOME-RUN LEADERS (Learning Level)**

Objectives: To interpret data from a bar graph
                   To complete a bar graph

Materials: Overhead transparency of the Favorite Sports bar graph (see appendix)
Baseball bat (borrow from physical education)
Home-Run Leaders activity sheet

Directions: Pick up the baseball bat and hold it for all to see. "How many of you have played baseball or softball and hit the ball with a bat? Are all bats the same?" (*no*) "How can they be different?" (*length, circumference, weight, color, made from wood or aluminum, the manufacturer of the bat*) "There are many differences in bats that we could explore, but what I want to know is what you might do in baseball that would give you a proud feeling?" (*Several possible responses, but wait for hitting a home run.*) "Yes, hitting a home run is something that is very popular in baseball. Name some baseball players who are good home-run hitters." (Take several responses.) "Who has hit the most home runs in professional baseball? You may not know his name, but he has the record for hitting the most home runs." (*Hank Aaron*) "We will explore home-run hitters more in a little while, but for now look at this graph." (Display the transparency of the Favorite Sports bar graph.)

"This is a bar graph, or a histogram. A bar graph displays data along a numeric scale. This graph shows the choices of favorite sport by the students at North Lake Elementary School. Each student was allowed to choose one sport. Approximately how many students chose soccer as their favorite sport?" (*180*) "How did you get your answer? Does anyone have a different answer? How did you get *your* answer? We seem to have several different answers. Why is it so hard to determine the exact answer?" (*The scale represents a wide range of numbers and it is difficult to determine the exact number.*)

Approximate the number of votes for basketball (*85*), football (*120*), skateboarding (*70*), and baseball/softball (*110*). Take several responses for each sport and have the students explain how they determined their answer. "Let's say that there were 90 votes for swimming. How would we add that data to the graph?" (*Add swimming to the horizontal axis and shade 2½ cells.*) Distribute the Home-Run Leaders activity sheet. Instruct the students to interpret the data from the graph by answering the questions and add data to the graph. Question 7 will require research to determine current totals. You may wish to assign two or three students to acquire this information and then report it to the rest of the class.

Answer Key: 1. 755; 2. 714; 3. 660; 4. 95; 5. 54; 6. 74; 7. 658. Answers will vary according to Bonds's current home-run total.

Related Activity: Each class member will survey as many people as possible to find their favorite radio station. Combine all of the data into one frequency table for the entire class. Provide pairs of students with a blank bar graph (see appendix) and instruct each pair to construct a bar graph using the class data. Give a reminder to include a title, a label for each axis, and an appropriate scale.

■ **4-4. SPORTING GOODS STORES (Learning Level)**

Objectives: To interpret data from a bar graph when each cell is equal to more than one
To interpret a cell that is not fully shaded

Materials: A recent *USA Today* newspaper, or graphs from a local newspaper
Sporting Goods Stores activity sheet

Directions: Hold up the *USA Today* newspaper and ask if anyone has seen the paper before. Show that the paper has four sections and describe each section. Point out the graph on the lower left corner of page 1. Describe the graph and the data it represents. State that graphs are used to give people a quick way of seeing data and that they make interpreting the data much easier. Show the graph on the first page of each section and describe the data to the students. Distribute the Sporting Goods Stores activity sheet. This activity allows the students to work with larger numbers and also interpret data when each cell equals more than one. Ask the students, "At what interval does the scale increase?" (*5,000*) Each fully shaded cell represents 5,000 responses. "Why does the graph start with 15,000 and why does it not include zero?" (*The smallest data are approximately 16,000, so starting at 15,000 saves time and space.*) "Approximately how many sporting goods stores were there in 1980?" (*31,000*) "Do we know exactly?" (*No. The data are large and we must use approximate numbers.*) "Is it very important to know if there were actually 30,950 sporting goods stores, or 31,025, or 31,060?" (*no*)

Allow the students to work in pairs or small groups to answer the questions and add the data from question 8 to the graph.

Answer Key: 1. 1985; 2. 36,000; 3. 1970; 4. 16,000; 5. 1990, 1995; 6. 1980, 1985, 1990, 1995; 7. 10,000; 8. 1980

Related Activity: Ask students to research different national fast-food chains on the Internet and look for the number of restaurants for each chain over the last 10 years. (One such Web site is: www.burgerking.com/company/facts.htm.) Have the students use the data to construct a bar graph for each fast-food chain. Emphasize a title for the graph, a label for each axis, and a consistent scale to accurately show the data.

■   **4-5. RUN, RUN, RUN! (Challenging Level)**

Objectives: To construct a bar graph from given data
To construct a bar graph with each cell equal to more than one

Materials: Run, Run, Run! activity sheet

Directions: Ask the students to name some fast land animals. Question students as to why they think the animal is fast or where they got their information. Ask how speed helps certain animals. (*capturing prey or escaping from a predator*) If they were going to construct a bar graph using the speed of certain land animals, what attributes of the graph should they include? (*title, label for each axis, scale*)

Distribute the Run, Run, Run! activity sheet. Review the data with the students and ask them to determine the scale for the graph. Have some students volunteer ideas for the scale and how they would write the numbers on the graph. Discuss several different options. Instruct the students to order the animals from greater to lesser speed and place them on the graph in that order. They should choose the scale that makes the most sense to them, and complete the bar graph on the activity sheet.

Answer Key: Answers will vary according to the scale chosen.

Related Activity: Have the students research on the Internet or in other resources (encyclopedias, almanacs, etc.) to find the five fastest land animals, the five fastest air animals, and the five fastest water animals. They should also find the speed for each animal. The students can then work in small groups and construct a bar graph for each category of animal.

■ **4-6. AVERAGE RAINFALL IN FLORIDA (Learning Level)**

Objective: To interpret data from a line graph

Materials: Overhead transparency of the Growth of a Bean Plant line graph (see appendix)
Overhead transparency of the School Fundraiser line graph (see appendix)
Average Rainfall in Florida activity sheet

Directions: Display the Growth of a Bean Plant line graph (frequency polygon), which shows the growth of a plant over a two-week period. "This is an example of a line graph, or frequency polygon. A line graph is best suited for displaying continuous data such as feet, centimeters, temperature, and ounces." The days are displayed on the horizontal axis, and the height of the plant on the vertical axis. Explain that line graphs are usually used to report the change in data, not necessarily the most and least. Ask students to determine the height of the plant on several days. Once they are able to read the graph, ask them how much the plant grew from one day to the next, or over a number of days. This is the typical use of a line graph. Pose a question about the direction of the line. Since it is constantly moving upward, it is showing consistent growth.

Display the School Fundraiser line graph. "The direction of the line might be different if we were graphing the amount of money collected each day for a school fundraiser. Let's say the school collected $200 on the first day. If the school collected $240 the following day, the line would move upward. However, if only $180 was collected on the next day, the line would move downward. The upward and downward movements show change in the data."

Distribute the Average Rainfall in Florida activity sheet. It is easy to see the months with the most rainfall and those with the least rainfall, but the line graph is usually used to report changes. Ask students to interpret the direction of the line from April to May (an increase) and the direction of the line from September to October (a decrease). Allow the students to interpret the graph by answering the questions.

Answer Key: 1. July; 2. May; 3. January, October, December; 4. It decreases, or becomes less; 5. It increases, or becomes more; 6. It is about the same; 7. 4½ in, 6 in minus 1½ in; 8. 2¼ in, 3¼ in minus 1 in; 9. 26 in; 10. 18 in

Related Acztivity: Place the students in pairs. Distribute several blank line graphs (see appendix) and ask the students to discuss and then draw the probable direction of the graph line. For example, try a line graph that shows a normal child's weight over the past five years. Since children usually gain weight each year, the graph line should move in an upward direction. A graph showing the amount of money earned each month from recycling drink cans should move up and down since there is no constant from one month to the next. Finally, a graph of the times for running a 200-meter race while one practices over the period of two months should move in a downward direction.

Upward   Inconsistent   Downward

■ **4-7. STUDENT ABSENCE (Learning Level)**

Objective: To interpret data from a line graph where the scale increases by more than one

Materials: Overhead transparency of the TV Watching Graph (see appendix)
Student Absence activity sheet

Directions: Display the TV Watching Graph, which shows the amount of TV watched by a student on a Thursday, Friday, Saturday, and Sunday night. Have the students determine the amount of TV that was watched on each night. (*120 minutes on Thursday, 240 minutes on Friday, 300 minutes on Saturday, and 180 minutes on Sunday*). Discuss how the data change from one day to the next and explore some reasons that the changes might occur.

Distribute the Student Absence activity sheet and review how to read a line graph. "Look to the scale on the vertical axis. How does the scale increase?" (*by tens*) "Locate October (Oct.) and move upward along its line until you reach the darker graph line. How many students were absent in October?" (*30*) Repeat for September. Since the graph line falls between two numbers on the scale, approximation is necessary. "How many students were absent in September?" (*15 or 16*) Allow the students to interpret the graph by answering the questions.

Answer Key: 1. 30, 70, 50, 10; 2. 15, 45, 35, 26; 3. November and February; 4. The number increased each month; 5. The number decreased each month; 6. illness, bad weather, holiday trips, etc.

Related Activity: Graph the student absences of your school. Have some of your students write a letter to your school office requesting the number of students absent for each month of the school year. Most schools will already have these data, so this should not add to the busy workload of the staff. The students will create a frequency table of the number of absences each month and then use the data to draw line graphs. The students can then form small groups and develop questions about the graphs. The groups will exchange and answer one another's questions.

■ **4-8. TERRIFIC TECH STOCK (Challenging Level)**

Objective: To create a line graph from given data

Materials: Overhead transparency of a blank line graph (see appendix)
At least 25 square overhead counters
Terrific Tech Stock activity sheet

Directions: Place the transparency of the blank line graph on the overhead. Write "Relationship of Side to Area of a Square" as the title of the graph. Label the horizontal axis "Length of Side" and the vertical axis "Area." Write "0" where the two axes meet and then "1," "2," "3," etc. along the horizontal axis. Write "2," "4," "6," etc. along the vertical axis. Explain that you will be graphing the relationship of the length of a side of a square to its area. Ask the students to define the term *area*. (*the number of square units to cover a surface*) Ask how to figure the area of a square. (*count the square units—length × width*)

Ask what would be the area of a square if each of its sides was zero units in length. (*zero square units*) We would not have a square. Label point (0,0). Place a square counter on the overhead. Ask what is the length of one side (*1 unit*) and area (*1 square unit*) of the square. "Run" along the horizontal axis until you reach 1 and then "jump" up to 1. Draw a dot, label it (1,1) and draw a line from (0,0) to (1,1). The next square would be 2 units on each side. Place four square counters on the overhead to form a square with 2 units on each side. Have the students determine the length of a side (*2 units*) and the area (*4 square units*). Run along the horizontal axis until you reach 2, then jump up to 4. Draw a dot, label it (2,4), and draw a line from (1,1) to (2,4).

Repeat the process with a square that measures 3 units on each side, and determine the area (*9 square units*). Since there is no 9 on the scale, ask students how to handle the problem. How will the students estimate where the point will go if the lines do not meet at an intersection? (*halfway between 8 and 10*) Mark the point (3,9). Continue with a square with 4 units on each side (*area = 16 square units and point is 4,16*) and a square with 5 units on each side (*area = 25 square units and point is 5,25*). At this time, stop and draw attention to the line. In which direction is it moving? (*upward*) Can the students predict where the line would be drawn for a square with 6 units on each side? (*area = 36 square units*) For a square with 7 units on each side? (*49 square units*) For a square with 10 units on each side? (*100 square units*) How are they calculating their answers, since they are not counting squares at this point? Will the line change direction? (*no*) Why not? (*Each time the side increases, the area also increases.*) Emphasize that we use line graphs to look at changes in the data. These data change by constantly increasing.

Distribute the Terrific Tech Stock activity sheet. Review the data with the students. Can they predict what direction the line might move? Why do they think this? What scale might the students use so all of the data will fit on the graph? After the discussion the students will construct the line graph to show the closing price data.

Answer Key: The graphs will vary according to the scale chosen. 1. upward; 2. The stock price doubled, so it changed. Accept reasonable answers for why it looks like the stock went up.

Related Activity: Choose five stocks that are reported in the newspaper or on the Internet. Have some of the students research the companies on the Internet and give a brief report about each (What do they do? How old are they? How big are they?) to the rest of the class. Each student will then choose one company and follow its stock trading price for two or three weeks. Each day choose a student to find the closing stock prices for the previous day for each of the companies. Post the prices for each day so the students can see if any changes are occurring. After two or three weeks, distribute a blank line graph to each student. Have the students title the graph and label each axis (horizontal will be Days and vertical will be Price), select an appropriate scale, and use the prices from their company to create a line graph. The students who chose the same company can meet to compare their graphs and interpret the direction of their line graph.

■ 4-9. NEW CARS (Beginning Level)

Objective: To interpret data from a circle graph

Materials: Overhead transparency of the Pizza Crust Preferences circle graph (see appendix)
Overhead transparency of the Summer Trip circle graph (see appendix)
New Cars activity sheet

Directions: "Raise your hand if you like pizza. That looks like just about everyone. What kind of pizza do you like?" (*Take several responses.*) "What type of crust do you like on your pizza?" (*Take several responses.*) "I have a graph that shows some students' preferences for the crust on their pizza. Before I display it, what does the word *preferences* mean?" (*a liking for something; a choice*) Display the graph on the overhead. "This is a circle graph. A circle graph uses sections of a circle to represent percentages of the data being shown. This circle graph shows the crust preferences of the fifth-grade students at Spotwood Elementary School. A circle graph uses regions, sections of the circle, to display the data. The circle is the whole and the regions are parts of the whole. The larger the region of the graph, the larger the value of that region. Look at the graph. Which is the largest region on the circle graph?" (*the stripes*) "Correct, the region that is shaded with stripes is the largest region. Which is the smallest region?" (*no shading*) "Correct, the section with no shading is the smallest region."

Draw the students' attention to the key that identifies each region. "Which crust is represented by stripes?" (*thin crust*) "Yes, it is thin crust. The stripes section is the largest region. Which type of crust received the most votes from the fifth-grade students?" (*thin crust*) "Correct! Which crust received the fewest votes?" (*pan*) "How do you know?" (*smallest region on the graph*) Continue, asking which crust received the second- and third-highest votes, and how the students knew the answers. "Circle graphs are very easy to read. Just remember that the size of the section tells us the value of that section."

Display the Summer Trip circle graph overhead. "This graph shows where the students from Spotwood Elementary School went on their summer vacations. What destination did most of the students travel to?" (*amusement park*) "What destination did the least number of students travel to?" (*the mountains*) Place one overhead on top of the other and display on the overhead. "What do you see about these graphs?" (*they both show the same size regions*) "The region that represents thin crust pizza and the region that represents amusement park are the same size. In the pizza survey 40 students chose thin crust. How many students do you think took a trip to the amusement park?" (*You will probably get an answer of 40.*) "Why do you think so?" (*The regions are the same size for both graphs.*) "That is logical thinking, but in this case it is not correct. Even though the two regions are the same size, the numbers they represent are not the same. A total of 100 students responded to the pizza survey. Of the 100 students, four-tenths, or 40, students preferred thin crust. A total of 300 students responded to the summer trip survey. Of the 300 students, four-tenths, or 120, students took a trip to the amusement park. You cannot compare two or more circle graphs just by looking at the size of the regions. The total number for each graph must be the same to compare the graphs using the size of the regions."

Ask the students what kinds of cars their families drive and if they have any idea what gas mileage the cars get. "Gas mileage represents the number of miles a car will run on a gallon of gasoline, or miles per gallon (mpg). It is an approximation, since many factors such as speed, hills, traffic, and the size of the car can cause changes in the gas mileage. Most car companies list their cars as getting a range of mileage, such as approximately 26 to 30 mpg."

Distribute the New Cars activity sheet and draw attention to the graph on the activity sheet. "We would not be able to interpret the graph without additional information, which is provided in the key. Here, different shadings represent different groups of vehicles that get certain gas mileage." Match each category in the key with its pie-shaped region on the graph. Allow the students to interpret the data by answering the questions.

Answer Key: 1. 21 to 25; 2. 31 and over; 3. 16 to 20; 4. no; 5. 21 to 25 and 26 to 30; 6. 10 to 15 and 26 to 30; 7. Answers will vary.

Related Activity: Have the students survey one another and members of other classes asking for their favorite TV show and favorite cookie. Enter the data into a computer database or statistics programs (such as AppleWorks), and create a bar graph and a circle graph for each set of data. Compare the circle and bar graphs of each data set and identify which categories are the most and least. Are the data different on the two graphs or are the data the same? (*The data remain the same. The graphs display the data in different ways.*)

Increase the favorite TV show data four times (multiply all data by 4). Use the computer to create a circle graph of the new data. Compare the new TV shows graph to the original cookie circle graph. "Are the graphs similar?" (*They should be.*) "Does each region mean the same number of responses on each graph?" (*No. There are four times as many responses on the new graph as on the original.*) Circle graphs, like other graphs, cannot be compared to one another unless the total number of responses is the same. Although two categories from two different graphs may have regions that are approximately ½ of the circles, they only represent percentages. One region may represent ½ of 100, while another region may represent ½ of 1,000.

■ 4-10. SCHOOL LUNCHES I (Learning Level)

Objective: To calculate a percentage of the total

Materials: Base-10 blocks (hundreds and ones)
Calculators
School Lunches I activity sheet

Directions: Write "%" on the board. "What is this?" (*percent*) "The term *percent* means 'for each hundred' or 'out of 100.'" (Write both phrases on the board.) "Let's say students were asked to vote for their favorite school lunch. If 10 percent of the students voted for spaghetti as their favorite lunch, it means that 10 students for each 100 students voted for spaghetti (point to the phrase), or 10 students out of 100 students voted for spaghetti (point to the phrase)."

Provide each student with one base-10 hundred flat and a supply of unit cubes. Refer to the flat. "What is the value of the flat?" (*100*) "How many individual squares are there?" (*100*) Place 10 ones (unit cubes) on the flat. "We said before that 10 percent of the students voted for spaghetti as their favorite lunch. That means 10 for each 100 or 10 out of 100. How many of the squares on your flat are covered?" (*10*) "Ten percent of your squares are covered."

Corn dogs received 25 percent of the votes for favorite school lunch. Have the students cover 25 percent of their flat. "How many ones did you use?" (*25*) "Why 25?" (*25 out of 100*) "When we calculate percent, we do not always have to have 100 votes or 100 cars. The percent tells how many it would have been out of 100. To calculate percent, we divide the part by the whole and then multiply by 100." Provide calculators for the students and distribute the School Lunches I activity sheet. Review the data for the favorite lunch and votes. Proceed to the first step. Guide the students through the steps to determine the percentage for hamburger. Make sure all of the students understand the process, then allow them to complete the percentages for the other four lunches and answer the questions.

Answer Key: *First Step:* 0.2, 20%; 0.25, 25%; 0.4, 40%; 0.1, 10%; 0.05, 5%; 1. 100%; 2. pizza; 3. pizza; 4. same data; 5. salad; 6. none; 7. pizza and sandwich; 8. hamburger, hot dog, and salad; 9. pizza and salad; 10. 15%; 11. 25%; 12. Answers will vary but should include some reference to "of 100" or "out of 100."

Related Activity: Survey the students on a topic and record the data on tally tables. Allow the students to convert the data to frequency tables and then calculate the percentage of the whole for the different responses. Possible topics could include the birth month of the students, their favorite ice cream flavor, their favorite drink, or the number of vowels in their first and last names.

■ 4-11. SCHOOL LUNCHES II (Learning Level)

Objectives: To calculate the number of degrees of a region of a circle
To construct a circle graph from given data
To interpret the data from the circle graph

Materials: Protractors
Overhead transparency of the blank circle graph (see appendix)
Large protractor or an overhead transparency of a protractor (see appendix)
Calculators
School Lunches II activity sheet

Directions: For this lesson the students should have had experience using a protractor to measure and draw angles. They should also have knowledge of percent and that there are 360 degrees in a circle. Ask the students their favorite color and record the results on a tally table. Convert the data to a frequency table. Distribute the calculators and, as a review, have the students determine the total responses and then calculate the percentage for each color. "In order to construct a circle graph, we have to find out how big each area or region will be. We do that by calculating the number of degrees in the angle that makes up the pie-shaped area. To calculate the number of degrees, divide the percentage by 100 and multiply that by 360. That gives the number of degrees in the angle. Why do we divide the percentage by 100?" (*It changes the percentage to a decimal. The value of it is still the same and can still be calculated as a percentage.*) "Why do you think we use 360?" (*There are 360 degrees in a circle.*) "Why do we multiply the decimal by 360?" (*It gives the percentage of the 360 degrees for that region.*) Calculate the degrees of the circle for each of the colors. Try to avoid decimals by rounding the degrees to the nearest whole, but be sure to have a total of 360 degrees.

Place the blank circle graph on the overhead. Use the overhead protractor and demonstrate how to draw the angles for each pie-shaped region using the center of the circle as the vertex for each. After the first one, ask the students to describe the steps for the other angles.

Organize the students into pairs. Distribute a protractor and the School Lunches II activity sheet to each pair. Review the data and the process for calculating percentages that has been completed in the first step. Have the students calculate the number of degrees for the hamburger lunch in the second step. (*72*) Allow the students to calculate the degrees of the circle for the remaining lunches. (*hot dog 90, pizza 144, sandwich 36, salad 18*) The total of all five lunches together should be 360 degrees. Instruct each pair of students to draw the 72-degree angle to represent the votes for hamburger. When you are satisfied that the pairs are able to draw the angle correctly, allow them to complete the circle graph. Remind them to color the key and the corresponding pie-shaped region the same color.

After the students complete the graph, they are to interpret the data by answering the questions. You may wish to end the lesson after the students draw the graphs, and have them answer the questions at another time.

Answer Key: *Second Step:* 20%, 0.2, 72; 25%, 0.25, 90; 40%, 0.4, 144; 10%, 0.1, 36; 5%, 0.05, 18. 1. pizza; 2. salad; 3. no; 4. hot dog; 5. pizza and sandwich; 6. pizza, hamburger, and salad; 7. All three lists are pizza, hot dog, hamburger, sandwich, salad; 8. All are the same since they are all formed from the same data.

Related Activity: The water of the world's oceans covers much of the world's surface. Scientists today tend to recognize only three main oceans: the Pacific Ocean, the Atlantic Ocean, and the Indian Ocean. The Pacific Ocean covers approximately 50 percent of the world's oceans, the Atlantic Ocean covers approximately 29 percent, and the Indian Ocean covers approximately 21 percent. Use the percentages to calculate the number of degrees of a circle for each ocean. Draw the correct angle for each ocean and color each angle a different color. Cut out the angles and paste them together to form a circle graph. Title the circle graph and provide a key to identify each ocean.

■ **4-12. CHOOSE THE GRAPH (Challenging Level)**

Objective: To choose the appropriate graph to fit the given data and situation

Materials: Choose the Graph activity sheet

Directions: A day or two before presenting this lesson, give the students an assignment to find graphs in newspapers or magazines and bring them to class the next day. Before the lesson, request that students who have several graphs share some with students who were unable to bring graphs. Write the terms "bar graph," "line graph," "picture graph," and "circle graph" on the board. Have the students tape their graphs under the correct type of graph. The students can examine all of the graphs to make sure they are all in the correct place.

Have the students identify attributes of the different types of graphs and write the attribute information under the respective graph. Include information of when and how the graphs are to be used. (See glossary.) Allow the students to use books and other resources if they need to find information about the graphs. Discuss how each type of graph differs from the other types. Distribute the Choose the Graph activity sheet. In pairs, allow the students to read each situation, discuss possible answers, and individually complete each section on the sheet.

Answer Key: 1. line graph, good for showing changes over time; 2. picture graph, compares amounts using symbols; 3. bar graph, able to show most and least; 4. circle graph, will easily show percentages

Related Activity: In pairs, have the students develop and write two situations that describe the use of graphs similar to the activity above. After completion, the pairs can trade their papers with other pairs and try to determine which graphs the others were writing about.

■ **4-13. COMPACT DISCS (Beginning Level)**

Objective: To calculate the mean of a data set

Materials: Dictionaries
Calculators
Compact Discs activity sheet

Directions: Write "average," "usual," "typical," and "mean" on the board. Have some students find and read aloud the definition for each of the words. Conduct a discussion about the meanings of the words *average*, *usual*, and *typical*, looking for similar ideas and how the words have similar meanings. Have a student read the definition for *mean*. He or she will probably read something that indicates bad-tempered or vicious. Ask if that has anything to do with math. Since it does not, is there another meaning that might be math oriented? Tie the definition of *mean* back to the ideas of average, usual, and typical.

Present the mean, or average, as a number that is used as the usual or typical for a set of data. The mean is calculated by totaling each value in the set of data and then dividing by the number of values. For example, Juan has 7 trading cards, Christi has 11 trading cards, and Kanesha has 12 trading cards. To find the mean number of trading cards for the three children, we total the amounts ($7 + 11 + 12 = 30$) and divide by the number of children (3). The mean, or average, number of trading cards for the three children is 10.

Write four or five current but different gasoline prices from your city or area on the board. "These are some of the prices of gasoline that I have seen locally. There are many places to buy gasoline in our city and there are many different prices for the gasoline. If someone asked me what was the price of gasoline in our city, which price would I tell them? The mean, or average, price of gasoline would be the typical or usual price for all of the city. Some gas prices would be higher, some would be lower, and some would be about the same. Instead of telling all of the prices, I could give the mean as one price that represents all of the places to buy gas in the city." Review the procedure to calculate the mean or average. Add all of the values and divide that by the number of values.

Distribute the Compact Discs activity sheet and calculators. Instruct the students to look at the table and read the problem. The questions in Part One can be answered one at a time as a group. The students can then individually calculate the means in the questions in Part Two.

Answer Key: *Part One:* 1. 28; 2. 4; 3. 26; 4. 3.25. *Part Two:* 1. 3; 2. 11; 3. 8.5; 4. 299.5; 5. 91.1

Related Activity: Ask the students how many CDs each owns. Record the data on the board or on chart paper. Have the students tell the steps to calculate the mean as you write what they say. Point out that many times, the mean is not a whole number or even part of the data set. Have the students write how they feel the mean describes the number of CDs they own.

■ 4-14. LUNCH CHOICES (Learning Level)

Objectives: To calculate the mean of a data set
To complete a data set according to given criteria

Materials: Calculators
Lunch Choices activity sheet

Directions: "We have been talking about the mean and finding the mean for different sets of data. To review, what is the mean, or average?" (*a number that is used as the usual or typical for a set of data*) Write "2, 4, 6" on the board. "If the data are 2, 4, and 6, what is the mean?" (*4*) "How did you get your answer?" (*2 + 4 + 6 = 12, 12 divided by 3 = 4*) Write "12, 5, 4, 7" on the board. "The data are 12, 5, 4, and 7. What is the mean?" (*7*) "How did you get your answer?" (*12 + 5 + 4 + 7 = 28, 28 divided by 4 = 7*)

"Let's look at the mean in a different way. Here is the problem. The mean or average is 4 and there are three numbers in the set of data." Write "4 { _ _ _ }" on the board. "What would be the total of those three numbers? There are three numbers in the data set and the mean is 4. Each of those numbers could be shown as 4." Write a 4 on each line. "What is the total value?" (*12*) "How did you get that answer?" (*4 + 4 + 4 or 3 × 4 = 12*) "We can always find the total by multiplying how many are in the data set by the average."

Write "5 { _ _ _ }" on the board. "The average is 5 and there are three numbers in the data set. What is the total?" (*15*) "How do you know?" (*5 + 5 + 5 or 3 × 5 = 15*) "Now, what other numbers would also work for this problem?" Have the students generate as many correct data sets as possible. (*3 + 5 + 7 = 15; 2 + 3 + 10 = 15; any three addends totaling 15.*) (See glossary.)

Draw six stick figures and label them child 1, child 2, etc. up to child 6. "The average number of ice pops eaten by six children is 3 pops. What data sets could there be?" Create as many data sets as possible totaling 18. Write the individual numbers under each stick figure. (*2 + 2 + 3 + 3 + 4 + 4 = 18 would be one of many solutions*)

Distribute the Lunch Choices activity sheet. The students will use the data presented in the table to answer the questions. Starting with question 6, the students will create possible sets of data.

Answer Key: 1. 87, 17.4; 2. 60, 12; 3. Thursday and Friday, numbers add up to 30; 4. Tuesday and Wednesday; 5. any sets of data that total 25; 6. 5 × 5 = 25; 7. any sets of data that total 54; 8. 9 × 6 = 54; 9. 50, 5 × 10 = 50; 10. any sets of data that total 50

Related Activity: Review the terms *median*, *mode*, and *range* (see glossary). Allow the students to collect data through surveys and then calculate the mean, the median, the mode, and the range of the data sets. Possible topics to survey could include the number of siblings in the household, the length of different people's feet, the height of individuals, or the number of computers in each classroom in the school.

■ 4-15. JUST YOUR AVERAGE MEANS (Challenging Level)

Objectives: To calculate the average of given data
To interpret the average

Materials: Calculators
A baseball or softball bat (borrow from physical education)
Just Your Average Means activity sheet

Directions: Take the bat and swing it a few times. "How many of you play baseball or softball? One of the things you get to do is hit the ball. What is it called when you come up to bat?" (*an at-bat*) "What is a hit?" (*get on base by hitting the ball*) "How can you tell if a player is a good batter?" (*look at the batting average*)

"Another way to look at the concept of average is as a measure. When we measure, we find out the value of something. It does not always mean with a ruler. One measure in baseball is called the batting average. When you divide the number of hits a batter gets by the number of at-bats (the number of times the batter tried to get a hit) you get the batting average. The higher the average, the better the batter is at getting hits. Because the number of hits will always be less than the number of at-bats, the batting average will always be less than one."

Distribute the calculators. Write " $\dfrac{40 \text{ hits}}{120 \text{ at-bats}}$ " on the board.

"The last time I played baseball or softball I had 40 hits in 120 at-bats. Let's figure my batting average. Enter 40 on your calculator and divide by 120. What is your answer?" (*0.3333333*) (If your students are familiar with rounding, include it in the instruction. If not, leave it for now.) "My batting average is three thirty-three." (Write "0.333" on the board.) "For batting averages, we usually use the three numbers after the decimal point and say it as if it were a whole number."

"Let's look at another example." Write " $\dfrac{70 \text{ hits}}{225 \text{ at-bats}}$ " on the board.

"Enter 70 on your calculator and divide by 225. What is your answer this time?" (*0.311*) "The batting average is three eleven. (Write "0.311" on the board.) "Which is a higher batting average, 0.333 or 0.311?" (*0.333*) "How do you know?" (*333 is greater than 311 so .333 is greater than .311.*) "Now I will let you find out about another good hitter. Use your calculators and answer the questions about Super Starr." Distribute the Just Your Average Means activity sheet. Go through the directions with the students to reinforce the concept and assure yourself of student understanding.

Answer Key: *Example:* 204, .314; 1. 154/451 = .341; 2. 66/202 = .327; 3. 72/218 = .330; 4. left-handed, .330 is greater than .327; 5. 138/420 = .329; 6. last season, .341 is greater than .329

Related Activity: Use newspapers or the Internet to explore batting averages for baseball players. Expand the search by looking for shooting percentages of basketball players (number of baskets divided by the number of shots) or completion rates of football quarterbacks (number of passes completed divided by the number of passes thrown).

■ **4-16. CREATING DATA SETS (Challenging Level)**

Objective: To complete a data set according to given criteria

Materials: Creating Data Sets activity sheet

Directions: Review the terms *median, mode, mean,* and *range* with the students. Write "2, 4, ___, 6, 9" on the board or on chart paper. Tell the students that this is a data set but that one datum (singular form) is missing. "If the median of the data set is 5, what number should be written in the space to make the data set correct, and why?" (*5, since the middle measure must be 5*) Write a 5 in the space and review why other numbers could not be used. Erase the 5 and use the same data set, but this time the mode is to be 9. "What measure should be written in the space so that the mode of the data set is 9, and why?" (*9, most frequent measure*) Write a 9 in the space and review why other numbers could not be used.

   Write "14, 12, 8, 7, _____, 12, 14" on the board. "What number should be written in the space so the mode of this data set is 14?" (*14*) "Why?" (*14 needs to be the most frequent*) Erase the 14. "What number should be written in the space so the range of the data set is 9?" (*5*) "Why?" (*The range is the highest measure minus the lowest. Since 14 is the highest measure, $14 - ? = 9$.*)

   Distribute the Creating Data Sets activity sheet. Review the directions and problem 1 with the students. Move to problem 3 and discuss the answers as a group. Pair the students and allow them to discuss and complete the rest of the problems.

Answer Key: 1. 35; 2. 15, $24 - 15 = 9$; 3. any number > 10 and ≤ 15, any number > 15 and ≤ 3; 4. 72 or 103, $96 - 72 = 24$ or $103 - 79 = 24$; 5. 14, 14, 14, most frequent; 6. 22, any number ≥ 22 and ≤ 27; 7. 11, 75 divided by 5; 8. 11, midway between 10 and 11

Related Activity: Place the students into small groups and have each group create three data sets with missing measures similar to the activity sheet. When completed, have the groups exchange papers and solve each other's problems. Allow discussion when groups disagree about answers.

■ **4-17. BASEBALL (Beginning Level)**

Objective: To interpret a stem-and-leaf plot

Materials: Overhead of a one-inch grid (see appendix)
                 Baseball activity sheet

Directions: Due to the length and complexity of this lesson, you may wish to present the content in two lessons. The first lesson could include creating the stem-and-leaf plot, and the second lesson could focus on interpreting the data.

   "What is a stem? (*part of a plant*) "How are stems and leaves connected?" (*leaves grow on stems*) "We have worked with picture graphs, bar graphs, line graphs, and circle graphs. Today we are going to look at another kind of a graph called a stem-and-leaf plot. It is a different kind of a graph and looks a little like a bar graph, but there are some special reasons that we use the stem-and-leaf plot."

   "Stem-and-leaf plots organize data and can be used to quickly see the range, mode, median, and mean of the data set. Frequently, stem-and-leaf plots show two-digit numbers but can be used to show higher numbers also. Let's take a look at one." Draw a vertical line near the left edge of the grid. Label the left side "Tens" and the right side "Ones." Draw another line in the center of the grid. Label the left side

"Stem" and the right side "Leaves." Remove the grid and place a blank transparency on the overhead. "Recently, some students took a science test. Here are their scores: 53, 89, 96, 77, 59, 64, 72, 85, 77, 64, 91, 80, 85, 93, 73, 87, 94, 55, 77, 70, 68, 60, 81, 78, and 84." Record the scores on the transparency as you are saying them.

"If we quickly wanted to know the mode, median, and mean of the test scores, we would have to find a way to display them and then figure out the statistics. A stem-and-leaf plot can help us." Move the scores toward the top of the overhead and place the grid below the numbers so both are showing. "When we look at the data, we can see that they are all two-digit numbers. What is the lowest score?" (*53*) "What is the highest score?" (*96*) "Our data set begins in the 50s and ends in the 90s." On the grid, write "5" in the cell under Tens. "Five tens will be for all of the scores in the 50s. The stem represents the same thing." On the same line, write "5" under Stem. "The stem represents the tens place."

Tens	Ones		Stem	Leaves			
5			5				

Move down one cell in the Tens column and write "6," then continue down with "7," "8," and "9." "These are the tens place digits for all of the rest of the scores. They represent 50, 60, 70, 80, and 90." Write "6," "7," "8," and "9" in the column for Stem. "The stem represents the tens place digit so these read 60, 70, 80, and 90."

"What is the first test score?" (*53*) Write a "3" under Ones and under Leaves. "The leaves represent the ones place. The stem represents 50 and the leaf 3, so the score of 53 is recorded. What is the next score?" (*89*) Point to the "8" under Tens and next to it write a "9" under Ones. Point to the "8" under Stem and next to it write a "9" under Leaves. "The stem represents 80 and the leaf 9, so the score of 89 is recorded. What is the next score?" (*96*) Add 96 to the Ones and Leaves columns. At this point, state that you will no longer be filling in the Tens and Ones columns. The information will be recorded under Stem and Leaves only. Fill in the next test scores by writing the numbers in the ones place under Leaves in the boxes to the right of the correct stem amount. Continue adding the data until all of the scores are recorded.

Tens	Ones		Stem	Leaves					
5	3		5	3	9	5			
6			6	4	4	8	0		
7			7	7	2	7	3	7	0	8
8	9		8	9	5	0	5	7	1	4
9	6		9	6	1	3	4			

"We now have all of the data but we still cannot use them properly." Write "Stem" and "Leaves" again to the right of the plot, but horizontally even with the data. "When we put the leaves in order, we can use the plot." Point to the first plot. "Here are the numbers 53, 59, and 55. Are they in numerical order?" (*no*) "What should the order be?" (*53, 55, 59*) Move over to the second plot. Write "5" under Stem and "3," "5," "9" in adjacent cells under Leaves. "Now the data for the 50s are in order. Let's look at the 60s." Write "6" under Stem and order the leaves from smallest to largest. (*0, 4, 4, 8*) Continue the procedure for the 70s, 80s, and 90s. Save the overheads for the next activity, "Canned Food Drive."

Stem	Leaves						
5	3	5	9				
6	0	4	4	8			
7	0	2	3	7	7	7	8
8	0	1	4	5	5	7	9
9	1	3	4	6			

"Here is the ordered plot, and now we can use it. It gives us a picture of what the data look like. If we say that the data are concentrated, then they fit nicely together. They are not spread out. If they were spread out, we would call them scattered. Which stem and leaf had the most scores?" (*70s and 80s*) "How many scores were in each?" (*7*) "Which had the least scores?" (*50s*) "How many were there?" (*3*) "What is the range of the data?" (*43*) "How did you get the answer?" (*highest score minus lowest score: 96 – 53*) "We can easily see the highest and lowest score on the plot. What is the mode?" (*77*) "How do you know?" (*three leaves of 7*) "Yes, it is very easy to see the mode of the data when using a stem-and-leaf plot."

"The median is also easy but you have to be careful. What is the median?" (*the middle measure*) "How do you find the middle measure if all of the data are ordered in a straight line?" (*count to determine the middle measure*) "We do the same thing, but the data are not in a straight line. Follow along. How many scores were in this data set?" Begin counting at 53, then to 55, then to 59, then back to 60, then 64, until you reach 96. "We have 25 scores. It is important to come back to the stem each time you reach the end of the leaves. That keeps you in numerical order. We have 25 scores. Which score is the middle measure?" (*the thirteenth*) Begin at 53 and count to the thirteenth score, emphasizing returning to the stem at the end of each row of leaves to keep in numerical order. "The median of the data set is 77."

Briefly review the steps of recording the data as stems and leaves on a plot and ordering the data onto a second plot. The ordered plot is used to determine the statistics. The instruction was given using a grid paper. The grid paper is not necessary if the students space the leaves by pretending that there is grid paper. All of the leaves should be approximately the same spacing apart and under the ones above them. This allows us to see the shape of the data and make some preliminary estimations of the statistics of the data set. Distribute the Baseball activity sheet and allow the students to work through the stem-and-leaf process, and then interpret the data by answering the questions.

Answer Key: 1. 60; 2. 100; 3. 16; 4. 5; 5. 8; 6. 104; 7. 53; 8. 104 – 53 = 51; 9. concentrated; 10. 65 or 82 or 90; 11. 80

Related Activity: Pair the students and provide each with a pair of dice of different colors. The students will designate one die as the tens and the other as the ones. The students will roll the dice and record the result as a two-digit number. For example, if they rolled a 4 with the tens die and a 2 with the ones die, the result would be 42. Each pair of students will roll the dice 100 times and record each result on a stem-and-leaf plot. They will then order the leaves and determine the range, mode, median, and approximate mean of their data set. When finished, they can compare their data with other pairs and discuss any similarities and differences.

■ **4-18. CANNED FOOD DRIVE (Learning Level)**

Objectives: To complete a stem-and-leaf plot
                  To interpret a stem-and-leaf plot

Materials: Overheads from the science scores stem-and-leaf plot from activity 4-17
                 Canned Food Drive activity sheet

Directions: Display the overhead of the science test scores. Remind the students of where they came from and ask them to give step-by-step directions of how to construct a stem-and-leaf plot. (Determine and write the numbers for the stem, and add the leaves as they occur. Order the leaves on a second plot.) Display the science test score plots. "Gaps in the data are where there are no data." Cover the leaves in the 60s with your finger or a piece of paper. "If there were no scores in the 60s, there would be a gap." Remove the finger or paper. "Are there any gaps in this data?" (*no*) "There are no gaps in this data. If we say that the data are concentrated, then they fit nicely together. They are not spread out. If they were spread out, we would call them scattered. Are these data concentrated or scattered?" (*concentrated*)

Distribute the Canned Food Drive activity sheet. The students will complete the stem-and-leaf plot and then use the plot to answer the questions.

Answer Key: 1. 28, 97; 2. 97 – 28 = 69; 3. concentrated; 4. only small gaps in the data, most of the scores are together; 5. 68; 6. 65; 7. 68.9 (any estimate between 65 and 71 would be acceptable)

Related Activity: Mount a long inch-measuring tape vertically on a wall and a large piece of grid paper near it. Mark the grid paper as follows:

Stem	Leaf
3	
4	
5	
6	

Each student will measure his or her height to the nearest inch and record the measure on the stem-and-leaf plot. The tens place of the student's height is the stem, and the leaf is the ones place. After all of the students have recorded their heights, produce a second grid and order the leaves. Then have the class discuss and interpret the range, the mode, the median, and any gaps in the data, and approximate the mean. Tell the students to remember their height and save the grid sheet for the next activity.

■ **4-19. WORLD WEATHER WATCH (Challenging Level)**

Objective: To construct and interpret a stem-and-leaf plot

Materials: World map or a globe
Ten little flags with tape at one end
World Weather Watch activity sheet

Directions: Choose eight or ten of the cities from the World Weather Watch activity sheet. Write a city on the board and ask who knows where the city is located. Once it is found on the map, allow a student to tape a flag at its location. Continue until all or most of the cities are located. You may wish to point out a few more of the cities.

Tell the students that they will look at the high temperature (Fahrenheit) of several cities from around the world on a recent spring day. They will use the temperatures to construct a stem-and-leaf plot and will use the plot to interpret the data by answering the questions.

Answer Key: 1. $91 - 60 = 31$; 2. 68; 3. 68; 4. no really extreme data; 5. 70.8 (any estimate from 67 to 73 would be acceptable); 6. not symmetrical, many data in 60s

Related Activity: Display the ordered grid sheet of the students' heights from the previous related activity. Place yarn or tape on the floor to produce the lines of the stem-and-leaf plot and the numbers 3, 4, 5, and 6 written with a dark marker on a sheet of 18-inch by 12-inch paper. Write the number for each leaf with a dark marker on 8½-inch by 11-inch paper. Tell the students that they will be making a living stem-and-leaf plot. Read the plot starting with the smallest value. As each student's height is announced, that student will sit in the corresponding place on the living plot. Remind them that even though there are no grid lines on the floor, correct spacing should be maintained.

The main drawback of a living plot or graph is that the students cannot observe the finished product since they are part of it. Use a video camera or regular camera to take pictures of the living stem-and-leaf plot. The students should hold their "leaf" right under their chins so all of the data and their faces are visible. The finished video or pictures can be viewed by the class and serve as reinforcement for stem-and-leaf plots.

4-1. Awards Assembly

Central Elementary School held an assembly to present awards to the third-, fourth-, and fifth-grade students in the school. The awards were for their schoolwork, attendance, behavior, help to others, and athletics. The picture graph shows the number of awards presented in each grade level. Use the data to answer the questions.

Number of Awards Presented

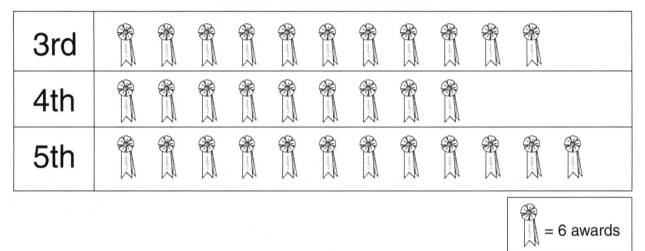

= 6 awards

1. How many awards were presented to fifth-grade students? _____

2. How many awards were presented to third-grade students? _____

3. How many awards were presented in total? _____

4. How many more awards were presented to third-grade students than to fourth-grade students? _____

5. How many more awards were presented to fifth-grade students than to fourth-grade students? _____

6. How many more awards would the fourth-grade students need to equal the number of awards for the fifth-grade students? _____

7. How many symbols should be added to the graph to make the number of awards for third-grade students *and* fourth-grade students, equal to the number of awards for fifth-grade students? _____

Name _____   Date _____

4-2. Play Ball!

Part One: The rules of many sports state the official number of players who are on the field or on the court at one time. Use the data listed below to construct a picture graph to show the official number of players for each team sport. Create your own symbol that will equal two players. Be sure to provide a key and to title the graph.

Sport	Players
Baseball	9
Basketball	5
Football	11
Field Hockey	11
Ice Hockey	6
Volleyball	6
Water Polo	7

Key:

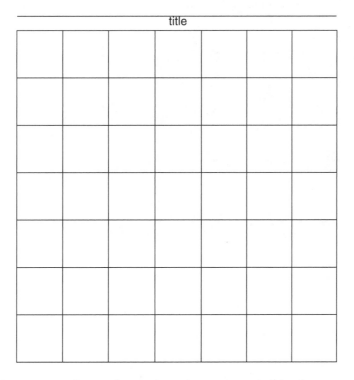

title

Part Two: Create three questions about the picture graph. Trade papers with a classmate and answer each other's questions.

4-3. Home-Run Leaders

Henry "Hank" Aaron is baseball's all-time leader in home runs. Babe Ruth had held the record for many years and many people felt that the record would not be broken. Hank Aaron not only hit as many home runs as Babe Ruth, he went on to hit more home runs. Use the bar graph that shows the number of home runs hit through the end of the 2003 baseball season to answer the questions below.

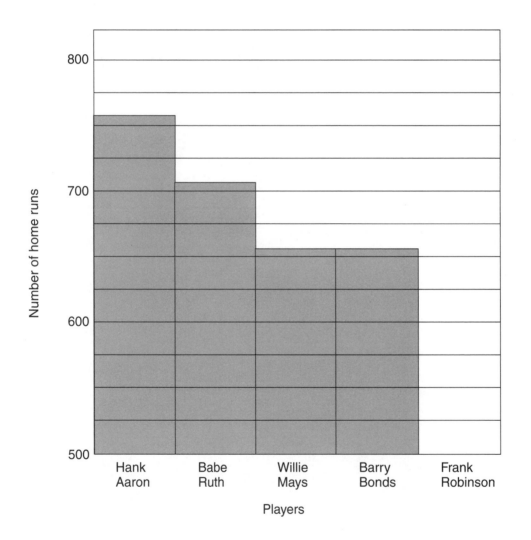

1. Approximately how many home runs did Hank Aaron hit? _____

2. Approximately how many home runs did Babe Ruth hit? _____

4-3. Home-Run Leaders (*continued*)

3. Approximately how many home runs did Willie Mays hit? _____

4. Approximately how many more home runs did Hank Aaron hit than Willie Mays? _____

5. Approximately how many more home runs did Babe Ruth hit than Willie Mays? _____

During his career Frank Robinson hit 586 home runs and is in fifth place in total home runs. Add Robinson's data to the graph.

6. Using the data from the graph, tell approximately how many more home runs Willie Mays hit than Frank Robinson hit? _____

7. Barry Bonds was still playing baseball through the end of the 2003 baseball season. How many home runs did Barry Bonds hit? _____ Check the Internet (www.mlb.com) or other resources such as almanacs for Bonds's current number of home runs. How many more home runs does Bonds need to have hit as many as Hank Aaron? _____

4-4. Sporting Goods Stores

The bar graph below shows the approximate number of sporting goods stores in the United States for 25 years. Bar graphs are also referred to as histograms. Use the bar graph to answer the questions.

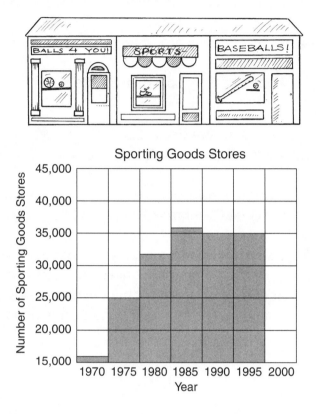

1. What year on the bar graph shows the largest number of sporting goods stores?

_____

2. Approximately how many sporting goods stores were there in that year?

_____

3. What year on the bar graph shows the least number of sporting goods stores?

_____

4. Approximately how many sporting goods stores were there in that year? _____

5. What two years show approximately the same number of sporting goods stores?

_____ and _____

6. Which years show more than 30,000 sporting goods stores in the United States?

_____ _____ _____ _____

7. Approximately how many more sporting goods stores were there in 1995 than 1975?

_____

8. Let's say that in the year 2000 there were approximately 33,000 sporting goods stores. Add to the bar graph to show this data. This would be approximately the same number of stores as what year on the bar graph? _____

4-5. Run, Run, Run!

The table shows the top speed of land animals in miles per hour (mph). Construct a bar graph for the set of data. Be sure to include a title for the graph, label each axis, and choose an appropriate scale.

Animal	Top speed in mph
Antelope	62
Cheetah	70
Elk	45
Gazelle	50
Horse	46
Lion	50
Zebra	40

4-6. Average Rainfall in Florida

Due to the climate, the state of Florida does not get the same amount of rainfall in each month during the year. Some months it is very wet and some months it is very dry. This line graph shows the average rainfall in Florida. Use the line graph to answer the following questions.

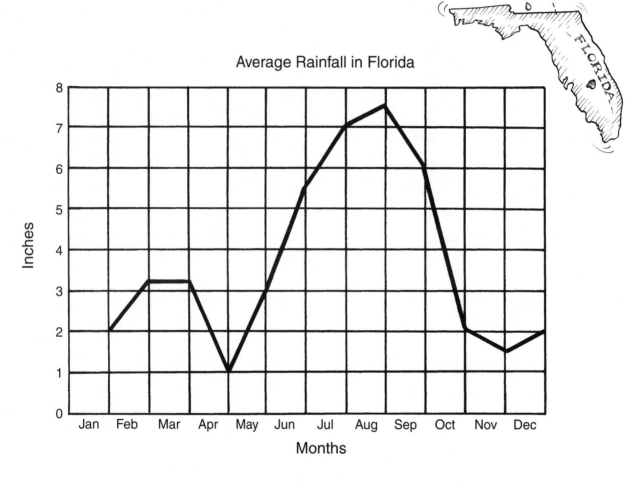

Average Rainfall in Florida

Months

© 2004 by John Wiley & Sons, Inc.

1. Which month averages 7 inches of rain? _____

2. Which month averages 3 inches of rain? _____

3. Which three months had the same average rainfall? _____

_____ and _____

4-6. Average Rainfall in Florida (continued)

4. How does the rainfall change from April to August?

_____

5. How does the rainfall change from August to October?

_____

6. How does the rainfall change from February to March?

_____

7. On average, approximately how much more rainfall does Florida get in September than in November?

_____

How did you get your answer?

_____

_____

8. On average, approximately how much more rainfall does Florida get in March than in April?

_____

How did you get your answer?

_____

_____

9. Florida's rainy season lasts four months. Approximately how much rainfall can Floridians expect during those four months?

_____

10. Approximately how much rainfall can Floridians expect during the other eight months?

_____

4-7. Student Absence

Line graphs, also called frequency polygons, are used to display information. They usually show how data change over a period of time. Although the most and least are easily seen, the main purpose of the line graph is to show change. Principal Liu wanted to look at the changes in students being absent from school through the school year. Use the graph that Principal Liu created to answer the questions below.

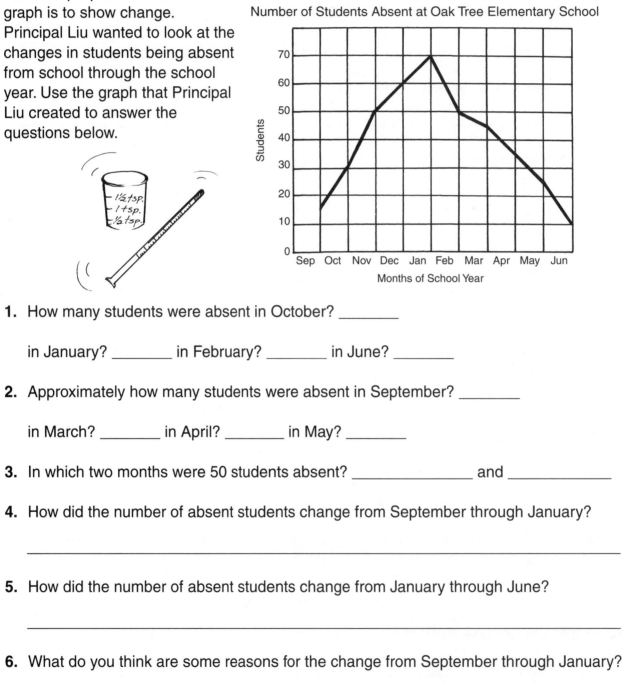

Number of Students Absent at Oak Tree Elementary School

Months of School Year

1. How many students were absent in October? _____

   in January? _____ in February? _____ in June? _____

2. Approximately how many students were absent in September? _____

   in March? _____ in April? _____ in May? _____

3. In which two months were 50 students absent? _____ and _____

4. How did the number of absent students change from September through January?

   _____

5. How did the number of absent students change from January through June?

   _____

6. What do you think are some reasons for the change from September through January?

   _____

4-8. Terrific Tech Stock

Listed below are the closing prices for stock in the Terrific Tech company for six months. Use the data to create a line graph. Remember to include a title for the graph, label each axis, and use an appropriate scale. Then use the line graph to answer the questions.

Month	Closing Price
January	$ 1.65
February	$ 2.37
March	$ 2.20
April	$ 2.43
May	$ 2.87
June	$ 3.24

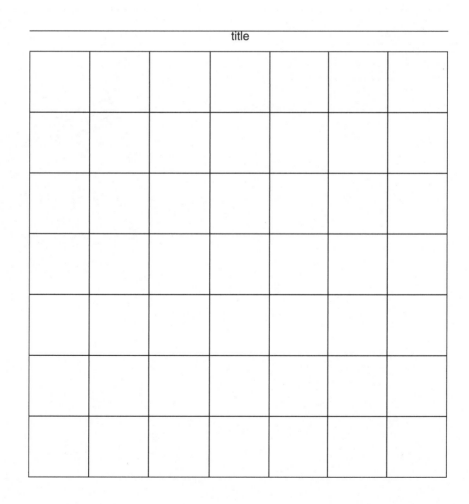

title

4-8. Terrific Tech Stock *(continued)*

1. What is the general direction of the line? _____

2. Did the price of the stock remain about the same for the six months or did it change quite a bit?

    _____

    Why do you think so?

    _____

    _____

    _____

    _____

    _____

    _____

Name _____   Date _____

4-9. New Cars

A magazine recently published the overall gas mileage for 100 models of new cars. (Miles per gallon is abbreviated as mpg.) The cars were grouped according to the following categories: 10 to 15 mpg, 16 to 20 mpg, 21 to 25 mpg, 26 to 30 mpg, and 31 mpg and over. A circle graph (also known as a pie chart) was constructed to show the data.

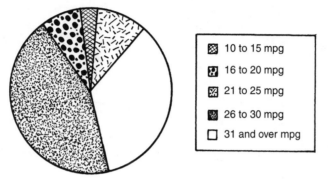

▨	10 to 15 mpg
▨	16 to 20 mpg
▨	21 to 25 mpg
▨	26 to 30 mpg
☐	31 and over mpg

The individual areas of the graph show the percentage of cars that are in each category. The larger the area, the larger the percentage of the whole and the larger the number in that category. Use the circle graph to answer the following questions.

1. The largest number of cars got from _____ to _____ mpg.

2. What were the miles per gallon of the next-largest number of cars? _____

3. Which category had the fewest number of cars? _____

4. Look at the areas of the circle graph. Is any one area larger than ½ of the circle? _____

5. Which two categories are approximately equal to ½ of the circle? _____ to _____ and _____ to _____

6. Which two categories are approximately equal? _____ to _____ and _____ to _____

7. If you were going to buy a car, which category would you choose from? _____

    Why? _____

    _____

4-10. School Lunches I

The students at Sunset Lakes Elementary School voted for their favorite lunch from five possible choices. The data are displayed below.

Favorite Lunch Votes

Hamburger	112
Hot Dog	140
Pizza	224
Sandwich	56
Salad	28
	Total 560

A circle graph can be used to display the data in an easy-to-read manner. Before a circle graph can be constructed, the data need to be converted into other forms. The first step is to find the percentage of the total votes for each lunch. Use a calculator to fill in the blanks. Then answer the questions.

Divide the number of votes for each lunch by the total number of votes and multiply by 100. This gives the percentage of votes for each lunch.

Hamburger: 112 divided by 560 = _____ × 100 = _____%

Hot Dog: 140 divided by 560 = _____ × 100 = _____%

Pizza: 224 divided by 560 = _____ × 100 = _____%

Sandwich: 56 divided by 560 = _____ × 100 = _____%

Salad: 28 divided by 560 = _____ × 100 = _____%

1. What is the total percentage for all five lunches? _____

2. Which lunch received the highest number of votes? _____

3. Which lunch received the highest percentage of votes? _____

4-10. School Lunches I (continued)

4. Why do you think the answers are the same? _____

_____

5. Which lunch received the lowest percentage of votes? _____

6. Which lunch received more than 50 percent of the votes? _____

7. Which two lunches together received 50 percent of the votes?

_____ and _____

8. Which three lunches together received 50 percent of the votes?

_____, _____, and _____

9. Hamburger and hot dog together received 45 percent of the votes. What other two lunches together also received 45 percent of the vote?

_____ and _____

10. How much more percent of the votes did pizza receive than hot dog? _____

11. How much more percent of the votes did hamburger and sandwich together receive than salad? _____

12. Explain in your own words what is meant by *percent*. _____

_____

_____

4-11. School Lunches II

The students at Sunset Lakes Elementary School voted for their favorite lunch from five possible choices. The data are displayed below.

Favorite Lunch Votes

Hamburger	112
Hot Dog	140
Pizza	224
Sandwich	56
Salad	28
	Total 560

First Step. The number of votes for each lunch was divided by the total number of votes and then multiplied by 100 to give the percentage of total votes for each lunch.

Hamburger	20%	Sandwich	10%
Hot Dog	25%	Salad	5%
Pizza	40%		

Second Step. There are 360 degrees in a circle. Use a calculator to find the number of degrees in each pie-shaped region of the graph by dividing its percentage by 100 and then multiplying by 360. This gives each lunch an area of the circle based on how many votes it received. Use the percentages from above.

Hamburger: _____% divided by 100 = _____ × 360 = _____ degrees

Hot Dog: _____% divided by 100 = _____ × 360 = _____ degrees

Pizza: _____% divided by 100 = _____ × 360 = _____ degrees

Sandwich: _____% divided by 100 = _____ × 360 = _____ degrees

Salad: _____% divided by 100 = _____ × 360 = _____ degrees

Third Step. Use a protractor to divide the circle by the number of degrees for each pie-shaped region. Color each lunch in the key a different color and then color the corresponding pie-shaped region the same color.

4-11. School Lunches II (continued)

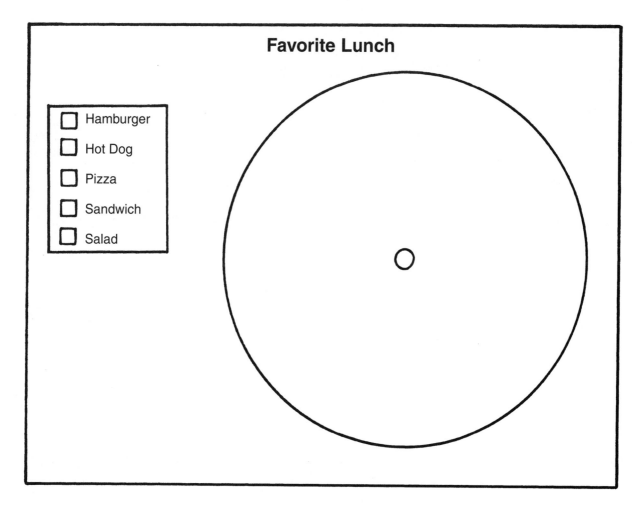

Favorite Lunch

- ☐ Hamburger
- ☐ Hot Dog
- ☐ Pizza
- ☐ Sandwich
- ☐ Salad

Use the circle graph to answer the following questions.

1. The largest area represents the lunch that received the most votes. Which lunch received the most votes? _____

2. The smallest area represents the lunch that received the fewest votes. Which lunch received the fewest votes? _____

3. Did any one lunch receive more than ½ of the votes? _____ If so, which one? _____

4. Study the circle graph. Which lunch received ¼ of the votes? _____

4-11. School Lunches II *(continued)*

5. Which two lunches together received just about ½ of the votes?

_____ and _____

6. Which three lunches together received just about ⅔ of the votes?

_____, _____, and _____

7. List the lunches in order from greatest to least by the different categories.

Votes Received	**Percentage**	**Degrees of the Circle**
_____	_____	_____
_____	_____	_____
_____	_____	_____
_____	_____	_____
_____	_____	_____

8. Are the lists the same or are they different? _____ Why do you think that happened?

_____

_____

_____

Name _____   Date _____

4-12. Choose the Graph

From the descriptions below, determine which type of graph would be best to use for each situation. The choices are:

- Bar graph
- Line graph
- Picture graph
- Circle graph

Then briefly tell why you feel that particular graph is best for the situation described.

1. Juan and his family have moved across the country. Juan wants to know more about the weather in his new home state. He is interested in the changes in the monthly rainfall. He finds the rainfall for each of the past 12 months listed in the newspaper and wants to display the data in an easy-to-read graph. Which type of graph should Juan choose to best display the data?

_____

Why do you think this is the best graph for this situation? _____

_____

2. Julie is in charge of displaying the number of books that her class reads at home for each month of the school year. She wants to compare each month to the other months, so she chooses the symbol of a book to represent every 10 books read by the class. Which type of graph should Julie use?

_____

Why do you think this is the best graph for this situation? _____

_____

4-12. Choose the Graph (continued)

3. Kanesha wants to survey the third-grade students in her school to find out their favorite TV show from six shows she has listed. Kanesha knows that by constructing a graph, she will be able to show which TV show is the most popular, which is the least popular, if any shows are tied for popularity, and if any shows receive no votes. Which type of graph should Kanesha use to display her data?

_____

Why do you think this is the best graph for this situation? _____

_____

4. Mr. Lu, the cafeteria manager, wants to serve lunches that the students enjoy. He has all of the students in the school vote for their favorite lunch from the following choices: pizza, hot dogs, hamburgers, fish, or salad. Mr. Lu figures that any lunch that receives more than 25 percent of the votes is popular. Which type of graph should Mr. Lu use to easily show which lunches receive enough percentage of the votes to be considered popular?

_____

Why do you think this is the best graph for this situation? _____

_____

4-13. Compact Discs

Seven children are comparing how many compact discs (CDs) each of them owns. The number of CDs owned by each child is shown in this table.

Child	CDs Owned
Antonio	6
Keisha	4
Michael	2
Sara	4
Lee	3
Maria	3
Hakeem	6

The *mean* is a number that is thought of as the "average," or "usual," or "typical." Follow the steps below to figure out the average number of CDs the children own.

Part One: Calculate the mean, or average

1. Add the number of CDs each child owns and write the total. _____

2. Divide the total number of CDs by the number of children (7). Write that result here. _____ This value is the mean, or the average number of CDs the children own. The average number of CDs owned by the children is 4 CDs.

    In this case, the mean of 4 is also one of the values in the original data set. This does not always happen. Take a look at the next set of data. Suppose eight children are now comparing the number of CDs each owns. This time the data have changed.

5 CDs	4 CDs	2 CDs	4 CDs	3 CDs	2 CDs	5 CDs	1 CD

3. What is the total number of CDs owned by the children? ___

4. Divide the total by the number of children. The average number of CDs owned by these children is _____. The value you have determined is the mean, but this time it is not one of the values in the original data set. This will probably happen often. The mean in this example is not any better or worse than other means. It is just not part of the original data.

4-13. Compact Discs (continued)

Part Two: Find the mean for the following data sets:

1. The number of pieces of candy each child has is 4, 2, 6, 1, and 2. The mean number of pieces of candy for the children is _____.

2. The number of points each basketball player scored in a game is 11, 15, 21, 9, 5, and 5. The mean number of points each player scored is _____.

3. The number of points each child scored in a game of darts is 7, 16, 3, 15, 9, 12, 4, and 2. The mean number of points the children scored is _____.

4. The number of times thrill-seekers rode the Big Monster roller coaster last summer is 224, 216, 328, and 430. The mean number of times the thrill seekers rode the roller coaster is _____.

5. The number of times jumping rope without a miss is 76, 124, 85, 56, 116, 102, 77, 98, 109, and 68. The average number of jumps without a miss is _____.

Name _____   Date _____

4-14. Lunch Choices

The students in Mr. Johnson's class collected data for one week to determine how many of them bought their lunch at school and how many brought their lunch to school. Use these data to calculate the average number of students who bought their lunch and the average number who brought their lunch during that week.

	Bought Lunch	Brought Lunch
Monday	17	13
Tuesday	20	9
Wednesday	13	15
Thursday	22	8
Friday	15	15

1. The total number of students who bought lunch at school was _____.

   The mean number of students who bought lunch at school during the week was _____.

2. The total number of students who brought their lunch to school was _____.
   The mean number of students who brought their lunch to school during the week was _____.

3. All of the students in the class were present on Monday. On what other days were all of the students present?

   _____

   How do you know? _____

4. On what day or days were students absent or not in the lunch count? _____

   _____

4-14. Lunch Choices (continued)

5. The mean or average is 5, and there are 5 numbers in the set of data. Fill in the spaces to make two correct sets of data.

____ + ____ + ____ + ____ + ____ = ____

____ + ____ + ____ + ____ + ____ = ____

6. Explain why you believe your sets of data are correct. _____

_____

7. The mean or average is 9, and there are 6 numbers in the set of data. Fill in the spaces to make two correct sets of data.

____ + ____ + ____ + ____ + ____ + ____ = ____

____ + ____ + ____ + ____ + ____ + ____ = ____

8. Explain why you believe your sets of data are correct. _____

_____

During a different week in Mr. Johnson's class the mean number of students who brought their lunch to school was 10. This means that, on average, 10 students brought their lunch to school each of the five school days.

9. How many students brought their lunch to school during the five-day school week?

_____

How did you get your answer? _____

_____

10. Create a data set to show how many students may have brought their lunch each day.

Monday _____ Tuesday _____ Wednesday _____ Thursday _____ Friday _____

4-15. Just Your Average Means

Super Starr is a baseball player who can bat either right-handed or left-handed, which is called switch-hitting. Looking back at the last baseball season, Super saw that he had collected 90 hits in 247 at-bats while hitting right-handed and 64 hits in 204 at-bats batting left-handed. Use a calculator to determine the following batting averages for Super. Divide the number of hits by the number of at-bats.

Last season batting right-handed:

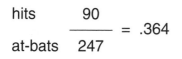

$$\frac{\text{hits}}{\text{at-bats}} \quad \frac{90}{247} = .364$$

Last season batting left-handed:

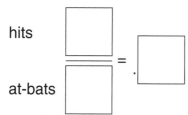

$$\frac{\text{hits}}{\text{at-bats}} \quad \frac{64}{\boxed{}} = .\boxed{}$$

Super is a better right-handed hitter than a left-handed hitter. His right-handed average of .364 is higher than his left-handed average of .314.

1. What is Super's batting average for last season (right-handed and left-handed) combined? Add the total number of hits and divide by the total number of at-bats.

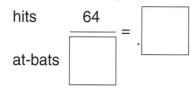

$$\frac{\text{hits}}{\text{at-bats}} \quad \frac{\boxed{}}{\boxed{}} = .\boxed{}$$

This tells us that on average, Super gets about 3 hits for every 10 times he comes to bat. It also tells us that on average, Super gets about 34 hits for every 100 times he comes to bat.

This baseball season Super had 66 hits in 202 at-bats right-handed and 72 hits in 218 at-bats left-handed. Calculate Super's right-handed batting average for this season and his left-handed batting average for this season.

2. This season batting right-handed.

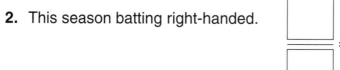

© 2004 by John Wiley & Sons, Inc.

4-15. Just Your Average Means (continued)

3. This season batting left-handed.

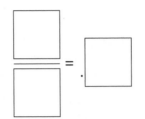

4. Was Super a better right-handed hitter or a better left-handed hitter this season?

_____

How do you know? _____

_____

5. Now calculate his total batting average for this season.

6. Did Super bat better last season or this season? _____

How do you know?_____

_____

4-16. Creating Data Sets

For each data set, fill in the number or numbers that make the sentence correct. Let's look at the first sentence and data set. The mode is the most frequent number in the data set. Which numbers occur most frequently? _____ and _____
What number should be added in the blank space to make 35 the most frequent piece of data? Then fill in the rest of the blanks.

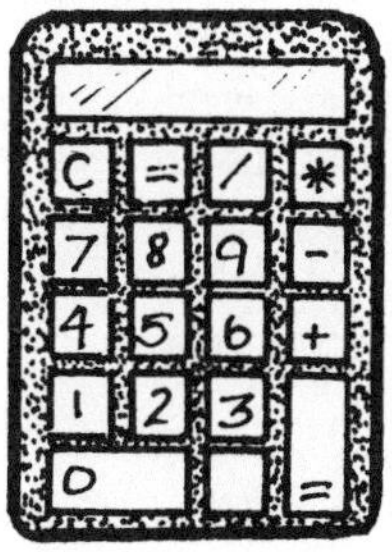

1. The mode is 35:   15, 35, 17, _____, 15, 23, 35

2. The range is 9:   24, 22, 18, 17, _____

   Why? _____

3. The median is 15:   8, 10, _____, 15, 23, _____, 31

   Why? _____

4. The range is 24:   88, 86, 96, 88, _____, 79

   Why? _____

5. The mode is 14:   18, _____, 16, 18, _____, 22, 10, _____, 13

   Why? _____

6. The median is 22:   14, 16, 19, 22, _____, _____, 27, 33

   Why? _____

7. The mean is 15:   19, 22, 11, 12, _____

   Why? _____

8. The median is 10.5:   3, 4, 8, 10, _____, 13, 17, 25

   Why? _____

4-17. Baseball

Tina recorded the number of games that several baseball teams won during the past season. She then used the data to construct a stem-and-leaf plot. Use the stem-and-leaf plot to answer the questions below.

Stem	Leaf
5	3
6	5 5
7	1 4 5 6 8
8	2 2 7
9	0 0 8
10	1 4

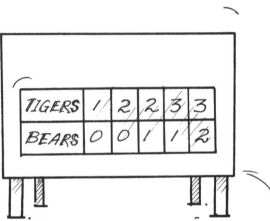

1. How much does the numeral 6 in the stem represent? _____

2. How much does the numeral 10 in the stem represent? _____

3. How many teams are shown in the stem-and-leaf plot? _____

4. How many teams won between 70 and 80 games? _____

5. How many teams won more than 80 games? _____

6. Atlanta won the most games. How many games did Atlanta win? _____

7. Florida won the least number of games. How many games did Florida win? _____

8. What is the range of the data set? _____ – _____ = _____

9. Are the data scattered or concentrated? _____

10. St. Louis and Houston won the same number of games. How many games could the two teams have won? _____ or _____ or _____

11. What was the median number of wins for these baseball teams? _____

© 2004 by John Wiley & Sons, Inc.

4-18. Canned Food Drive

Stem-and-leaf plots organize data and allow for quick interpretation. The following data represent the number of cans of food collected by each class at Westside Elementary School during the holiday canned food drive.

46, 78, 28, 97, 74, 56, 68, 67, 83, 75, 88, 68, 91, 84, 78, 49, 65, 46, 68

Since the data are not organized, it would be difficult to understand them.

In this set all of the data are two-digit numbers, so the stem will represent the tens place. The data vary from the 20s through the 90s.

Stem	Leaf	Stem	Leaf
2		6	
3		7	
4		8	
5		9	

The next step is to plot the leaves by writing the ones-place digit next to the appropriate tens place. One class collected 46 cans, so a 6 is written as a leaf next to the 40. Another class collected 78 cans, so an 8 is written as a leaf next to the 70. The data of 28, 97, and 74 have been written in and have been crossed off. Write in the rest of the data and cross off each number as you use it.

46, 78, 28, 97, 74, 56, 68, 67, 83, 75, 88, 68, 91, 84, 78, 49, 65, 46, 68

Stem	Leaf	Stem	Leaf
2	8	6	
3		7	8 4
4	6	8	
5		9	7

4-18. Canned Food Drive (continued)

Now rewrite the data ordering each leaf from least to most.

Stem	Leaf	Stem	Leaf
2		6	
3		7	
4		8	
5		9	

Use the ordered stem-and-leaf plot to analyze the data.

1. What is the smallest value? _____ What is the largest value? _____

2. What is the range of the data set? _____ – _____ = _____

3. Are the data concentrated or scattered? _____

4. Why do you think so? _____

   _____

5. The mode is the most frequent score. The mode for the data set is _____.

6. The median is the middle score. The median of the data set is _____.

7. Without using a calculator, estimate the mean of the data set. The mean of the data set is _____.

4-19. World Weather Watch

Listed below are the high temperatures for a recent spring day in several locations around the world. Construct a stem-and-leaf plot from the data and then determine the central tendencies using the plot.

Acapulco	91	Cairo	68	Madrid	64
Amsterdam	62	Copenhagen	63	Moscow	75
Athens	75	Dublin	66	Nice	68
Bangkok	89	Frankfurt	65	Oslo	60
Beijing	78	Geneva	68	Paris	68
Beirut	82	Helsinki	60	Rome	71
Berlin	66	Hong Kong	80	Sydney	68
Bermuda	70	Jerusalem	80	Tokyo	73
Bogotá	64	London	71	Zurich	68

Stem	Leaf	Stem	Leaf	Stem	Leaf

1. What is the range of the temperatures? _____

2. What is the median temperature? _____

3. What is the mode of this data set? _____

4. Identify any extreme data that might affect the mean. _____

5. Estimate the mean temperature. _____

6. Describe the amount of symmetry in the plot. _____

_____

Section 5

PROBABILITY

Activity	Concept	Knowledge Level
5-1. In All Likelihood	Likelihood	Learning
5-2. Chance	Chance	Learning
5-3. Fair or Unfair	Fair Games	Learning
5-4. The Match Game	Fair Games	Challenging
5-5. More or Less	Probability as Ratio	Learning
5-6. The Ready Ratio	Probability as Ratio	Learning
5-7. Thinking	Probability	Learning
5-8. More Probability	Probability	Challenging
5-9. Number Cube	Number Cubes/Dice	Learning
5-10. Dice Outcomes	Dice	Learning
5-11. Some Sums	Dice Likelihood/Chance	Challenging
5-12. Odd or Even	Dice/Fair Game	Challenging
5-13. Flip Them	Counters/Coins	Learning
5-14. Clever Triangles	Pascal's Triangle	Challenging
5-15. Spinning Spinners	Spinners	Learning
5-16. Tally and Win	Spinners	Challenging
5-17. We All Scream for Ice Cream	Permutations	Beginning

161

Teacher Directions

■ **5-1. IN ALL LIKELIHOOD** (Learning Level)

Objective: To determine the likelihood of an event occurring

Materials: Several green and yellow cubes (or any two colors) and a paper bag for you and all the students
In All Likelihood activity sheet

Directions: Write the word "likelihood" on the board or overhead and ask several students to explain what the word means to them. (*the chance of a certain thing happening*) State that the thing that could happen is called an event, and write that word on the board. Ask what it means if an event is certain to happen. (*It will happen.*) Have several students describe events that are certain to happen. (*It gets dark at night. A dropped ball will fall downward. Etc.*) Then ask what it means if an event is impossible (*it will not happen*) and obtain examples. (*Cows will fly. Flowers will talk to us tomorrow. Etc.*)

Distribute the bags and the cubes to the students and allow a short period of time for the students to explore the materials. "I am going to place some of these cubes into the bag and then, without looking, I will pull one cube from the bag. I want to be certain that I pull a green cube. That is the event, pulling a green cube from the bag. What cubes should I put into the bag so I will be certain to pull a green cube?" (*all green cubes*) "Why will that make it certain?" (*must pull a green if only green cubes are in the bag*) Place four green cubes into the bag and ask the students to do the same. Have everyone pull out a cube to prove the point. Empty the bag. "What cubes should I put into the bag so it is impossible to pull a green cube?" (*all yellow; no cubes would also be correct but we do want cubes in the bag*) "Why will that make the event impossible?" (*cannot pull a green cube if there are only yellow cubes in the bag*) Have the students place yellow cubes into the bag and, without looking, pull out one cube to prove the point.

Write "very likely," "maybe," and "very unlikely" on the board. Have the students describe what each means and give several examples of each. To further reinforce the concepts, ask the students to also give nonexamples of each term. (Nonexample of very likely: *I will ride a lion to school tomorrow.*) Emphasize that very likely is not certain and that very unlikely is not impossible. "Although some events are certain or impossible, most events are either very likely to happen, may happen, or are very unlikely to happen." Have the students place 4 green cubes and 1 yellow cube into the bag as you demonstrate the action. "I am going to reach into the bag and, without looking, pull out one cube. Would pulling out a green cube be very likely, a maybe, or very unlikely?" (*very likely*) "Why?" (*four green cubes and only one yellow*) "Would we always pull a green cube?" (*no*) "Why not?" (*A yellow cube could be pulled.*) Have all of the students pull a cube without looking. Total the number that pulled each color of cube. There should be about four times as many green as yellow. "Would pulling a yellow cube be very likely, a maybe, or very unlikely?" (*very unlikely*) "Why?" (*only one yellow cube out of five*) Place the cubes back into the bag and pull again. There should be only a few yellow cubes. Replace the cubes.

"How could I change the cubes in the bag so maybe I would pull a green cube and maybe I will not?" (*equal number of each color*) Have the students place an equal number of green and yellow and have everyone pull a cube again. The numbers of each color should be fairly even. "In review, events that are impossible cannot happen and events that are certain will happen. Many other events either are very likely to happen, may happen, or are very unlikely to happen." Distribute the In All Likelihood activity sheet. The students will determine the likelihood of events occurring and justify their answers.

Answer Key: 1. very likely—more red than blue; 2. maybe—equal numbers of each color; 3. very unlikely—more blue than red; 4. gray, black—gray is the largest quantity and black is the least; 5. purple, yellow—purple is the largest quantity and yellow is the least; 6. yellow or purple, orange—yellow and purple are the largest quantities and orange is the least

Related Activity: Divide your class into groups of three having, as much as possible, a high, middle, and low math achiever in each group. Each group will receive a bag with 15 3 × 5 index cards inside. Instruct the students to use crayons to mark the cards as follows: 4 cards marked "green," 2 cards marked "yellow," 3 cards marked "blue," and 6 cards marked "purple." This is similar to problem 8 of the In All Likelihood activity. Review with the students which card would be the most likely to be drawn (*purple*) and which card would be the least likely to be drawn (*yellow*). Ask which is the second and third most likely to be chosen (*green and blue*).

The students will then conduct an experiment to see how the results of the experiment compare to the likelihood of the color being chosen. The students will take turns drawing a card from the bag without looking, and recording the result. The card is returned to the bag and mixed with the others before the next turn. Each student will have four turns pulling a card (12 turns for each group of students). When they are finished, compile the data into a class tally table and compare the results to the likelihood of the color. (*1—purple, 2—green, 3—blue, 4—yellow*) The students can discuss why the order was the same or if there were any differences in the order. Refrain from teaching about chance, since this is the next lesson. Allow the students to discuss chance if they originate the idea. Save the class tally table for activity 5-2.

■ 5-2. CHANCE (Learning Level)

Objective: To describe the effect of chance upon likelihood

Materials: Several yellow cubes and one green cube (or any two colors) and a paper bag
Class tally table from activity 5-1
Chance activity sheet

Directions: Without the students seeing, place a piece of tape on the green cube. Do not let the students see the tape as you teach the lesson. Have the students watch as you place four yellow cubes and the green cube into the bag. Ask which is the more likely color to be pulled from the bag (*yellow*). Reach into the bag and feel around until you identify the tape and pull out the green cube. Ask why they think that happened and generate several student responses. Write "chance" on the board and have the students describe what the word means (when something happens that we did not expect to happen). Place the green cube back into the bag. Ask how many think the yellow cube will be pulled this time. Repeat the process a few times, pulling the green cube each time. Point out that this is how chance could happen, then reveal the "secret."

Relate chance back to the terms *likely* and *unlikely*. Have students describe a few events that are likely to happen and write a couple on the board. Ask if they are certain to happen. (*no*) What else could happen? (*something else happens*) When we expect an event to happen and a different event happens, it is by chance. Have the students describe a few events that are unlikely to happen. For each event, have the students state what else could happen and why something else could happen. (*chance*)

"Some people think of chance as luck. The green cube is drawn due to being lucky or unlucky. Mathematicians do not see chance as lucky or unlucky. It is simply something that happens that we did not expect." Review the class tally table from related activity 5-1. "We would have expected the most frequent color chosen to be purple, followed by green, blue, and yellow. If the order of the class tally table was different from the likelihood, then it was by chance. If the order was the same, chance did not play a significant role in the totals. However, not everyone pulled green most frequently. When a different color was pulled most frequently, it was by chance." Pair the students and distribute the Chance activity sheet. The students will conduct the experiments together and answer the questions.

Answer Key: 1. When an event occurs that was not expected; 2. Answers will vary; 3. Answers will vary.

Related Activity: Review the term *event* as something that can happen. Introduce *outcome* as the result of the event. If there were red and green cubes in a bag, the event would be pulling a red cube. The outcome would be whatever cube was pulled out. Give each student a coin or two-color counter. Identify heads and tails on the coin. "If I flipped this coin, what outcomes could there be?" (*heads or tails*) "What is the likelihood of flipping a head? Is it very likely, maybe, or not likely." (*maybe*) "Why is that?" (*one event and only two possible outcomes*) "If I flipped the coin ten times and recorded my results, how many heads do you think I would get and how many tails?" (*Accept all answers, but lead toward the answer of 5 heads and 5 tails.*) "What would be a reason to not get 5 heads and 5 tails?" (*chance*)

Instruct each student to flip his or her coin ten times and record the results. Then construct a class tally table using the student data. Note any individual totals that may have been affected by chance. Convert the tally table into a frequency table and compare the total results to the likelihood of flipping a head. The heads total and tails total should be equal. If they are not, it was due to chance.

■ **5-3. FAIR OR UNFAIR (Learning Level)**

Objectives: To determine if an event is fair or unfair
To correct an unfair situation

Materials: Ball and piece of paper to serve as a target
Bag with 5 red blocks and 2 blue blocks
Fair or Unfair activity sheet

Directions: Place the piece of paper on the floor a good distance (possibly across the room) from you. Hold the ball and tell the class that all of you are going to play a game. The competition is you against the class. You and the students will take turns rolling the ball at the target. Each time the ball stops on the target, the class gets one point. Each time the ball misses the target, you get two points. You will probably hear protests and grumbling, but ask if the game is fair or unfair, and why the students think so. (*unfair, more chance to miss yet greater points, target too far,* etc.) Generate as many reasons as possible that the game is unfair.

"All right, let's think about another game. We'll play a board game. You have to move around on the spaces, and the first one who gets to the finish line wins." Show the 5 red blocks and count them as you put them into the bag. Show the 2 blue blocks and count them as you put them into the bag. "I will pull a block from the bag without looking. Each time I pull a red block, I move my marker one space. Each time I pull a blue block, you move your marker one space. The block is returned to the bag before the next turn. Is this a fair game?" (*no*) "Why not?" (*more red blocks than blue*) "How can we make it a fair game?" (*equalize the number of blocks*)

Have individual students describe games that they play at home, at recess, or at physical education. Ask them to declare if the games are considered to be fair and the reasons they believe this. List these on the board. Consider ways to make the games unfair and list those on the board. Then look for general categories of why games are fair (*equal turns, equal scoring, equal chances,* etc.) and unfair (*unequal scoring, unequal chances,* etc.).

Distribute the Fair or Unfair activity sheet. The students will determine if the games are fair or unfair, and state why.

Answer Key: 1. yes; 2. no; 3. Both have equal chances with the die and can only move one space no matter what number is rolled; 4. yes; 5. either girl; 6. equal area on the spinner; 7. no; 8. Ricardo; 9. more area on the spinner for numbers 1 and 3; 10. The spinner will be redrawn with four equal areas; 11. no; 12. Ricardo; 13. more cards with even number; 14. Answers will vary, but should be odd numbers.

Related Activity: Organize the students in pairs. Distribute a deck of playing cards and three sheets of paper to each pair. The students will decide who is player A and who is player B, and draw a tally table on one of the papers to keep track of their points. The cards will be shuffled and placed facedown in a pile. The players will take turns turning the cards over one at a time. If the card is a heart, player A gets three points. If the card is a club, a spade, or a diamond player B gets one point.

Before they start playing, each player will take one of the other pieces of paper and write down if he or she thinks the game is fair, and why. The game will continue until one player has 25 points. When all have completed the game, ask several students to share why they thought the game was fair or unfair and the outcome of their game. Then compile the class data and see how many times player A won versus how many times player B won. Discuss what the data show about the fairness of the game. (The game is fair. Each suit in the deck has 13 cards. There is a club, a spade, and a diamond for each heart. The likelihood is that each time a heart is turned over, the three points are equalized by three one-point cards.)

■ 5-4. THE MATCH GAME (Challenging Level)

Objective: To determine if an event is fair or unfair

Materials: Bag with 2 red cubes and 1 blue cube
3 yellow cubes, 2 purple cubes (or other colors), and a bag for each pair of students
The Match Game activity sheet

Directions: Review the concept of fair and unfair events for games by listing student responses about why events are considered fair (*equal turns, equal scoring, equal chances,* etc.) and why events are considered unfair (*unequal scoring, unequal chances,* etc.). Show the two red cubes and one blue cube as you place them into the bag. Tell the students about a new game. You will reach into the bag and, without looking, pull out one cube. Then you will do it a second time. If the colors match, the students get a point. If the colors do not match, you get a point. Replace the cubes after each second pull.

Ask for students' opinions about the fairness of the game and then demonstrate the game at least 10 times with the students keeping the score. You should be comfortably ahead. Ask why this is so and see if the students can figure out the possible combinations that can be pulled from the bag. Designate the cubes as R1 for the first red cube, R2 for the second red cube, and B1 for the blue cube.

Write R1 on the board and ask what the second cube could be (*R2 or B1*). Write the following statements on the board:

Are R1 and R2 a match? (*yes*)

Are R1 and B1 a match? (*no*)

Ask what could be the second cube if R2 was the first cube (*R1 or B1*). Continue, writing the following statements:

Are R2 and R1 a match? (*yes*)

Are R1 and B1 a match? (*no*)

Finally, what could be the second cube if B1 was the first cube? (*R1 or R2*) Continue writing:

> Are B1 and R1 a match? (*no*)
>
> Are B1 and R2 a match? (*no*)

Point to the yes and no answers and ask the students if it is a fair game. (*no*) "Why?" (*There are two outcomes that match and four outcomes that do not match.*) "Many times, what appears to be fair turns out to be not fair if we look at it very closely."

Pair the students. Distribute the Match Game activity sheet, purple and yellow cubes, and a bag to each pair. Instruct the students that there are two sets of cubes that can be used in the game. They are to decide which set of cubes will make a fair game. The students will play the match game two times, once with the cubes in Set 1 and once with the cubes in Set 2. They will then predict which set of cubes makes the game fair and justify their prediction. Finally, the students will work through the activity to determine if their prediction was correct.

Answer Key: 1. 4, 8; 2. no, only 4 times matching to 8 times not matching; 3. 6, 6; 4. yes, equal number of matches for both players; 5. Answers will vary.

Related Activity: Write "Chance" and "Skill" on the board, leaving room between the words. Ask the students to describe how these words might relate to games. (*Chance games are those where luck is involved, and skill games are those where what the player does decides the outcome.*) Write "Chess" under "Skill." "Why would chess be considered a skill game?" (*You need to know the rules and the strategies. There is little luck in chess.*) Write "War" under "Chance." "Why would the card game War be a chance game?" (*You have to get the right cards to win. There is not much strategy involved.*) Write "Both" between "Chance" and "Skill" and "Monopoly" under "Both." "Why would the board game Monopoly include both chance and skill?" (*It helps to have skill in the game but rolling the dice is chance. Sometimes you get a good roll, other times, not.*) Have the students generate additional games for the lists, describing why they think the games are chance games, or skill games, or both.

■ 5-5. MORE OR LESS (Learning Level)

Objective: To classify an event as less likely, equally likely, or more likely to occur

Materials: Large coin or two-sided counter
Overhead of a 3-region spinner (see appendix)
Overhead fraction bars
More or Less activity sheet

Directions: Show the coin to the students and identify both sides. "How likely would it be to toss a head with this coin? Would it be less likely, equally likely, or more likely?" (*equally likely*) "Yes, it would be equally likely, but why?" (*only two outcomes, either could come up*) "We can say how likely it would be by using a ratio. A ratio is a relationship of numbers. They go together and, in this case, show the likelihood of an event occurring."

Write "$\frac{1}{2}$" on the board. "This is a ratio. It shows how two numbers go together." Hold up the coin. "How many outcomes can there be by flipping this coin?" (*2*) Point to the 2 in the ratio. "How many ways can I get a head?" (*1*) Point to the 1 in the ratio. "The ratio shows us that there are two different outcomes and one of them is the event that I was looking for. It is not read as one-half, it is read one out of two. It also means that I should be able to produce that event one out of every two times that I try it. In other words, if I flip the coin twice, I *should* get a head once. Not *will*! I *should* get a head once." Flip the coin until you get a head. If you got the head within two flips, that demonstrates the likelihood. If it took longer, it is due to chance.

Display the 3-region spinner. "What is the probability of spinning a 2? How many outcomes are there?" (*3*) Write "⅓" on the board. "How many ways can I get a 2?" (*1*) Finish the ratio to show ⅓. "The ratio shows 1 out of 3. I should be able to spin a 2 once out of three spins." Spin the spinner until you get a 2. Did it occur within the likelihood of 3 spins or did it take longer due to chance?

Point to the ½ and ⅓. "I called these ratios. You may be thinking that they are fractions. A ratio is a relationship between two numbers. Ratios can be written in fraction form. Here (*point to* ½) the ratio is 1 out of 2. The good thing about ratios is that they behave like fractions. Their values are the same, we can take them to simplest terms, and we can combine them. Once you know fractions, you know a lot about ratios."

Place the whole from the fraction bars on the overhead and draw a line the length of the bar. Write "0" at the left end and "1" at the right end.

"The probability of an event occurring is a ratio between the number 0 and 1. What is the probability that I will walk on the ceiling right now?" (*0*) "If an event is impossible, the probability is 0. What is the probability that I am breathing air right now?" (*1*) "If the probability is 1, it is certain to happen. If I had a bag with two red cubes in it, the probability of pulling out a green cube is 0. It cannot happen. The probability of pulling out a red cube is 1. It has to happen." Remove the fraction bar.

"In between the 0 and the 1 are many probabilities." Take the ½ fraction bar and lay it next to the line even with the left side. Make a mark on the line at the right side of the ½ bar. Then remove the bar and write "½" under the mark.

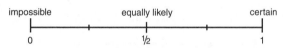

"Zero shows that it is impossible and 1 shows that it is certain. What does 1 out of 2 show? How likely is the event to occur?" (*equally likely*) Write "equally likely" above ½. Place the ¼ fraction bar on the line even with the left side. Make a mark at the right end, write "¼," and remove the bar.

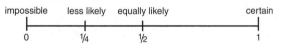

"Here is the ratio 1 out of 4. Is it very likely to occur or less likely to occur?" (*less likely*) "Why?" (*should only happen once in four tries; closer to zero*) "The closer a ratio is to 0, the less likely it is to occur. It is not impossible, only less likely to occur." Write "less likely" above ¼.

Place either a ¾ bar on the line or three ¼ bars to equal ¾. Repeat the questions and finally write "more likely" above ¾.

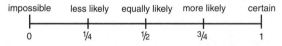

"The closer the ratio is to 1, the more likely it is to occur." Distribute the More or Less activity sheet to the students. As a review, go through the description and the diagram with the students. The students will then determine the likelihood of an event occurring by using the probability ratio.

Answer Key: 1. less likely; 2. closer to 0; 3. more likely; 4. closer to 1; 5. more likely; 6. ⅘, closer to 1; 7. ¾, closer to 1; 8. ½; 9. equally likely; 10. halfway between 0 and 1; 11. ¾; 12. more likely; 13. closer to 1; 14. ⅕; 15. less likely; 16. closer to 0

Related Activity: Pair the students and instruct each to use a marker to write their first and last names in fairly large letters on a piece of paper. One partner will hold a sharpened pencil approximately two feet above the paper and drop the pencil onto the name. The other will determine where the pencil hits by watching the mark that the pencil point makes. Before students begin, they should answer the following questions:

- What is the probability of hitting a vowel in your first name? How likely is it to occur?

- What is the probability of hitting a vowel in your last name? How likely is it to occur?

- The five most common letters in written English are E, T, A, O, and N. What is the probability of hitting one of these letters in either name? How likely is it to occur?

Once the questions have been answered, the students can take turns dropping the pencil and recording the data. They can count any drops close to the letter as hits. After several tries, the students can compare their data to the probabilities.

■ **5-6. THE READY RATIO (Learning Level)**

Objectives: To determine the probability of an outcome occurring
To classify an event as less likely, equally likely, or more likely to occur

Materials: 3×5 index cards with 0, 1, ¼, ⅓, ½, ⅔, and ¾ written on them
Tape
The Ready Ratio activity sheet

Directions: Place the cards on the board using some tape. Draw this figure on the board.

Review the concept of a ratio (*relation between two numbers; looks like a fraction; behaves like a fraction; is not a fraction*) and how the numbers are determined (*top number is the number of ways an event can occur; bottom number is the total number of possible outcomes*). Pull the 0 card from the board and ask what probability it represents (*zero, impossible*). Have a student tape it where it belongs on the number line (*see More or Less activity sheet*). Pull the 1 card and ask what probability it represents (*one, certain*) and allow a student to place it on the line.

Tell the students that you will be reading a problem and that the answer is shown on one of the cards. Choose a student to identify the card, state why the ratio fits the problem, tape the card on the correct place on the line, and state if it is less likely to occur, equally likely to occur, or more likely to occur, and why.

- What is the probability of picking a brown chip from a bag that contains 1 white chip and 3 brown chips? (*¾; more likely*)

- What is the probability of flipping a yellow with a two-color counter? (*½; equally likely*)

- What is the probability of spinning an odd number on a three-region spinner that has the numbers 1, 2, and 3? (*⅔; more likely*)

- What is the probability of choosing a girl's name from a list of six boys' names and two girls' names? (*²⁄₈, ¼; less likely*)

- What is the probability of pulling a green cube from a bag that contains a yellow cube, a purple cube, and a green cube? (*⅓; less likely*)

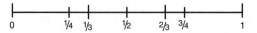

Distribute The Ready Ratio activity sheet. The students will determine and interpret the ratios.

Answer Key: 1. $\frac{1}{2}$; 2. both; 3. equally likely; 4. halfway between 0 and 1, or equal chance of the outcomes; 5. $\frac{1}{6}$; 6. 0; 7. less likely; 8. only one event of six outcomes, or closer to 0; 9. $\frac{3}{5}$; 10. more likely; 11. closer to 1

Related Activity: Without the students seeing, place 5 red, 3 green, and 1 orange cubes (or other colors) in a bag. Construct a tally table on the board and list the colors red, green, and orange. Tell the students that there are 9 cubes in the bag and that the colors are red, green, and orange. Pass the bag around the room and allow each student to draw one cube from the bag, without looking. Record the color chosen on the tally table and have the cube returned before the bag is passed to the next student.

When every student has had the opportunity to draw a sample, draw one yourself and add your tally to the table. Total the number for each color on the tally table. Divide the class into small groups. Their assignment is to use the sample totals to predict the number of each color in the bag. Remind them that there are only 9 cubes in the bag and that the colors are red, green, and orange. Each group can report and explain how they determined their prediction to the rest of the class. (It is probable that the total tallies for each color will be in proportion to the 5 red, 3 green, and 1 orange cubes in the bag.) Finally, the bag can be opened and the actual numbers revealed.

■ **5-7. THINKING (Learning Level)**

Objective: To determine the probability of events occurring

Materials: 3 blue cubes, 4 red cubes, 2 green cubes, and a bag
Thinking activity sheet

Directions: Select a student to record some information on the board. Display the bag and count the cubes by color as you drop them into the bag. Ask the student to record the total for each color for all to see. "Without looking into the bag, what is the probability of pulling a blue cube?" (*$\frac{3}{9}$, or $\frac{1}{3}$*) "Explain how you got your answer." (*3 blue cubes out of a total of 9 cubes*) Now the next question. "Without looking, what is the probability of pulling a blue *or* a red cube from the bag?" (*$\frac{7}{9}$*) "Explain how you got your answer." (*3 blue cubes plus 4 red cubes out of a total of 9 cubes*)

"When we are not looking for a particular event and use the word 'or,' we use the probability of each event and add them. The probability of pulling a blue cube was $\frac{3}{9}$." Have the student write "$\frac{3}{9}$" on the board. "The probability of pulling a red cube was $\frac{4}{9}$." Have the student write "+ $\frac{4}{9}$" on the board. "Probabilities are ratios, but remember that they behave like fractions. What do we get when we add $\frac{3}{9}$ and $\frac{4}{9}$?" (*$\frac{7}{9}$*) Have the student write "= $\frac{7}{9}$" on the board.

"What is the probability of pulling a red *or* a green cube?" (*$\frac{6}{9}$*) "Explain how you got your answer." (*4 red cubes plus 2 green cubes out of a total of 9 cubes*) Have the student write "$\frac{4}{9}$ + $\frac{2}{9}$ = $\frac{6}{9}$" on the board. "Is $\frac{6}{9}$ in simplest form?" (*no*) "What is the simplest form?" (*$\frac{2}{3}$*) Have the student write "$\frac{2}{3}$" on the board. "The probability of $\frac{2}{3}$ says that it should occur 2 out of 3 times. Let's try it." Close the bag, shake the cubes, and pull one cube. Record the color, replace the cube, and pull again. Record the color, replace the cube, and pull again. The probability is that you pulled a red or green cube 2 of the 3 tries. Distribute the Thinking activity to the students. Stress that the students should fully answer the why questions.

Answer Key: 1. yes, two ways to spin a 3 out of 8 outcomes; 2. yes, three ways to spin a 1 out of 8 outcomes; 3. yes, five ways to spin a 3 or a 1 out of 8 outcomes; 4. $\frac{3}{8}$, two ways to spin a 2 and one way to spin a 4 out of 8 outcomes

Related Activity: You may present this activity as it is stated below, or you can provide a bag of candy, allow the students to count and create the frequency table, and create similar questions to suit that particular candy. The candy must have a variable such as color, shape, or size.

Sour Hearts Candy Colors	
Red	14
Green	7
Yellow	25
Blue	24
Orange	27

Mr. Gonzalez opened a bag of Sour Hearts candy and sorted the pieces by color. Mr. Gonzalez and the class then constructed a frequency chart to show the data.

Use the chart to answer the following questions. What is the probability of shaking a candy from the bag without looking and

■ getting a red or a blue candy? ($^{38}/_{97}$)

■ getting a yellow or orange candy? ($^{52}/_{97}$)

■ getting a green, a red, or a yellow candy? ($^{46}/_{97}$)

■ not getting a blue candy? ($^{73}/_{97}$)

■ not getting a green candy? ($^{90}/_{97}$)

■ 5-8. MORE PROBABILITY (Challenging Level)

Objective: To determine the probability of an event occurring

Materials: Several red, blue, or green cubes (or any three colors) and a bag
More Probability activity sheet

Directions: Have the students watch as you place 4 red cubes, 3 blue cubes, and 2 green cubes into the bag. Write the colors and quantities on the board so the students can refer to them. "What is the probability of pulling a red cube from the bag?" ($^4/_9$) "What does this mean?" (*There is a probability of pulling a red cube 4 times out of 9 tries.*) "What is the probability of pulling a green cube from the bag?" ($^2/_9$) "What is the probability of pulling a red *or* green cube?" ($^6/_9$)

If students give the correct answer for pulling a red or green cube, ask them to explain how they figured it out. (*The number of ways the event can occur is 4 + 2, or 6. The total possible outcomes is still 9.*) If they cannot give and explain the answer, explain the process by asking the ways that each event can occur and the number of outcomes. Ask them to explain what $^6/_9$ means. (*should occur 6 out of 9 times*) "Is $^6/_9$ in simplest terms?" (*no*) "What would the simplest term be?" ($^2/_3$) "And what does $^2/_3$ mean?" (*should happen 2 out of every 3 times*)

Call three students to help you. Allow one to reach into the bag and, without looking, pull a cube. Record the color on the board. Return the cube to the bag and allow the next student to pull a cube. Record the color, return the cube to the bag, and allow the third student to pull a cube. Compare the outcomes to the probability of $^2/_3$ for pulling a red or green cube. "If we repeated this, we would have six students pull a cube. According to the probability, how many red or green cubes would we expect to pull?" (*4*) Choose three more students to repeat the process. Discuss the outcomes according to probability. Finally, choose three more students for a total of nine pulls. Discuss the outcomes according to the probability of $^6/_9$.

"Now let's look at a different way to think about probability. There are 15 students competing on an obstacle course. There is an expectation that $^2/_3$ of the students will make it through the course. That would mean that $^1/_3$ are not expected to make it. Here is how we look at the probability this time. If 3 students run the obstacle course, how many are expected to finish?" (*2*) "How do you know?" (*The probability is $^2/_3$.*) "This means that for every 3 students who run the course, 2 will finish. Will that happen every time 3 students run the course?" (*no*) "What other outcomes could happen with those three students?" (*all 3 finish; none finish; only one finishes*)

"So once again chance plays a part in the outcomes. What is expected does not always happen. If 6 students run the course, how many would you expect to finish?" (*4*) "Why?" (*2 out of every 3 would be 4 out of 6*) "And if 9 students run the course, how may would you expect to finish?" (*6*) "Why?" (*2 out of every 3*) "Now go back to the 15 students. Each student who finishes gets a medal. If 15 students run the course, how many medals should be ordered?" (*10*) "Why?" (*2 out of 3*)

"Will they need 10 medals each time 15 students run the course?" (*no*) "What might happen?" (*more or less could finish*) "Why wouldn't we order 15 medals for each group of 15 students?" (*cost*) "So we are talking about probabilities that can give us an approximate number. How many medals we actually order is a decision that we have to make." Distribute the More Probability activity sheet. The students will determine the probability of events occurring by answering the questions.

Answer Key: 1–3. Answers will vary according to your class enrollment; 4. $\frac{10}{22}$, or $\frac{5}{11}$; 5. $\frac{7}{22}$; 6. $\frac{12}{22}$, or $\frac{6}{11}$; 7. $\frac{6}{26}$, or $\frac{6}{13}$; 8. $\frac{11}{26}$; 9. $\frac{13}{26}$, or $\frac{1}{2}$; 10. 40; 11. 1 out of every 2; 12. Answers will vary.

Related Activity: The parents who sell drinks for the baseball team surveyed 20 students to find out their choice of soft drink. The results showed that 12 liked cola. The parents expect about 100 students to attend the baseball game. According to the probability, how many cans of cola should the parents have for sale at the game so the students can have one drink of their choice? (60: 5 × 20 = 100, 5 × 12 = 60)

■ **5-9. NUMBER CUBE (Learning Level)**

Objectives: To determine the probability of rolling a number on a number cube or die
To conduct an experiment

Materials: Two number cubes or a pair of dice for each student
Number Cube activity sheet

Directions: Review the concept of chance and probability. (See the teacher directions for 5-2 and 5-5 for concept information.) Shake a number cube or die in your hand and then hold it so two fingers are touching any two opposite sides. "Who knows the sum of the two numbers that my fingers are touching? No guessing allowed! Only those who positively know can answer." (*7*) Allow the students who know the answer to explain to it to the others. (*Any two opposite sides always add up to 7 on a legal die.*) If they do not know, encourage the students to explore their number cube or die and see what sums come up when considering any two opposite sides. This information is trivia. It will not affect the outcome, but if students are going to construct number cubes for games or experiments in the future, the cubes should be correctly constructed.

"What is the probability of rolling a 2 with the cube?" ($\frac{1}{6}$) "How do you know?" (*number of ways an event can occur over the total number of possible outcomes*) "If I roll two cubes, how many possible different sums could we get for the outcomes?" (*11, 2–12*) "What sum do you think would be rolled most often? What sum do you think would be rolled least often?" Take several responses and reasons why for both questions but do not acknowledge any as being correct or incorrect. "After answering some questions about number cubes, you will conduct an experiment. Predict what sum you think will occur the most times, then roll the cubes 36 times and record your results. Finally, compare your results to your prediction." Distribute the Number Cube activity sheet and allow the students to answer the questions and conduct the experiment. Save the completed activity sheets for the following related activity.

Answer Key: 1. $\frac{1}{6}$; 2. $\frac{1}{6}$; 3. $\frac{1}{6}$; 4. $\frac{3}{6}$, or $\frac{1}{2}$; 5. $\frac{3}{6}$, or $\frac{1}{2}$; 6. 0; 7–9. Answers will vary.

Related Activity: Redistribute the Number Cube activity sheets to the students. Have them write a total for each sum from their experiment. Draw a large table on the board and write in the sums from 2 to 12. Have the students enter the number of times they rolled each sum on the table. When all of the data have been recorded on the table, use calculators to convert the data to a class frequency table for the experiment. Have the students discuss why they think certain sums occurred more or less often than others. Save the class data for activity 5-10.

■ **5-10. DICE OUTCOMES (Learning Level)**

Objective: To determine the outcomes from rolling a pair of dice

Materials: Overhead of the Dice Outcomes Matrix (see appendix)
Dice Outcomes activity sheet

Directions: Review the data from the previous related activity and several of the student ideas as to why certain sums occurred most or least often. "We will come back to this in a little while and see which reasons will explain why certain sums occurred more and less often." Write the numeral "1" on the board. Roll a pair of dice. "If one of the dice shows a 1, how many different outcomes could there be on the second die?" (*6*) "What could they be?" (*1, 2, 3, 4, 5, 6*) Write the outcomes next to the 1 as shown.

"When the dice are rolled and one of them is a 1, how many different sums could occur?" (*6*) "What are they?" (*1 + 1 = 2, 1 + 2 = 3, 1 + 3 = 4, 1 + 4 = 5, 1 + 5 = 6, 1 + 6 = 7*) "Yes, when one of the dice is a 1, there could be six possible sums."

Roll the dice again. Write a "2" on the board. "If one of the dice shows a 2, how many different outcomes could there be on the second die?" (*6*) "What could they be?" (*1, 2, 3, 4, 5, 6*) Write the outcomes next to the 2 as you did with the 1. "When the dice are rolled and one of them is a 2, how many different sums could occur?" (*6*) "What are they?" (*2 + 1 = 3, 2 + 2 = 4, 2 + 3 = 5, 2 + 4 = 6, 2 + 5 = 7, 2 + 6 = 8*) "Yes, when one of the dice is a 2, there could be six possible sums, the same as when one of the dice was a 1." Roll the dice again and write "3" on the board. "How many different outcomes would there be if one of the dice was a 3?" (*6*) Write the outcomes next to the 3 in similar fashion. "What would the sums be?" (*4, 5, 6, 7, 8, 9*) "When a pair of dice are rolled and one of them is a 1, then there are 6 possible sums. When a pair of dice are rolled and one of them is a 2, then there are 6 possible sums. The same is true if one of them is a 3. What is your prediction for the number of sums that could occur if one of them is a 4?" (*6*) "Why?" (*still only 6 outcomes on the second die*) "That sounds correct to me!"

Place the Dice Outcomes Matrix on the overhead. State that the left vertical column represents the first die and the top horizontal row represents the second die. Demonstrate that if the first die in the vertical column is a 4 and the second die is a 3, where the two meet is the sum of 7. Show another example using 5 and 6 = 11. Ask what is the sum and where would it be written if the dice showed 5 and 3. Distribute the Dice Outcomes activity sheet. The students will fill in the matrix and answer the questions. To further reinforce the sums of dice, the students will then fill in the second matrix by drawing pips (dots) for each die. Save the completed activity sheet for activity 5-11.

Answer Key: 1. 36; 2. 7; 3. 6; 4. 6 and 8; 5. 5 and 9; 6. 4 and 10; 7. 3 and 11; 8. 2 and 12

Related Activity: Supply each student with a die. Review the probability of rolling a 6 with the die. ($\frac{1}{6}$) Each student will toss a die until a 6 is rolled and keep track of how many times it took. The student will record the data and repeat the process four more times. Title a large piece of paper "How Many Times to

Roll a 6" and write the numbers 1 through 20. The students will compile their data by placing tally marks next to the numbers to show how many times it took to roll a 6 in each of their trials. After all of the data have been compiled, the students can discuss the results in terms of probability of the event, rolling a 6, occurring.

■ 5-11. SOME SUMS (Challenging Level)

Objectives: To conduct an experiment
To compare the results to the probabilities

Materials: Pair of dice or number cubes for each student
Completed Dice Outcomes activity sheet
Some Sums activity sheet

Directions: "When you roll two dice or number cubes, several events (something that can happen) can occur. Look at one die or cube. When you roll the die, six total events can occur so the probability of a number occurring is $\frac{1}{6}$, or 1:6." Write $\frac{1}{6}$ and 1:6 on the board. "Another way to write a ratio is like this." (Point to 1:6.) "It means the same thing as $\frac{1}{6}$. It is the probability of the event occurring one time out of six tries."

Continue, "We have seen that when rolling a pair of dice, for each number on one die, any of six numbers can occur on the second die." Write the following on the board:

If the First Die Is:	The Second Die Could Be:
1	1 2 3 4 5 or 6
2	1 2 3 4 5 or 6
3	1 2 3 4 5 or 6
4	1 2 3 4 5 or 6
5	1 2 3 4 5 or 6
6	1 2 3 4 5 or 6

"The probability of a number occurring on the first die is 1:6." Write "1:6" under the first die column. "The probability of a number occurring on the second die is 1:6." Write "1:6" under the second die column. "Multiplying 6 × 6 gives us the total of 36 possible outcomes that could occur when two dice are rolled. To find out the probability of a sum occurring, we figure out how many different ways that sum could occur."

Distribute the completed Dice Outcomes activity sheets to the students. "The first matrix (the addition table) on this sheet shows the 36 different outcomes from rolling a pair of dice. Look at the matrix. How many different ways can we roll a sum of 4?" (*3*) "What are they?" (*1 + 3, 2 + 2, 3 + 1*) "The probability of rolling a sum of 4 is 3:36." Write this on the board. "There are three ways to get a sum of 4 and there are 36 possible outcomes that could occur. How many different ways can we roll a sum of of 9?" (*4*) "What are they?" (*3 + 6, 4 + 5, 5 + 4, 6 + 3*) "The probability of rolling a sum of 9 is 4:36." Write this on the board. Have the students determine the probability of rolling the sum of 2 (*1:36*), 3 (*2:36*), 5 (*4:36*), 6 (*5:36*), 7 (*6:36*), 8 (*5:36*), 10 (*3:36*), 11 (*2:36*), and 12 (*1:36*). Write these on the board as the students identify them.

Distribute the Some Sums activity sheet and a pair of dice to each student. The students will conduct an experiment and compare their results to the probability of those outcomes.

Answer Key: 1. Answers will vary; 2. Events will usually occur according to probability if there are enough tries; 3. Answers will vary; 4. Events will usually occur according to probability if there are enough tries, but they don't have to; 5. Answers will vary, but should be something like probability is a measure of how likely it is that an event will occur.

Related Activity: Pair the students. Provide each pair with two dice and 22 two-color counters (or counters of two different colors, such as red and yellow). One of the players will write the numbers 2 through 12 in a row on a sheet of paper.

| 2 | 3 | 4 | 5 | 6 | 7 | 8 | 9 | 10 | 11 | 12 |

The players will roll the dice and predict which sums will come up most frequently. One player will place 11 red counters on the numbers and the other player will place 11 yellow counters on the numbers. On any number, the students can place up to three counters, or they do not have to place any counters on that number. The players will take turns rolling the dice. Each player will remove one of his or her counters from the number that equals the sum on the dice. If a player has more than one counter on that number, he or she may remove only one counter each time that sum is rolled. The first player to remove all 11 counters is the winner. The pair can discuss which strategies might be most helpful to winning and play the game again.

■ 5-12. ODD OR EVEN (Challenging Level)

Objectives: To determine the total possible outcomes
To determine the fairness of a game

Materials: Pair of dice for each student
Odd or Even activity sheet

Directions: Review the concept of fair games with the students and list ideas that make games fair (*equal chances, equal turns, equal scoring,* etc.). Tell the students that they will be playing a game that involves a pair of dice. Each time the sum of the dice is even, player A moves one space. Each time the sum of the dice is odd, player B moves one space. Pair the students, designating player A and player B, and allow the pairs to try the game for several minutes. Each pair will decide if this is a fair game. As the students discuss why the game is fair or unfair, they should come to the conclusion that there are six even sums (2, 4, 6, 8, 10, 12) and five odd sums (3, 5, 7, 9, 11). They will probably agree that the game is unfair since there are more even sums than odd sums. If the conclusion is not evident, then point it out.

Distribute a pair of dice and the Odd or Even activity sheet to each student. Students are to answer questions 1, 2, and 3, and then continue the activity. The answer to question 4 may be a bit of a surprise to the students. (*It is a fair game. Although the numbers of odd and even sums are not equal, the numbers of ways to roll the odd and even sums are equal.*)

Answer Key: 1. 2, 4, 6, 8, 10, 12; 2. 3, 5, 7, 9, 11; 3. Answers will vary; 4. yes, same number of possible rolls for each

Related Activity: The game is the same as the one described in the directions for this activity, except this time the numbers on the dice are multiplied. Predict whether this is a fair game or not, and why. Determine the number of possible outcomes that are even (*27*) and the number that are odd (*9*). "Is it a fair game?" (*no*) "If it is not a fair game, how could the game be made fair by making a change in the number of spaces that each moves?" (*There are 27 even sums and 9 odd sums. Since there are three times as many even sums as odd sums, each time there is an odd sum, the player gets to move three spaces.*)

■ 5-13. FLIP THEM (Learning Level)

Objective: To determine the possible outcomes of flipping three counters

Materials: 2 copies each of head and tail of coin (see appendix)
3 two-color counters for each student
Flip Them activity sheet

Directions: "Today we are going to discuss probabilities involving flipping coins and counters. If I flipped one coin, how many outcomes could there be?" (*2*) "What are they?" (*head or tail*) Write "1 coin" on the board and tape a copy of a head and a tail under it. "So one coin will give two possible outcomes. What is the probability of flipping a head?" ($\frac{1}{2}$) "What is the probability of flipping a tail?" ($\frac{1}{2}$) Write "2 coins" on the board. "Now if I flipped two coins, what are the possible outcomes?" (*H and H, H and T, T and H, T and T*) As the students generate the responses, tape the correct coin combinations under "2 coins." Have the students determine the probability of flipping two heads ($\frac{1}{4}$), two tails ($\frac{1}{4}$), or a head and a tail in any order ($\frac{2}{4}$, *or* $\frac{1}{2}$). "So, flipping one coin will give two possible outcomes and flipping two coins will give four possible outcomes."

Write "3 coins" on the board. Have the students generate possible outcomes for flipping three coins. Tape the coins to show the possibilities under "3 coins." Stop after three or four responses. Tell students you are going to let them figure out the rest of the outcomes. Distribute three two-color counters and the Flip Them activity sheet to each student. The students will use the counters to figure the possible outcomes and then answer the questions. The activity shows red and yellow as the colors of the two-color counters. If your counters are different colors, instruct the students to make changes on their activity sheet.

Answer Key: 1. 8; 2. 1; 3. $\frac{1}{8}$; 4. $\frac{3}{8}$; 5. $\frac{3}{8}$; 6. $\frac{1}{8}$; 7. 16; 8. Outcomes increased from 2 to 4 to 8. Next would be 16.

Related Activity: Four trucks are going to race. Pair the students. The students will take turns flipping 3 coins (or two-color counters). If all three of the coins are heads, truck 1 moves one space. If there are two heads and one tail, truck 2 moves one space. If there are two tails and one head, truck 3 moves one space. If all three of the coins are tails, truck 4 moves one space. The first truck to move 10 spaces wins.

Before the students begin, they should write down which truck they predict will win the race and why they think so. They will run the race twice and compare their results to their prediction. When they are finished, compile the data into a class chart showing how many races each truck won. Have the class discuss the results. (The probability is that truck 2 and truck 3 will win three times as many races as truck 1 and truck 4. The probability of getting two heads and one tail is $\frac{3}{8}$, as is getting two tails and one head. The probability of getting three heads or three tails is $\frac{1}{8}$.)

■ 5-14. CLEVER TRIANGLES (Challenging Level)

Objectives: To determine a pattern
To continue a pattern

Materials: Red and yellow overhead counters
Clever Triangles activity sheet

Directions: Place the students in pairs and distribute the Clever Triangles activity sheet to each student. Instruct the students to study the pattern with their partners and each fill in the rest of the white triangles to complete the pattern. Allow sufficient time for the students to complete the sheet. If some pairs do not see the pattern, other students can explain the pattern to them. See the answer key for the pattern and correct answers.

"We give credit for this arrangement of numbers to a man named Blaise Pascal. Pascal was a mathematician who lived in the 1600s and studied probability. This triangle of numbers has a lot to do with the probability that we have been working with. The key to this arrangement is the rows of numbers. These rows go horizontally across. The first row is at the top and has the numbers 1 and 1. We all know that 1 + 1 is 2. Think back to flipping one coin. How many possible outcomes could there be?" (2) "And what were the outcomes?" (*H or T*)

"Look at the triangle on your papers. The first row of Pascal's triangle shows this. If we flipped one coin, we could get one head (point to either 1 in the first row) or one tail (point to the other 1 in the first row). The one head or one tail gives us two possible outcomes. On the left side of your triangle, even with row one, write '1 coin' and on the right side of your triangle, even with row one, write '2 total outcomes.' Now think about when we flipped two coins. How many different outcomes could we get?" (4) "What were they?" (*HH, HT, TH, TT*). "Look at row two of the triangle. The numbers are 1, 2, 1, which equal 4. When we flipped two coins, how many ways could we get two heads?" (*1; point to one of the 1's in row two*) "How many ways could we get two tails?" (*1; point to the other 1*) "How many ways could we get a head and a tail in any order?" (*2; point to the 2 in row two*) "On the left side of your triangle, even with row two, write '2 coins' and on the right side of your triangle, even with row two, write '4 total outcomes.'

"How many coins would be flipped in row three?" (*3 coins*) "How do you know?" (*1 coin to 2 coins to 3 coins*) "Correct! There is a progression from 1 to 2 to 3 coins. How many total outcomes are there when three coins are flipped?" (8) "How do you know?" (*1 + 3 + 3 + 1*) "Correct! The numbers in row three add up to 8." Point to a 1. "This shows that an outcome can only occur one way. When flipping three coins, what is an outcome that can only occur one way?" (*HHH or TTT*) "What is another outcome that can only occur one way?" (*TTT or HHH*) Point to a 3. "This shows that an outcome can occur three ways. What outcome can occur three ways?" (*2 heads and 1 tail or 2 tails and 1 head*) Point to the other 3. "What other outcome can occur three ways?" (*2 tails and 1 head or 2 heads and 1 tail*) "On the left side of your triangle, even with row three, write '3 coins' and on the right side of your triangle, even with row three, write '8 total outcomes.'"

Instruct the students to use the triangle to answer the questions on the activity sheet.

Answer Key: The triangle can be interpreted by looking at the horizontal rows. Add two adjacent numbers and put the sum in the triangle below. The vertices of those three triangles touch each other. *4th row:* 1, 4, 6, 4, 1; *5th row:* 1, 5, 10, 10, 5, 1; *6th row:* 1, 6, 15, 20, 15, 6, 1. *Questions:* 1. 4; 2. 16; 3. HHHH or TTTT; 4. HHH, T or TTT, H; 5. HH or TT; 6. HHTT, HTHT, HTTH, THHT, THTH, TTHH; 7. 32; 8. 64

Related Activity: Distribute a copy of Flipping Four Coins (see appendix) to each student. A partially completed version is also available (see appendix) if you feel this would benefit your students. Place the students in pairs if you feel that would be helpful. "If you flipped four coins, there are 16 different outcomes that could occur. Two of the outcomes have a probability of $\frac{1}{16}$ each. The probability of flipping 3 heads and 1 tail is $\frac{4}{16}$, which means that there are four ways this can occur. The probability of flipping 1 head and 3 tails is also $\frac{4}{16}$. There are four ways this can occur. Finally, there are six ways of flipping 2 heads and 2 tails."

Instruct the students to determine the 16 different outcomes for flipping four coins by using the probabilities and clues in the illustration. They should use "H" for head and "T" for tail.

Answer Key:

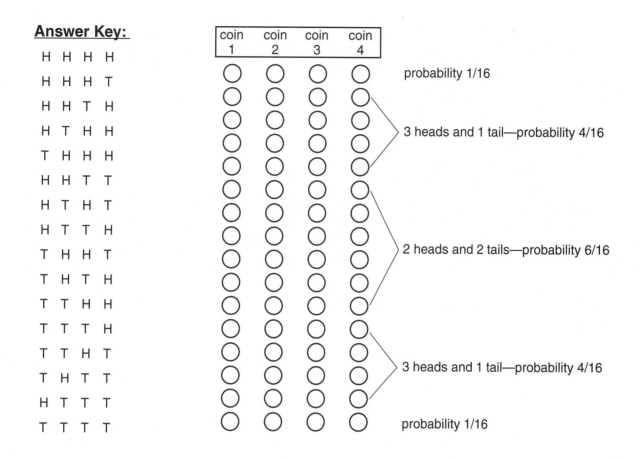

H	H	H	H
H	H	H	T
H	H	T	H
H	T	H	H
T	H	H	H
H	H	T	T
H	T	H	T
H	T	T	H
T	H	H	T
T	H	T	H
T	T	H	H
T	T	T	H
T	T	H	T
T	H	T	T
H	T	T	T
T	T	T	T

probability 1/16

3 heads and 1 tail—probability 4/16

2 heads and 2 tails—probability 6/16

3 heads and 1 tail—probability 4/16

probability 1/16

■ **5-15. SPINNING SPINNERS (Learning Level)**

Objective: To determine the outcomes for independent events

Materials: 2 red, 2 blue, 2 green, and 2 yellow overhead counters
Overhead transparency of two bags (see appendix)
Spinning Spinners activity sheet

Directions: Review the concept of not looking for a particular event (see activity 5-7). "The word *or* is used when any of two or more events would be satisfactory." Place the transparency on the overhead and put 1 red, 2 blue, and 2 green counters inside the bag. "Without looking, what is the probability of pulling a red *or* a blue counter from the bag?" (³⁄₅) "Please explain why it is ³⁄₅." (*Red is ¹⁄₅ and blue is ²⁄₅, which added together makes ³⁄₅.*) "And what does ³⁄₅ mean in terms of pulling a counter from the bag?" (*You should get a red or blue counter 3 out of 5 times.*)

"Now we are going to look at independent events." Write "independent events" on the board. "Independent events happen separately. They do not depend on each other. Many times we use the word *and* when talking about independent events." Rearrange the counters so there are 1 red, 1 blue, and 1 green in each bag. "What is the probability of pulling a red counter from one bag *and* then pulling a green counter from the other bag?" Allow the students time to reflect on the question. They may think that it is ¹⁄₃ + ¹⁄₃, but remind them that we added the ratios when we said *or*. We are using *and* now.

"What possible outcomes could we get?" Start with one counter in the first bag (red, blue, or green) and the possibilities from the second bag (red, blue, or green). Chart the outcomes for all of the students to see: RR, RB, RG BR, BB, BG GR, GB, GG.

"How many possible outcomes do we have?" (*9*) "How many of them are red and green?" (*1*) "What about GR? Isn't that red and green?" (*No. Order is important. Red and green is not the same as green and red.*) "What is the probability of pulling a red marker from the first bag and then a green marker from the second bag?" ($^{1}/_{9}$)

"When we use *and*, the way we figure the probability changes. The probability of pulling a red from the first bag is $^{1}/_{3}$." Write "$^{1}/_{3}$" on the board or overhead. "The probability of pulling a green from the second bag is $^{1}/_{3}$." Leave a space and write "$^{1}/_{3}$" on the board or overhead. "The probability of pulling a red from one bag and then a green from the other bag is $^{1}/_{9}$. What can be done with the ratios of $^{1}/_{3}$ and $^{1}/_{3}$ to get $^{1}/_{9}$? Remember, ratios are just like fractions." (*Multiply the ratios.* $^{1}/_{3} \times ^{1}/_{3} = ^{1}/_{9}$) If the students are not familiar with multiplying fractions, demonstrate the process of multiplying the numerators and then the denominators to produce $^{1}/_{9}$. "Look back at the chart. There were nine different outcomes and only one of them was red and green, which is what the probability is telling us."

Add a yellow counter to each bag. "Would adding the yellow counters to the bag change the probability of pulling a red from one bag and then a green from the other?" (*Yes.* Take several responses and have the students state the reasons they believe the probability would change or not change.) "What is the probability of pulling a red from this bag?" ($^{1}/_{4}$) "And what is the probability of pulling a green from this bag?" ($^{1}/_{4}$) "So for this set of counters, what is the probability of pulling a red from this bag and a green from the other?" ($^{1}/_{16}$)

"When we use the word *or*, we add the individual probabilities. When we use the word *and*, we are dealing with independent events and we multiply the probabilities."

Distribute the Spinning Spinners activity sheet. Students will generate possible outcomes and determine probabilities.

Answer Key: 1. 1 + 1, 1 + 2, 1 + 3, 2 + 1, 2 + 2, 2 + 3, 3 + 1, 3 + 2, 3 + 3; 2. $^{3}/_{9}$, or $^{1}/_{3}$; 3. $^{5}/_{9}$; 4. 16; 5. 1 + 1, 1 + 2, 1 + 3, 1 + 4, 2 + 1, 2 + 2, 2 + 3, 2 + 4, 3 + 1, 3 + 2, 3 + 3, 3 + 4, 4 + 1, 4 + 2, 4 + 3, 4 + 4; 6. 5; 7. $^{4}/_{16}$, or $^{1}/_{4}$; 8. 8; 9. $^{1}/_{8}$; 10. $^{3}/_{8}$; 11. $^{3}/_{8}$; 12. $^{1}/_{8}$

Related Activity: At Wonder Pizza you can get a personal pizza with your choice of pepperoni, sausage, onion, or mushrooms as toppings. How many different personal pizzas with at least one topping can you get at Wonder Pizza? (*16*) Make a chart to show all the different pizzas. Use the letters P, S, O, or M to label the toppings, such as:

Answer Key: P, S, O, M, PS, PO, PM, SM, SO, OM, PSO, PSM, POM, SOM, PSOM

■ 5-16. TALLY AND WIN (Challenging Level)

Objectives: To predict outcomes
To conduct experiments to evaluate the predictions

Materials: 3-region spinners and 4-region spinners for each student (see appendix)
Overhead transparency of two 3-region and two 4-region spinners (see appendix)
2 paper clips for each student
Tally and Win activity sheet

Directions: Place the transparency of the two 3-region spinners on the overhead. Explain that both will be spun and the two numbers will be added. Ask what sums are possible. (*2, 3, 4, 5, 6*) Ask what sums are most likely to be spun and why the students think so. Take several responses. Place the transparency of the two 4-region spinners on the overhead. Ask what sums are possible (*2, 3, 4, 5, 6, 7, 8*) and which are most likely to be spun.

Distribute 2 paper clips, a 3-region spinner, a 4-region spinner, and a Tally and Win activity sheet to each student. Demonstrate how to use the clips to make spinners. See the appendix. This may take a little time, and some students may need individual help. The students will predict the most likely outcomes and conduct experiments to evaluate the predictions.

1. Place the rounded end of one clip over the center of the spinner.

2. Bend the outside of another clip to a right angle.

3. Place the end on the center of the spinner. Hold in place, spin the first clip.

Answer Key: 1–8. Answers will vary.

Related Activity: Organize the students in pairs and provide each pair with 5 two-color counters and a cup. The students will take turns shaking the counters in the cup, tossing the counters out and recording the results. Before they begin, discuss the number of possible outcomes for flipping one counter (*2*), two counters (*4*), three counters (*8*), and four counters (*16*). Can the students determine the total number of possible outcomes for flipping five counters? (*32. See row five of activity 5-14.*)

Before they begin, have the students predict which combination of counters they think will occur most often (*5 red; 4 red, and 1 yellow; 3 red and 2 yellow; 2 red and 3 yellow; 1 red and 4 yellow; or 5 yellow*) and write down the reasons they think so. The students will toss the counters 32 times and record the results each time. When all have completed the activity, conduct a group discussion about the reasons behind the predictions and the possible reasons the results supported or did not support the predictions.

■ 5-17. WE ALL SCREAM FOR ICE CREAM (Beginning Level)

Objective: To determine the arrangements of a permutation

Materials: 18 4-inch by 6-inch pieces of construction paper with "Hakeem" written on 6 of the papers, "Lee" written on 6 other papers, and "Kanesha" written on the last 6 papers
We All Scream for Ice Cream activity sheet

Directions: "Three students are going to receive awards at an assembly. They are to stand next to each other while the principal reads the awards. The students wonder who should stand next to whom. The students are Hakeem (tape a paper with Hakeem on the board), Lee (tape a paper with Lee to the right of Hakeem), and Kanesha (tape a paper with Kanesha to the right of Lee). This is one way that they could stand; Hakeem on the left, Lee in the middle, and Kanesha on the right. What are different ways that the students could stand?" As different arrangements are given, tape those papers onto the board.

Hakeem, Lee, Kanesha	Hakeem, Kanesha, Lee
Lee, Hakeem, Kanesha	Lee, Kanesha, Hakeem
Kanesha, Lee, Hakeem	Kanesha, Hakeem, Lee

"We can see that there are six different arrangements or ways that they can stand. Could they stand Lee then Hakeem then Hakeem?" (*no*) "Why not?" (*only one Hakeem*) "Correct! These special arrangements are called permutations." Write "permutations" on the board. Although the word *permutations* is being introduced, there is not an expectation that the students will use the word. The concept of arrangement will be emphasized. "Only one of each element of the set can be in each arrangement. We use special arrangements, permutations, when we are looking at a particular order.

"I am going to make a sandwich with ham, cheese, and tomato. I am very particular about the way I arrange my sandwich. What different ways could I arrange my ham, cheese, and tomato?" As the students respond, write the arrangements on the board. (*HCT, HTC, CHT, CTH, TCH, THC*) After all six arrangements are discovered, pick one out as your favorite way to arrange your sandwich. "Could I have ham, cheese, and cheese as one of these arrangements?" (*no*) "Why not?" (*only one of each element in the arrangement*)

"Raise your hand if you like ice cream. What are some of your favorite flavors?" (*take several responses*) "This activity sheet is about a girl who likes certain flavors of ice cream and she likes them in a certain order. You will find the six arrangements that can be made from her flavors of ice cream." Distribute the We All Scream for Ice Cream activity sheet.

Answer Key: MC MC FR FR RR RR

FR RR RR MC FR CC

RR FR MC RR MC FR

Related Activity: In 2001, the following were four very expensive cities in which to live: Tokyo, Moscow, Hong Kong, and Beijing.

These were also four very expensive cities in which to live for the year 2000, but in a different order. Find all of the 24 possible ways these cities could be ordered from 1 through 4. Use T = Tokyo, M = Moscow, H = Hong Kong, and B = Beijing. The first few have been done for you.

	1st	2nd	3rd	4th
1.	T	M	H	B
2.	T	M	B	H
3.	T	B	M	H
4.	T	B	H	M
5.	T	H	B	M

Answer Key:

	1st	2nd	3rd	4th		1st	2nd	3rd	4th		1st	2nd	3rd	4th
1.	T	M	H	B	9.	M	H	B	T	17.	H	M	T	B
2.	T	M	B	H	10.	M	H	T	B	18.	H	M	B	T
3.	T	B	M	H	11.	M	B	T	H	19.	B	H	M	T
4.	T	B	H	M	12.	M	B	H	T	20.	B	H	T	M
5.	T	H	B	M	13.	H	B	M	T	21.	B	M	H	T
6.	T	H	M	B	14.	H	B	T	M	22.	B	M	T	H
7.	M	T	H	B	15.	H	T	B	M	23.	B	T	M	H
8.	M	T	B	H	16.	H	T	M	B	24.	B	T	H	M

5-1. In All Likelihood

1. You are going to explore the likelihood of an event happening. A bag contains 3 red cubes and 1 blue cube. With your eyes closed, what is the likelihood of pulling a red cube out of the bag? (very likely, maybe, or very unlikely?) _____

   Why do you think so? _____

   _____

2. Now the bag contains 2 red cubes and 2 blue cubes. With your eyes closed, what is the likelihood of pulling a red cube? (very likely, maybe, or very unlikely?) _____

   Why do you think so? _____

   _____

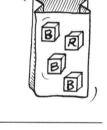

3. This time the bag contains 1 red cube and 3 blue cubes. With your eyes closed, what is the likelihood of pulling a red cube from the bag this time? (very likely, maybe, or very unlikely?) _____

   Why do you think so? _____

   _____

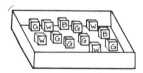

4. A box contains 4 white blocks, 6 gray blocks, and 2 black blocks. Keisha reaches in without looking and pulls out a block. Which color block is she most likely to pick? _____

   Which color block is she least likely to pick? _____

   Why do you think so? _____

   _____

5-1. In All Likelihood (continued)

5. A box contains 4 green blocks, 2 yellow blocks, 3 blue blocks, and 6 purple blocks. Ricardo reaches in without looking and pulls out a block.

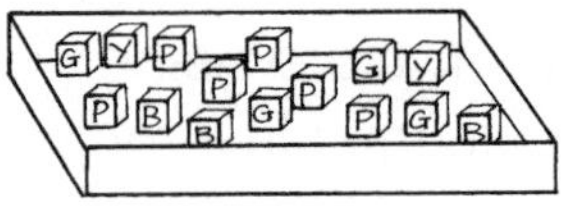

Which color block is he most likely to pick? _____

Which color block is he least likely to pick? _____

Why do you think so? _____

_____

6. A box contains 4 red blocks, 6 yellow blocks, 3 orange blocks, and 6 purple blocks. Sara reaches in without looking and pulls out a block.

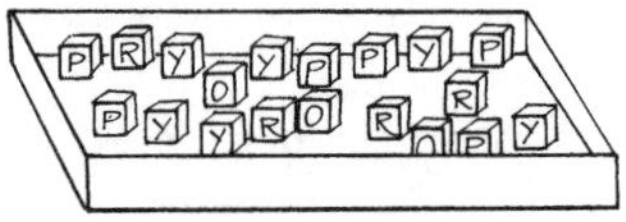

Which color block is she most likely to pick? _____

Which color block is she least likely to pick? _____

Why do you think so? _____

_____

Name _____   Date _____

5-2. Chance

When something happens that isn't planned, we call it chance. We can think that one event will occur, but by chance a different event occurs. For example, you have 5 red crayons and 1 blue crayon in a bag. If you pull one out, it will likely be red. But sometimes you pull out the blue one. It happens by chance.

Conduct an experiment. Place 5 red crayons and 1 blue crayon in the bag, close your eyes, and pull out one crayon. It is likely that it will be a red crayon. There is a chance, however, that it will be blue. Do this 6 times. Each time you take a crayon out, put it back for the next draw. Record your data on the chart below.

Trial	Color of Crayon
1	
2	
3	
4	
5	
6	

How many times did you pull out a blue cube? _____ It is likely that you did it one time. If you pulled out the blue cube more than one time, or not at all, it was by chance.

1. Describe in your own words what chance means. _____

   _____

   _____

2. Conduct the experiment again, but make predictions before you begin. This time you will do 12 trials. How many times do you predict you will pull a red crayon? _____
   How many times do you predict you will pull a blue crayon? _____
   Record your predictions in a chart like the one above.

3. How many times did you pull a red crayon during the second experiment? _____
   How many times did you pull a blue crayon during the second experiment? _____
   Were your predictions correct? _____

183

5-3. Fair *or* Unfair

Keisha and Sara are going to play a game that involves rolling a die or number cube. If a 1, 2, or 3 is rolled, then Keisha moves her marker one space on the board. If 4, 5, or 6 is rolled, then Sara moves her marker one space on the board. The first one around the board wins. Sara feels that since she has the larger numbers she will win.

1. Is this game fair? _____

2. Do you think Sara has a better chance to win the game than Keisha? _____

3. Why do you think so?_____

_____

Keisha and Sara decide to play another game. This time they are going to use a spinner like the one on the right to decide who moves her marker one space on the board. If the spinner stops on 1 or 2, Keisha moves her marker one space. If the spinner stops on 3, then Sara moves her marker one space.

4. Is this game fair? _____

5. Who has a better chance to win the game? _____

6. Why do you think so?_____

_____

Ricardo and Michael are going to play a game. If the spinner stops on 1 or 3, then Ricardo moves one space. If the spinner stops on 2 or 4, then Michael moves one space.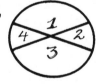

7. Is this game fair? _____

8. Who do you think will win the game? _____

9. How do you know?_____

_____

5-3. Fair or Unfair (*continued*)

10. If the game is unfair, redraw the spinner to make it a fair game.

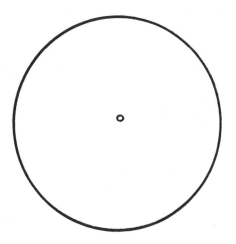

In another game, the boys shuffle the cards and place them facedown. The cards are turned over one by one. If the card shows an even number, Ricardo moves one space. If the card shows an odd, number Michael moves two spaces.

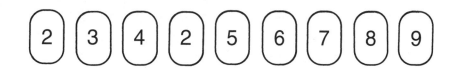

11. Is this game fair? _____

12. Who do you think will win the game? _____

13. How do you know? _____

_____

14. If the game is unfair, add a number to one more card to make it a fair game.

5-4. The Match Game

You and a friend are going to play a game and you both want it to be fair. You will look at two ways to play the game and decide which one will be fair to both of you.

Some purple and yellow cubes are placed in a bag. One player reaches into the bag and, without looking, pulls out two cubes. If the cubes match in color, then you move one space. If they do not match, your friend moves one space. The cubes are then placed back into the bag before the next player pulls out two.

Look at the two sets of cubes that could be placed into the bag.

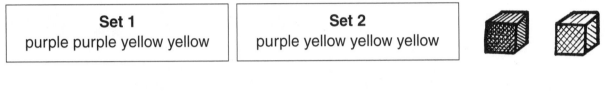

Set 1 purple purple yellow yellow	**Set 2** purple yellow yellow yellow

Which set of cubes do you think will make the game fair? _____ Why? _____

_____

_____

Now let's take a closer look at the sets of cubes. In Set 1 we will call the first purple cube P1 and the second purple cube P2. We will call the yellow cubes Y1 and Y2. Look at the table below. The cubes in the left column represent the first cube that could be pulled. The top row represents the second cube that could be pulled.

second cube

first cube	P1	P2	Y1	Y2
P1	—	yes	no	no
P2	yes	—	no	no
Y1	no	no	—	yes
Y2				

5-4. The Match Game (*continued*)

If P1 is chosen first, then looking across the row, P2 would match, Y1 would not match, and Y2 would not match. Of course, P1 could not be the first and second cube to be pulled, so nothing is recorded there. If P2 is the first cube pulled, then P1 would match, and neither Y1 nor Y2 would match. Review the row if Y1 is chosen first and then complete the row if Y2 is chosen first.

1. Examine the table. How many times did the cubes match? _____ How many times did the cubes not match? _____

2. Is this a fair game? _____ Why? _____

   _____

   _____

In Set 2 the purple cube is P1 and the yellow cubes are Y1, Y2, and Y3. Fill in the table below, showing if the first and second cubes match.

second cube

	P1	Y1	Y2	Y3
P1				
Y1				
Y2				
Y3				

first cube

3. Examine this table. How many times did the cubes match? _____ How many times did the cubes not match? _____

4. Is this a fair game? _____ Why? _____

   _____

   _____

5. Was your prediction correct? _____

5-5. More or Less

The likelihood that an event is going to occur is also known as the probability. Probability is a measure of how likely an event is to happen. Some events are more likely to occur and some are less likely to occur. An outcome is the result of the event. If the event is tossing a coin and getting a head, the outcome is how the coin comes up—heads or tails.

The probability of pulling a red cube from a bag that contains 3 red cubes and 1 blue cube, the event, is ¾, or 3 out of every 4 times. This means if we try 4 times, we should pull a red cube 3 times. The probability looks like a fraction and behaves like a fraction, but it is really a ratio. A ratio is a relationship of numbers. A probability of ¾ is a relationship that represents 3 out of every 4 times.

The probability of an event occurring lies between the numbers 0 and 1. A probability of 0 shows that the event is impossible, and a probability of 1 shows that the event is certain. The closer a probability is to 0, the less likely it is to occur; the closer a probability is to 1, the more likely it is to occur.

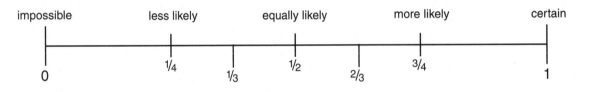

1. Is an event with a probability of ⅓ less likely to occur, equally likely to occur, or more likely to occur?_____

2. Why do you think so? _____

3. Is an event with a probability of ¾ less likely to occur, equally likely to occur, or more likely to occur?_____

4. Why do you think so? _____

5. Is an event with a probability of ⅘ less likely to occur, equally likely to occur, or more likely to occur? _____

6. Why do you think so? _____

5-5. More or Less (continued)

7. Which is more likely to occur, an event with a probability of ¾ or an event with a probability of ⅓? _____ Why do you think so? _____

_____

8. What is the probability of spinning a 2 on the spinner below? _____

9. Is it less likely to occur, equally likely to occur, or more likely to occur? _____

_____

10. Why do you think so? _____

_____

11. What is the probability of pulling a green marble from a bag that contains 1 blue marble and 3 green marbles? _____

12. Is it less likely to occur, equally likely to occur, or more likely to occur? _____

_____

13. Why do you think so? _____

_____

14. What is the probability of shuffling 1 ace and 4 kings and turning over an ace? _____

15. Is it less likely to occur, equally likely to occur, or more likely to occur? _____

_____

16. Why do you think so? _____

_____

Date _____

5-6. The Ready Ratio

The likelihood that an event is going to occur is also known as the probability. Probability is a measure of how likely an event is to happen. An outcome is the result of the event. If the event is rolling a 4 on a number cube, the outcome is the number that is rolled. One way to write a probability is like this:

$$\frac{\text{The number of ways an event can occur.}}{\text{The total number of possible outcomes.}}$$

The probability looks like a fraction and behaves like a fraction, but is really a ratio. The closer the ratio is to 1, the greater the probability is of the event occurring.

1. What is the probability of flipping a two-color counter and getting a certain color? _____

2. Is the ratio closer to 0 or to 1? _____

3. Is the event less likely to occur, equally likely to occur, or more likely to occur?

     _____

4. Why do you think so? _____

5. What is the probability of rolling a 4 on a six-sided number cube? _____

6. Is the ratio closer to 0 or to 1? _____

7. Is the event less likely to occur, equally likely to occur, or more likely to occur?

     _____

8. Why do you think so? _____

9. What is the probability of pulling a red crayon from a bag that contains 3 red crayons and 2 blue crayons? _____

10. Is the event less likely to occur, equally likely to occur, or more likely to occur?

     _____

11. Why do you think so? _____

5-7. Thinking

Antonio and Christi are working on some problems dealing with the probability of spinning certain numbers on the spinner.

Problem: What is the probability of spinning a 3?

  Antonio thinks the spinner is divided into eight equal sections and two of those parts are 3, so the probability of spinning a 3 is ²⁄₈, or ¼.

1. Do you agree with Antonio's thinking, and why? _____

_____

Problem: What is the probability of spinning a 1?

  Christi thinks three of the eight parts are numbered 1, so the probability of spinning a 1 is ³⁄₈.

2. Do you agree with Christi's thinking, and why? _____

_____

Problem: What is the probability of spinning a 3 or a 1?

  Christi and Antonio think that since the probability of spinning a 3 is ²⁄₈ and the probability of spinning a 1 is ³⁄₈, then the probability of spinning a 3 or a 1 is ⁵⁄₈.

3. Do you agree with Christi and Antonio's thinking, and why? _____

_____

4. Write how Antonio and Christi would think about the probability of spinning a 2 or a 4.

_____

_____

Name _____   Date _____

5-8. More Probability

To choose the helper of the week for your class, your teacher puts each student's name on a piece of paper and places the papers in a bowl. After mixing them up, your teacher reaches in and pulls out the name of a student who will be helper for the week. Use the students in your classroom for the data.

1. What is the probability the helper will be a girl? _____

2. What is the probability the helper will be a boy? _____

3. What is the probability the helper of the week will be you? _____

A piggy bank contains 7 dimes, 5 nickels, and 10 quarters.

4. What is the probability of shaking a quarter out of the bank? _____

5. What is the probability of shaking a dime out of the bank? _____

6. What is the probability of shaking a dime *or* a nickel out of the bank? _____

A bag contains 7 red candies, 4 green candies, 5 yellow candies, 8 brown candies, and 2 blue candies. Without looking, what is the probability you will reach in and pull out:

7. a blue *or* green candy? _____

8. a green *or* red candy? _____

9. a brown *or* yellow candy? _____

In the school Bike-a-Thon, the principal figures there is a probability that one of every two fourth-grade students will ride far enough to win a T-shirt. There are 80 fourth graders who will participate in the Bike-a-Thon.

10. How many fourth graders will probably earn T-shirts? _____

11. Explain how you got your answer. _____

_____

_____

12. To be safe, how many T-shirts do you feel the principal should order so all fourth grade students who ride far enough get a T-shirt, and there are not a lot of T-shirts left over?

_____

_____

192

Name _____   Date _____

5-9. Number Cube

Carefully examine a number cube and determine the number of possible outcomes that could occur by rolling the number cube. Use the cube to answer questions 1–6.

1. What is the probability of rolling a 1? _____

2. What is the probability of rolling a 4? _____

3. What is the probability of rolling a 5? _____

4. What is the probability of rolling an even number? _____

5. What is the probability of rolling an odd number? _____

6. What is the probability of rolling a 0? _____

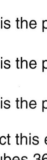

To conduct this experiment, you will need two number cubes or a pair of dice. You will roll the cubes 36 times and add the two numbers each time. Before you begin, however, predict what sum you believe will occur the most times. _____ Now roll the cubes 36 times and record a tally next to the sum each time it occurs.

Sum	Tally
2	
3	
4	
5	
6	
7	
8	
9	
10	
11	
12	

7. What sum or sums occurred the most amount of times?

_____

8. What sum or sums occurred the least amount of times?

_____

9. Was your prediction correct? _____ Why do you think it was or was not?

_____

_____

_____

5-10. Dice Outcomes

Here is an addition table. A few of the sums have been filled in for you. Study the table and fill in the remaining sums.

+	1	2	3	4	5	6
1	2	3				
2		4	5			
3		5				
4			7	8		
5						11
6	7				11	

1. How many total sums are there? _____

2. Which sum occurs the most? _____

3. How many times does it occur? _____

4. Two sums occur five times each. They are _____ and _____ .

5. Two sums occur four times each. They are _____ and _____ .

6. Two sums occur three times each. They are _____ and _____ .

7. Two sums occur two times each. They are _____ and _____ .

8. Two sums occur only once each. They are _____ and _____ .

There are 36 outcomes when rolling a pair of dice. Fill in the pips (dots) on the table to show the 36 outcomes.

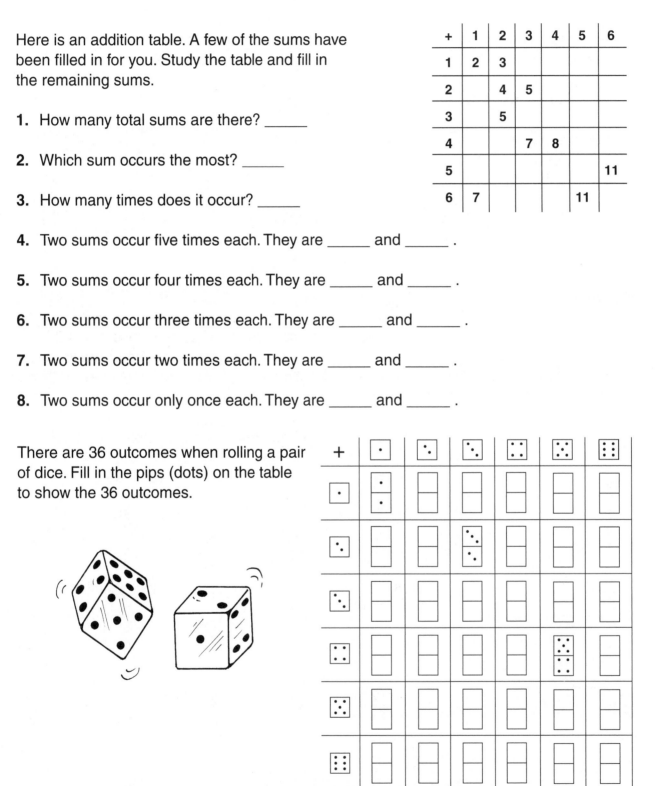

5-11. Some Sums

Probability is a measure of how likely it is that an event will occur. But probability is not absolute. Sometimes the events will occur according to the probability and sometimes they will not. Sometimes the unexpected occurs, but if we conduct the event enough times, the outcome usually occurs according to the probability.

The following experiment looks at the probability of an event occurring and the effect of chance. Roll a pair of dice or number cubes 36 times. Mark a tally to record each sum that comes up. Write your results in the form of a ratio and compare your results to the probability of that sum occurring. An example is given.

Sum	Tally	Probability of the Sum Occurring	Results of 36 Rolls
2	//	1:36	2:36

Sum	Tally	Probability of the Sum Occurring	Results of 36 Rolls	Results of 72 Rolls
2		1:36	_____: 36	_____:36
3		2:36	_____:_____	_____:_____
4		3:36	_____:_____	_____:_____
5		4:36	_____:_____	_____:_____
6		5:36	_____:_____	_____:_____
7		6:36	_____:_____	_____:_____
8		5:36	_____:_____	_____:_____
9		4:36	_____:_____	_____:_____
10		3:36	_____:_____	_____:_____
11		2:36	_____:_____	_____:_____
12		1:36	_____:_____	_____:_____

1. How many of your results from 36 rolls are close to the probabilities? _____

2. Why do you think they were close to the probabilities? _____

_____

5-11. Some Sums (continued)

Do the experiment again and combine the results. Since there will be 72 rolls, divide each tally result by 2 and write the result as a ratio of 36. For example, if there were 10 tallies, divide by 2 and write the ratio as 5/36. Then compare the ratios to the probabilities. For example:

Results of First Trial	Sum	Probability of Sum	Tally	Results of Second Trial	Total	Divide by 2 for Results
3 of 36	2	1:36	/	1 of 36	4 of 36	2 of 36

Results of First Trial	Sum	Probability of Sum	Tally	Results of Second Trial	Total	Divide by 2 for Results
____ of 36	2	1:36		____ of 36	____ of 72	____ of 36
____ of 36	3	2:36		____ of 36	____ of 72	____ of 36
____ of 36	4	3:36		____ of 36	____ of 72	____ of 36
____ of 36	5	4:36		____ of 36	____ of 72	____ of 36
____ of 36	6	5:36		____ of 36	____ of 72	____ of 36
____ of 36	7	6:36		____ of 36	____ of 72	____ of 36
____ of 36	8	5:36		____ of 36	____ of 72	____ of 36
____ of 36	9	4:36		____ of 36	____ of 72	____ of 36
____ of 36	10	3:36		____ of 36	____ of 72	____ of 36
____ of 36	11	2:36		____ of 36	____ of 72	____ of 36
____ of 36	12	1:36		____ of 36	____ of 72	____ of 36

3. How many of your results from 72 rolls are close to the probabilities? _____

4. Why do you think the results are closer to the probabilities (or not closer if the results are not closer)?

_____

Probability is a study of numbers and chance. The numbers will not always behave as they are supposed to, but if the event is repeated enough times, the outcome eventually will follow the rules of probability.

5. In your own words, define probability. _____

_____

5-12. Odd or Even

You and your best friend are going to play a game. Your friend explains the rules. Two dice will be rolled and the two numbers added together. Each time the sum is even, your friend moves one space forward. Each time the sum is odd, you move one space forward.

1. Write the possible even sums. _____

2. Write the possible odd sums. _____

3. Do you think this is a fair game? _____ Why? _____

_____

Take a closer look at the game. For each even sum, write all of the possible ways to roll that sum. The sum of 4 has been done for you. Then do the same thing for the odd sums.

Even Sum	Possible Rolls		Odd Sum	Possible Rolls
_____	_____		_____	_____
4	3 + 1, 2 + 2, 1 + 3		_____	_____
_____	_____		_____	_____
_____	_____		_____	_____

4. Count the total possible rolls for the even numbers and the total for the odd numbers.

Now do you think this is a fair game? _____ Why? _____

_____

5-13. Flip Them

You will need several two-color counters or coins to work through this activity. If you flip one counter, there could be two outcomes: a red or a yellow. The probability of flipping a two-color counter and getting a red is 1/2. This means that you should get a red one out of every two flips.

Take a second counter. What is the probability of flipping two counters and getting two reds? Use your two counters to show the following outcomes:

- The first counter is red and the second counter is red.

- The first counter is red and the second counter is yellow.

- The first counter is yellow and the second counter is red.

- The first counter is yellow and the second counter is yellow.

There are four possible outcomes when flipping two counters, and only one of the outcomes is two red counters. So the probability of flipping two counters and getting two reds is 1/4.

Take a third counter. What is the probability of flipping three counters and getting three reds? Finish listing all of the possible outcomes below.

First Counter	Second Counter	Third Counter
red	red	red
red	red	yellow
red	yellow	red
red		

1. How many possible outcomes are there when flipping three counters? _____

2. How many of the outcomes show three reds? _____

3. What is the probability of flipping three counters and getting three reds? _____

© 2004 by John Wiley & Sons, Inc.

Name _____   Date _____

5-13. Flip Them (*continued*)

4. What is the probability of flipping three counters and getting two reds and one yellow, in any order? _____

5. What is the probability of flipping three counters and getting one red and two yellows, in any order? _____

6. What is the probability of flipping three counters and getting three yellows? _____

Fill in the chart using the above information and answer questions 7 and 8.

Number of Counters Flipped	Number of Possible Outcomes
1	_____
2	_____
3	_____

7. Write your prediction for the number of possible outcomes for flipping four two-color counters. _____

8. Why do you think so? _____

_____

_____

5-14. Clever Triangles

Study the design below. The numbers form a pattern. Determine the pattern and fill in the rest of the numbers. Then answer questions 1–8.

1. How many coins would be flipped in row 4? _____

2. How many total outcomes would there be in row 4? _____

3. What outcome in row 4 could only happen one way? _____

4. What outcome in row 4 could happen four ways? _____

5. What outcome in row 4 could happen six ways? _____

6. Show the six ways this could happen. Use H for heads and T for tails. Remember to show four coins in each of the six ways.

_____

_____

_____

7. How many total outcomes would there be in row 5? _____

8. How many total outcomes would there be in row 6? _____

Name _____   Date _____

5-15. Spinning Spinners

For each set of spinners below, write all of the possible outcomes and then determine the probability of the event happening.

1. Both spinners are spun and the two numbers that come up are added together. Finish writing all of the possible outcomes here.

Spinner One		Spinner Two		Spinner One		Spinner Two		Spinner One		Spinner Two
1	+	1		_____	+	_____		_____	+	_____
1	+	2		_____	+	_____		_____	+	_____
1	+	_____		_____	+	_____		_____	+	_____

2. What is the probability that the sum will be a 4? _____

3. What is the probability that the sum will be even? _____

4. Both spinners are spun and the two numbers that come up are added together.

    How many possible outcomes could there be? _____

5. Write all of the possible outcomes.

    _____

    _____

    _____

5-15. Spinning Spinners (*continued*)

6. What sum is most likely to occur? _____

7. What is the probability of that sum occurring? _____

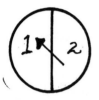 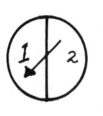 

8. All three spinners are spun and the three numbers that come up are added together. How many possible outcomes could there be? _____

9. What is the probability that the sum will be 3? _____

10. What is the probability that the sum will be 4? _____

11. What is the probability that the sum will be 5? _____

12. What is the probability that the sum will be 6? _____

Name _____   Date _____

5-16. Tally and Win

You and your partner will each need a 3-region spinner (with the numbers 1, 2, and 3). You will each spin, add the two numbers, and record that sum on the tally table until one of the sums has ten tallies.

1. Before you begin, what sum do you predict will get the ten tallies first? _____

2. Why do you think so? _____

Now conduct the experiment.

Sum	Tallies
2	
3	
4	
5	
6	

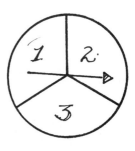

3. Which sum got ten tallies first? _____ Was your prediction correct? _____

4. Why do you think your prediction was or was not correct? _____

You and your partner will conduct the experiment again, but this time you will use 4-region spinners (with the numbers 1, 2, 3, and 4). You will each spin, add the two numbers, and record that sum until one of the sums has ten tallies. Use your knowledge from the three-region spinner experiment to answer questions 5 and 6.

5. Before you begin, what sum do you predict will get the ten tallies first? _____

6. Why do you think so?_____

Construct a tally table and begin the experiment.

7. Which sum got ten tallies first? _____ Was your prediction correct? _____

8. Why do you think your prediction was or was not correct? _____

5-17. We All Scream for Ice Cream

Julie goes to her favorite ice cream shop to have a triple-scoop cone. Her three favorite flavors are Fudge Ripple, Mint Chocolate, and Rocky Road. She is a lover of ice cream, so it is important for Julie to have the scoops in the proper order.

Since there are three choices of ice cream, there can be six different ways to arrange the scoops so there is one scoop of each flavor on each cone. Show the different cones that Julie can choose from. Remember, only one scoop of each flavor on each cone. Use the flavor key for the abbreviations for the ice cream flavors.

Flavor Key	Fudge Ripple FR	Mint Chocolate MC	Rocky Road RR

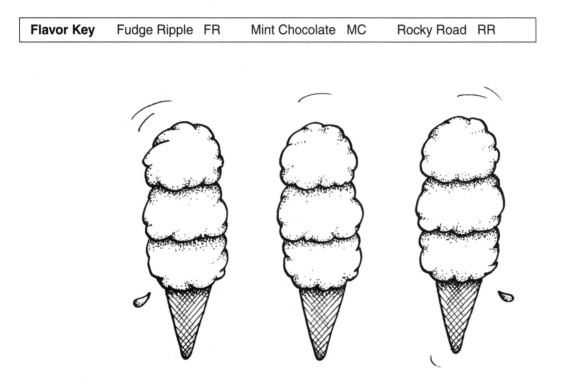

Section 6

ALGEBRA

Teacher Directions

■ **6-1. CHOOSE THE BEST** (Learning Level)

Objectives: To choose an equation to match a symbolic representation
To draw a symbolic representation of equations

Materials: Overhead transparency of Set Rings (see appendix)
Overhead counters
Overhead pens
Choose the Best activity sheet

Directions: Review, or introduce, an equation as a number sentence that uses an equal sign to show that two expressions have the same value. Have the students generate several examples of equations. (*3 + 5 = 8, 17 = 9 + 8, 24 – 17 = 7, 3 × 15 = 45*, etc.) Show some nonexamples of equations to further develop the concept. (*4 × 7, 9, ¹/₂*, etc.)

Place the Set Rings transparency onto the overhead and use a piece of paper to cover the transparency so only the top representation is showing. Point to the top representation. "This is a representation. We call it a representation because it represents, or stands for, something. It shows something that we are trying to describe. What do you see in this representation?" (*two set rings or set hoops inside another set ring*) "What might I be trying to show with this representation?" (*two sets of something that are together*)

Place one counter in each of the smaller rings. Point to one ring, then the other. "Here is a set of one and here is a set of one. Both of the sets are inside the larger set. For now let's pretend that each counter is a piece of candy. Listen to this story. 'Sara had one piece of candy. Her father gave her another piece of candy.' How does the representation relate to the story?" (*a set of one and another set of one making a set of two*) "What math sentence, or equation, could we use that would match this representation?" Write "1 + 1 = 2" under the symbolic representation. Have the students explain why the equation would match the representation.

"Think of another story and equation that could be shown by this representation." (*2 × 1 = 2 or 2 ÷ 2 = 1*) As the students respond with the equations, write them under the representation. "This symbolic representation (point to it) can represent, or stand for, three different equations. A set of one plus a set of one. Two groups of one. Two divided into two equal groups. It is very useful!"

Slide the paper down the transparency to reveal the second representation. Place two counters into each of the smaller rings. "Lee had two bags. Each bag contained two cookies. Does this story match the representation?" (*yes*) "Why?" (*two groups of two*) "What equation would match the story and the representation?" Write "2 × 2 = 4" under the representation as the student responds. "What other stories and equations would match this representation?" (*2 + 2 = 4 or 4 ÷ 2 = 2*) Write the equations under the representation as the students explain why they are correct. "This symbolic representation (point to it) can also represent, or stand for, three different equations. A set of two plus a set of two. Two groups of two. Four divided into two equal groups. It is also very useful!"

Display the last representation. Place three counters in each of the three rings. Have the students choose an equation that matches the representation and justify their answer. (*3 + 3 + 3 = 9, 3 × 3 = 9, 9 ÷ 3 = 3*) Then have them describe why 9 – 3 = 6 does not match. (*There are 9 left inside the set ring, not 6. This representation does not show subtraction.*) Distribute the Choose the Best activity sheet. The students will choose the equations that match the representation and justify their answers. They will then create a representation to show specific equations.

Answer Key: 1. c, two sets of three; 2. a and c, two sets of two; 3. a, b, and c, three sets of two; 4. 4 + 4 + 4 = 12, 3 × 4 = 12, 12 ÷ 3 = 4; 5. three sets of five

Related Activity: Pair the students. Distribute a set of Cuisenaire rods, four 12-inch pieces of yarn, a 36-inch piece of yarn, and a pencil and paper to each pair. One of the pair will use the Cuisenaire rods and yarn to create a representation. The other will write equations that match the representation. After agreement about the equations, the partners can switch roles and continue for several rounds.

■ **6-2. CONTINUE THE PATTERN (Learning Level)**

Objectives: To continue a pattern
                    To identify specific elements of a pattern

Materials: Overhead counters of different colors
                  Continue the Pattern activity sheet

Directions: Use the counters to create an AAB AAB pattern (*red, red, blue, red, red, blue,* [or other colors]) on the overhead. Ask the students what would come next (*red*) and why. (*AAB pattern*) Ask the color of the 5th figure in the pattern. (*red*) If the pattern was continued, what would be the 13th figure? (*red*) Have several students describe different strategies for determining the 13th figure. Next, ask what would be the 36th figure and elicit different strategies for determining the 36th figure.

Write "1, 4, 7, 10, 13" on the board. Ask the students for the next three numbers in the pattern. (*16, 19, 22*) Have a student explain the pattern. (*+3*) Write "98, 92, 86, 80" on the board and have the students give the next three numbers in the pattern and explain the pattern. (*74, 68, 62; –6*) Now repeat the process with "0, 1, 3, 6, 10." (*+1, +2, +3, +4*, etc.)

Distribute the Continue the Pattern activity sheet. The students will continue patterns, identify specific elements, and explain their thinking.

Answer Key: 1. ◯ ; 2. ◯ ; 3. ◯ , 4 sets of 5 figures and 2 more; 4. ▢ , 10 sets of 5 figures; 5. 9, 6, 3; 6. 736, 640, 544; 7. 64, 128, 256, double; 8. 31, 63, 127, double and +1; 9. ⊞⊞ , 22 squares, starts with 4 squares and increases by 2

Related Activity: Michael gets paid for doing jobs in his neighborhood. He wants to save some of the money. Michael saved $1 the first week. He saved $2 the second week. He saved $4 the third week, and $7 the fourth week. If Michael continues this pattern, how much will he save in the ninth week? (*$37*) What is the total Michael will save in the nine weeks? (*$129*)

■ **6-3. REASONING (Challenging Level)**

Objectives: To continue a pattern
                    To identify specific elements of a pattern

Materials: Reasoning activity sheet

Directions: Write "TV VCR DVD CD TV" on the board. "What do you notice about the words that I wrote on the board?" (*All are shortened forms of words.*) "That is true, but what I did is make a pattern of words. Sometimes we make patterns using figures, sometimes we make patterns using numbers, and sometimes we make patterns using words. This is the complete pattern. What would be the next word in the pattern?" (*VCR*) "Correct. If the pattern was continued, what would be the fourteenth word?" (*VCR*) "How do you know?" (Responses will vary.)

Have the students work in pairs to create a pattern using words. Then they will assume that the pattern continues and determine a specific element in the pattern, such as the 23rd word. Ask three or four pairs to write their patterns on the board and ask for the specific elements. The rest of the class will determine the word, respond, and describe how they knew. This can be repeated with different pairs as long as you feel that the students are attending.

Distribute the Reasoning activity sheet. The students will continue the patterns and describe the patterns.

Answer Key: 1. spring, counted, or 2 sets of 5 and 4 more; 2. summer, 6 groups of 5 then 1 more; 3. M T W T F S (days of the week); 4. F M A M J J A S O N D (months of the year); 5. ⬛ ⬛ ⬛, upper left, upper right, lower right, lower left; 6. 10, 15, 21, 28, 36, 45, 55

Related Activity: A very wise person hires you to work for her for 10 days. She will pay you one of three ways:

1. $1 the first day, $2 the second day, $3 the third day, and continue the pattern up to 10 days.

2. $7 a day for each of the ten days.

3. $.10 the first day, $.20 the second day, each day doubling what you were paid the day before.

Which do you think you would choose? Why? (*Answers will vary.*) Figure out each option. (*$55, $70, $102.30*) Which do you choose now? Why?

■ **6-4. PATTERNS AND RATIOS (Learning Level)**

Objectives: To write a ratio three different ways
To use ratio to complete a table

Materials: Patterns and Ratios activity sheet

Directions: Have a student stand in front of the group. "How many hands does he [or she] have?" (*2*) On the board write "1 student, 2 hands." "There is a relationship between these two numbers. The relationship is one to two. What is the relationship called?" (*a ratio*) "A ratio is a relationship between two sets. In this case, one set is student and the other set is hands. There are three different ways that I can write a ratio. Who can come to the board and write one of the ways?" Continue until all three ways (*1 to 2, 1:2, ½*) are shown. "Each one of these different ways of writing the ratio says the same thing, one to two."

Have a second student join the standing student. "The ratio is one student to two hands. How many hands would two students have?" (*4*) "How did you get your answer?" (*counting, 2 × 2, 2 + 2, etc.*) "There are now two students and four hands. Is the ratio still one to two?" (*yes*) "Why?" (*²⁄₄ = ½, 2 to 4 = 1 to 2, etc.*) The students may sit down. "Using the ratio of one to two, how many hands would three students have?" (*6*) "And four students?" (*8*) "If there were ten hands, how many students would there be?" (*5*) "Why?" (*⁵⁄₁₀ = ½, or other descriptions of the same idea*) "How many students would there be if there were sixteen hands?" (*8*)

"What is the ratio of tricycles to the number of wheels?" (*1 to 3*) "Who can come to the board and write the ratio three ways?" (*1 to 3, 1:3, ⅓*) Draw a T chart on the board like the one on the right.

Tricycles	Wheels
1	3

"How many wheels would two tricycles have?" (*6*) Fill in 2 and 6 on the chart. "How many wheels would three tricycles have?" (*9*) Fill in 2 and 6 on the chart, then add 9 under Wheels. "If there were 9 wheels, how many tricycles would there be?" (*3*) Add 3 to the chart under Tricycles. Add 12 and 15 under Wheels and have students fill in 4 and 5 under Tricycles.

Tricycles	Wheels
1	3
2	6
3	9
4	12
5	15

Distribute the Patterns and Ratios activity sheet. The students will use the ratio to complete the tables and write the ratios in three different ways.

Answer Key: 1. books: 16, 20, 40; 2. balls: 12, 15—players: 10, 15, 50; 3. 2 to 25, 2:25, $\frac{2}{25}$, 4 = .50, 6 = .75, 10 = 1.25, 16 = 2.00, 20 = 2.50; 4. Answers will vary; 5.

4	8	12	16	20	24
5	10	15	20	25	30

, answers will vary

Related Activity: Allow the students to research data around the school that can be used in ratio problem solving such as: School lunches cost $1.50. How much will eight lunches cost? The students can solve each other's problems and then construct T charts to verify their answers.

■ 6-5. PROPERTIES (Learning Level)

Objective: To describe and identify properties of addition and multiplication

Materials: Overhead transparency of Property Problems (see appendix)
Overhead pens
Properties activity sheet

Directions: Knowledge of the properties of addition and multiplication are necessary for this activity. If the students do not have this knowledge, return to this activity after introducing and reinforcing the concepts.

Review the properties of addition and multiplication, asking the students to describe and give examples of the properties.

Commutative property of addition: The order of the addends does not affect the sum.

$$3 + 5 = 5 + 3$$

Commutative property of multiplication: The order of the factors does not affect the product.

$$3 \times 5 = 5 \times 3$$

Associative property of addition: When three or more numbers are to be added, the grouping of the addends does not affect the sum.

$$(3 + 5) + 7 = 3 + (5 + 7)$$

Associative property of multiplication: When three or more numbers are to be multiplied, the grouping of the factors does not affect the product.

$$(3 \times 5) \times 7 = 3 \times (5 \times 7)$$

Identity property of addition: The "no change" property. Any addend plus zero equals that addend. The identity element is zero.

$$3 + 0 = 3$$

Identity property of multiplication: The "no change" property. Any factor times one equals that factor. The identity element is one.

$$3 \times 1 = 3$$

"These are the properties of addition and multiplication. We can use these properties for different purposes, and one of them is to help us solve problems." Place the Property Problems transparency on the overhead. "Problem 1 shows one of the properties. Which property would that be?" (*commutative property of addition*) Write "commutative" in the space on the transparency. "What number would be in the box?" (*3*) Write "3" in the box. "Why would this be correct?" (*The order of the addends does not affect the sum.*)

"Now look at problem 2. Which property is being represented?" (*identity property of addition*) Write "identity" in the space. "What number would we write in the box to represent the identity property?" (*0*) "Why zero?" (*It is the identity element.*) Continue with problem 3. (*associative property of multiplication, 3 in the box, the way the factors are grouped does not affect the product*)

"Problem 4 also represents a property. Study the representation carefully. When you think you have an answer, whisper it to the person sitting next to you and see if you agree." (*identity property of addition*) "What equation would match this representation and show the identity property?" (*7 + 0 = 7*) Ask a student to explain why the identity property and equation are correct. Continue the process with problem 5, which is represented with Cuisenaire rods. Problem 5 represents the commutative property of addition, which can also be shown as r + g = g + r.

Distribute the Properties activity sheet to the students. The students will describe the properties, identify the properties, and represent the properties.

Answer Key: *Part One:* 1. The order of the addends does not affect the sum, $a + b = b + a$; 2. The order of the factors does not affect the product, $a \times b = b \times a$; 3. The "no change" property. Any addend plus zero equals that addend, $a + 0 = a$; 4. The "no change" property. Any factor times one equals that factor, $a \times 1 = a$; 5. When three or more numbers are to be added, the grouping of the addends does not affect the sum, $(a + b) + c = a + (b + c)$; 6. When three or more numbers are to be multiplied, the grouping of the factors does not affect the product, $(a \times b) \times c = a \times (b \times c)$. *Part Two:* 1. 3, commutative; 2. 1, identity; 3. 4, associative; 4. 9, identity; 5. 5 and 3 or 3 and 5, associative

Related Activity: The students will use a computer drawing program (AppleWorks and Microsoft Word are two examples) to create representations of different properties. The representations can be made into booklets of six or eight problems that the students can use to reinforce their knowledge of representations and properties. Answer keys can be made and the students can check their own work.

■ **6-6. FACT FAMILIES (Learning Level)**

Objective: To create a family of facts for a set of numbers

Materials: 18 counters for each student
Fact Families activity sheet

Directions: Ask what the word "family" means and take several responses. Then ask how the word "family" relates to numbers. Either review, or introduce, the idea that some numbers are related to each other and can be seen as belonging to the same family. Distribute the counters. Write "6, 7, 13" on the board. Relate that this set of numbers can form a family of facts. Instruct the students to make a group of 6 counters and a group of 7 counters. Ask a student to provide a basic fact that would represent the counters. (*6 + 7 = 13*) Ask for another basic fact that would represent the counters. (*7 + 6 = 13*) Group the 13 counters together and move 6 away. What basic fact would be represented by the counters? (*13 – 6 = 7*) Place the 13 counters back together and move 7 away. What basic fact is being represented? (*13 – 7 = 6*) Write "5, 6, 11" on the board. Have the students give the four basic facts for this set of numbers. (*5 + 6 = 11, 6 + 5 = 11, 11 – 5 = 6, 11 – 6 = 5*)

Write "3, 6, 18" on the board. Have the students use all of their counters to represent a basic fact for this set of numbers. They may try various combinations for the sum of 18, but remind them that the set of numbers includes 3 and 6, and 3 + 6 does not equal 18. Draw attention to any students who have formed 3 groups of 6 or 6 groups of 3 with their counters. Write "3 × 6 = 18" and "6 × 3 = 18" on the board. Instruct the students to place the 18 counters back together then to divide the counters into 3 equal groups. The basic fact is 18 ÷ 3 = 6. Then have the students place the counters back together and divide them into 6 equal groups. The basic fact is 18 ÷ 6 = 3. Write "4, 6, 24" on the board and have the students give the four basic facts for this set of numbers. (*4 × 6 = 24, 6 × 4 = 24, 24 ÷ 4 = 6, 24 ÷ 6 = 4*)

Distribute the Fact Families activity sheet. The students will form fact families.

Answer Key: 1. 5, 7, 5, 7; 2. 5, 7, 5, 7; 3. 7 × 8 = 56, 8 × 7 = 56, 56 ÷ 7 = 8, 56 ÷ 8 = 7; 4. 8 + 9 = 17, 9 + 8 = 17, 17 – 8 = 9, 17 – 9 = 8; 5. only one multiplication and one division fact, square numbers; 6. 2,2,4 3,3,9 4,4,16 5,5,25 7,7,49 9,9,81; 7. Answers will vary.

Related Activity: For this activity, no paper, pencils, markers, or calculators allowed. Pose this problem to the students in writing. Which would you rather have: twenty $10 bills + ten $5 bills + 5 $1 bills OR ten $20 bills + five $10 bills + one $5 bill? Why? (*They both equal $255. The commutative and associative properties are involved here.*)

■ **6-7. HOW MUCH DO THEY WEIGH? (Learning Level)**

Objective: To determine values to form equalities

Materials: A balance scale secured in a balanced position, two cubes and a sphere
2 9-inch by 12-inch pieces of construction paper folded in half, "15 pounds" written on one, "22 kilograms" written on the other
1 copy of Scale for each student (see appendix)
5 3-inch by 5-inch index cards for each student
Pattern blocks
How Much Do They Weigh? activity sheet

Directions: Place the "15 pounds" paper on one side of the scale and a cube on the other side. "We have 15 pounds on this side of the scale. Since the scale is balanced, it must mean that there are 15 pounds on this side also. How much would the cube weigh?" (*15 pounds*) "Why?" (*The scale is balanced, so equal weight must be on each side.*) Remove the cube and replace it with the sphere. "Looking at the position of the balance scale, how much does the sphere weigh?" (*15 pounds*) "Why?" (*The scale is balanced, so equal weight is on each side.*)

Remove the sphere. Then place a cube and a sphere on one side of the scale and keep the "15 pounds" paper on the other side of the scale. "We have 15 pounds on this side of the scale. Since the scale is balanced, it must mean that there are 15 pounds on this side also. Could this be correct? We just said that the cube and the sphere each equaled 15 pounds." (*Does not seem to be correct.*) "With these problems, each time you see the scale the weight of the shapes could be different. The shapes are used to show the different weights."

"So on this scale, the cube and the sphere weigh a total of 15 pounds together. If the cube weighed 10 pounds, how much would the sphere weigh?" (*5 pounds*) "How did you know?" (*10 + 5 = 15 or 15 − 10 = 5*) "That is correct. Together they weigh 15 pounds and the cube weighs 10 pounds so the sphere must weigh 5 pounds. Now let's make a change. The total weight on each side of the scale is still 15 pounds, but now the cube weighs 7 pounds. How much would the sphere weigh?" (*8 pounds*) "How do you know?" (*7 + 8 = 15 or 15 − 7 = 8*)

Remove the "15 pounds" paper and the shapes. Place the "22 kilograms" paper on one side of the scale, and two cubes and a sphere on the other side of the scale. "How much do these shapes weigh together?" (*22 kilograms*) "There are two cubes on this side of the scale. They are the same shapes, so they weigh the same. Any time you have two or more of the same shapes, they always weigh the same. If the sphere weighs 4 kilograms, how much does each cube weigh?" (*9 kilograms*) "How do you know?" (*22 − 4 = 18, 18 ÷ 2 = 9*)

"Remember, each time we have a different problem, the weight of the shapes can change. Let's say that now the sphere weighs 12 kilograms. How much does each cube weigh?" (*5 kilograms*) "How do you know?" (*22 − 12 = 10, 10 ÷ 2 = 5*)

Place the students in pairs. Distribute five index cards, several pattern blocks, and a copy of Scale to each student. The students will write different weights on the cards. One student from each pair will create a problem by placing the weight (the index card) on one side of the scale and pattern blocks on the other side. The students will challenge their partners to find the solution to the problem. The partners will switch roles back and forth for several turns.

Distribute the How Much Do They Weigh? activity sheet. "In each problem, you are given the total weight on the scale and the weight of some of the shapes. You are to figure out the weight of the other shapes. Make sure your total weight is the same on each side of the scale."

Answer Key: 1. 15 g, 12 + 8 + 15 = 35 or 35 − 12 = 23, 23 − 8 = 15; 2. 3 pounds, 16 − 10 = 6, 6 : 2 = 3; 3. 4 oz, 3 oz, cylinder 6 oz and spheres 2 oz each, cylinder 8 oz and spheres 1 oz each; 4. sphere: 1, 2, 3, 4, 5, 6, cylinder: 12, 10, 8, 6, 4, 2; 5. As the weight of each sphere increases by 1 oz, the weight of the cylinder decreases by 2 oz.

Related Activity: Find the values of each figure. All of the squares are the same number. All of the circles are the same number. The square and the circle are different numbers. The sum for each row or column is written at the end of the row or column. (Answer; ◯ = 1, ▢ = 5)

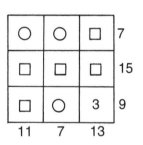

■ 6-8. MS. ROSA'S CHALLENGE (Challenging Level)

Objective: To determine values to form equalities

Materials: Ms. Rosa's Challenge activity sheet

Directions: Draw a balance scale (⎯⎯△⎯⎯) on the board and review the ideas of what it means when the scale balances. (*The values on each side of the scale are equal.*) Draw a cube on one side of the scale and three spheres on the other side. Write "cube" and "sphere" next to each other. Draw a horizontal line under the words and a vertical line between them to form a T chart. "Look at the scale. We have a cube on one side and three spheres on the other side. It is balanced. How much could each cube and each sphere weigh to make the scale

Cube	Sphere
3	1
6	2
9	3
12	4
15	5

balance?" As answers are offered, record them on the T chart. As they respond, ask the students to explain why they think their numbers make sense.

"There is only one scale, one cube, and three spheres. How could all of these answers be correct?" (*Since no values are given for the shapes, there are many possible answers.*) Distribute the Ms. Rosa's Challenge activity sheet. "This activity sheet allows you to come up with your own answers. The numbers have to make sense and the values on each side must be equal for the scales to balance. If they balance, your answers have to be correct." Allow the students to determine the weights to form equalities and justify why their numbers make sense.

Answer Key: 1–4. Answers will vary.

Related Activity: The following involves three balance scales and some figures. Distribute a copy of The Challenge (see appendix) to the students and discuss what is happening on each scale. Allow the students to work in pairs if you feel it would be helpful, or they can work by themselves. The challenge is to determine which one figure (square, circle, or rectangle) will balance scale 3. The students will also justify their answers.

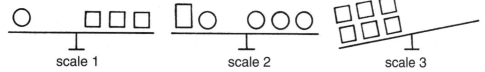

scale 1   scale 2   scale 3

Answer Key: rectangle—One circle equals three squares (scale 1), one rectangle equals two circles (scale 2), so two circles or one rectangle equals six squares.

■ **6-9. SYMBOLS (Learning Level)**

Objective: To state inequalities and equalities correctly

Materials: Blank transparencies and overhead pen
Overhead counters
Symbols activity sheet

Directions: "When we compare the quantities of two sets, we create one of three relationships. What are those relationships?" Write " =, >, <" on the overhead. (If the students know the three symbols and can identify the relationships, skip the next three paragraphs.

Place two sets of three counters on the top third of the transparency. (○ ○ ○   ○ ○ ○) "Here are two sets that I am comparing. What is the relationship between these counters?" Take several responses until you get the response "*they are equal.*" "Yes, these two sets are equal and I can show that by using this symbol called an equal sign." (○ ○ ○ = ○ ○ ○) Write under the sets as you state, "Three is equal to three. The equal sign shows the equal relationship between these sets."

Place a set of three counters and a set of two counters in the middle third of the transparency. (○ ○ ○   ○ ○) "I am comparing these two sets. What is the relationship between these two sets?" You are looking for the response "*is greater than.*" "Yes, this set is greater than the other set. We show that by using this symbol." (○ ○ ○ > ○ ○) Write under the sets as you state, "Three is greater than two. The greater than symbol shows the unequal relationship between these sets."

Now place a set of two counters and a set of three counters on the bottom third of the transparency. (○ ○   ○ ○ ○) "I am comparing these two sets. What is the relationship between these two sets?" You are looking for the response "*is less than.*" "Yes, this set is less than the other set. We show that by using this symbol." (○ ○ < ○ ○ ○) Write under the sets as you state, "Two is less than three. The less than symbol shows the unequal relationship between these sets."

"These symbols are important because they will help you write and solve equations as you study algebra. The symbols are parts of number sentences and it is very important to use all of the words in their meanings." Write "15 ○ 15" on a different transparency. "What is the relationship between these two numbers?" (*equal*) Write an equal sign inside the circle and ask a student to read the number sentence. As the student responds, write, "Fifteen is equal to fifteen." Write "13 ○ 11" on the transparency. Ask for the relationship and write ">" inside the circle. Ask a student to read the sentence while you write, "Thirteen is greater than eleven." Finally, write "10 ○ 14" on the transparency. Ask for the relationship and write "<" inside the circle. Ask a student to read the sentence while you write, "Ten is less than fourteen."

Distribute the Symbols activity sheet. The students will use the correct symbol to complete the number sentence and then state the inequality or equality in words.

Answer Key: *Part One:* 1. =, is equal to; 2. <, is less than; 3. >, is greater than; 4. =, is equal to; 5. <, is less than; 6. >, is greater than. *Part Two:* 1. <, 27 is less than 35; 2. <, 49 is less than 54; 3. >, 56 is greater than 54; 4. <, 78 is less than 84. *Part Three:* 1. 13 or more, 42 is less than _____; 2. 3, 21 is equal to 21; 3. 19 or more, _____ is greater than 63

Related Activity: Place the students in groups of three. Each group will decide on a strategy for solving the problem, solve the problem, and then create a method to prove their answer to the rest of the class. Different groups can demonstrate different methods for solving and proving their answers.

1. Three times a number is greater than 21. What could that number be? (*any number > 7*)

2. A number minus six is less than 9. What could that number be? (*any number < 15*)

3. Two times a number plus 5 is 21. What could that number be? (*8*)

■ **6-10. WORDS FOR THE OPERATIONS (Beginning Level)**

Objective: To match words or phrases to the correct operation

Materials: Transparency of Operations (see appendix)
Words for the Operations activity sheet

Directions: "When we perform operations on numbers, sometimes symbols are used to tell us what to do and sometimes words tell us what to do. There are several ways to say the same thing, so it is wise to know as many as we can. If I said 'plus,' what operation would I use?" (*addition*) "If I said 'minus,' what operation would I use?" (*subtraction*) "And if I said 'times'?" (*multiplication*) "These words we know. However, other words can tell us the same thing."

Cover the Operations transparency with a piece of paper and place it on the overhead. Slide the paper down to reveal problem 1, but not the equation or the representation. "Look at the words in number 1. 'The sum of 4 and 3 is.' What operation would that suggest to you?" (*addition*) "Why do you think so?" (*The sum is addition.*) "What equation can be written from 'The sum of 4 and 3 is'?" (*4 + 3 = 7*) "How might we represent the equation with a drawing?" (*a set of 4 and a set of 3 joined together*) Move the paper down to reveal the equation and the representation. Slide the paper down to reveal problem 2. Have the students determine the operation and the equation. Reveal the equation and have a student draw a representation for the equation on the transparency. Continue in the same manner with problems 3, 4, 5, and 6.

Distribute the Words for the Operations activity sheet. Draw the students' attention to the words under the four operations. You may wish to have students take turns reading each column aloud. Review the steps for the first problem, which has been completed.

Answer Key: 1. addition, 2 + 3 = 5; 2. subtraction, 5 – 3 = 2; 3. multiplication, 4 × 6 = 24; 4. division, 8 ÷ 2 = 4; 5. addition, 7 + 3 = 10; 6. multiplication, 7 × 3 = 21; 7. subtraction, 9 – 4 = 5; 8. division, 18 ÷ 9 = 2; 9. multiplication, 2 × 6 = 12; 10. addition, 3 + 8 = 11; 11. division, 10 ÷ 2 = 5; 12. subtraction, 12 – 3 = 9; 13. multiplication, 3 × 6 = 18; 14. addition, 5 + 9 = 14; 15. multiplication, 5 × 4 = 20; 16. subtraction, 11 – 6 = 5

Related Activity: Pair the students. Provide each student with a copy of Words for the Operations Practice (see appendix; since there are two sets on the page, each student receives a half page) and a pair of dice. One of the partners will roll the dice, state the roll (7), roll again, and state that roll (9). The other partner will choose an operation and use the Words for the Operations Practice sheet to create a problem involving the numbers. (*9 decreased by 7 is . . .*) The first partner has to solve the problem. (*2*) He or she may also use the sheet if necessary. The partners can take turns exchanging roles each time.

■ **6-11. DISCOVER THE RULE (Learning Level)**

Objective: To determine the input, output, and rule of a function

Materials: Overhead transparency of Input/Output Tables (see appendix)
Overhead pen
Discover the Rule activity sheet

Directions: For this activity, the students should be familiar with the terms *input* and *output,* and should understand how to determine the output number from the input number.
Introduce the word *function* as a rule between the input numbers and the output numbers. When following the function, each input number has one—and only one—output number. Display the Input/Output Tables on the overhead. Draw the students' attention to the headings of Input and Output in the first table. Have the students describe the terms. (*Input is the number to which the function is applied. After the function has been applied, the result is the output.*) Instruct the students to study the table and determine the function. (*+9*) Write the function in the appropriate space and have the students explain how they determined the function. Have students use the function to provide the output for inputs 3 (*12*) and 5 (*14*).
Point out that the next number given is the output of 19. What is the input? (*10*) Discuss different ways to determine the input if the output and function are known. (*19 – 9 = 10 should be the most common way.*) Fill in the input of 10 and then 15 after the students explain how they determined the answer.
Draw the students' attention to the second table. Review the first three rows and ask the students to determine the function. This will probably be difficult for them. Tell them that sometimes the function involves two operations. This function involves multiplication and addition. (*× 2, + 5*) Once the function is identified, have the students determine the missing values as you write them in the table. Be sure to have the students explain how they determined their answers.
Distribute the Discover the Rule activity sheet. The students will determine the function and complete the tables.

Answer Key: *Part One:* 1. input: 10, 12; output: 28; function: ×2; 2. input: 16, 20; output: 13; function: −5. *Part Two:* 1. input: 6, 7; output: 12; function: 1. ×2, −4; 2. input: 16, 18; output: 17, 20; function: ÷2, +10. *Part Three:* 1–2. Answers will vary.

Related Activity: 1. Use Cuisenaire rods to explore the function and to fill in the missing spaces on the horizontal table.

input	red	green	purple			black
output	green	yellow		blue	orange and white	

Answer: $(\times 2, -1)$

input	red	green	purple	yellow	dark green	black
output	green	yellow	black	blue	orange & white	orange & green

■ **6-12. GRAPH IT! (Challenging Level)**

Objective: To graph a function

Materials: Geoboards and geobands for each student
1 Copy of Coordinate Grid (see appendix section 3) for each student
Overhead transparency of Coordinate Grid (see appendix section 3)
Overhead pen
Graph It! activity sheet

Directions: Display the Coordinate Grid transparency. Review the concept of coordinates, two numbers that describe a specific location on the grid by using the *x*-axis and the *y*-axis. Write "(4,5)" below the grid. Demonstrate the idea of running along the *x*-axis until you get to 4 and then jumping up 5. Draw a dot at that point and label it "(4,5)." Now write "(2,5)" and demonstrate how to find that point by running along the *x*-axis until you get to 2 and then jumping up 5. Place a dot there and label it "(2,5)." Continue the process for coordinates (2,2) and (4,2). Use a straightedge to connect the dots and form a rectangle. Erase the transparency or display a second transparency.

Distribute the geoboards and geobands. Draw a T chart below the grid. Label the left side "*x*" and the right side "*y*." Write "(2,1)" next to the T chart. The numbers in a coordinate correspond to the *x*, *y* on the chart. Write "2" on the chart under *x*. State that the 2 in the coordinate is the number on the *x*-axis and the number on the T chart. Have the students use their geoboards as a coordinate grid and locate (2,1). They will start at the lower left pin, run along the *x*-axis until they get to the second pin, then jump up one pin. Place a geoband around that pin. Write "(4,3)" as a coordinate, then transfer the number to the chart. Have the students run along the *x*-axis until they get to 4 and then jump up 3. Stretch the geoband around this pin. Finally write "(3,5)" as a coordinate and on the chart. Have the students locate (3,5) on their geoboard and stretch the geoband around that pin. The resulting figure should be a triangle.

x	y
2	1
4	3
3	5

Distribute the Graph It! activity sheet and Coordinate Grid sheet. Point out the function table and tell the students that they are going to plot a function. They will end up with a figure, but you are not going to tell them what the figure is. Draw attention to the second table. This is the same type of function table that they have been using, but instead of the words "Input" and "Output," *x* and *y* have been substituted. It is still a function table, but the numbers will serve as the coordinates that will be plotted on the grid.

Answer Key: *Part One:* output, 7, 8, 9, 10, 11. *Part Two:* 1. straight line.

Related Activity: Use a computer program that has graphing capabilities (AppleWorks is one). Decide on a function, input the *x* and *y* data, and graph the data. Unless there is an error in the data, the result should always be a straight line. Each time the line crosses another coordinate, those numbers would work for the function also.

■ 6-13. MORE FUNCTIONS (Challenging Level)

Objectives: To determine the output through multiple functions
To determine functions

Materials: Overhead transparency of Multiple Functions (see appendix)
Overhead pen
More Functions activity sheet

Directions: Review the concept of a function (*a rule*) and that the function is applied to the input to produce the output. "Sometimes the input goes through several functions before the output is final." Display the Multiple Functions overhead. "Here we see that three separate functions are used on the input before the output is final. Let's go through the steps together. In the first row, we start with 5, and the first function multiplies that by 3. What value do we have now?" (*15*) Write "15" to the right of the function box to help the students see the process. "The second function is + 4. What do we add 4 to?" (*15*) "Why to 15 and not to 5?" (*Already performed first function and the product is 15.*) "What is the sum?" (*19*) Write "19" to the right of the +4 function box. "The third function is –5. What value are we taking 5 from?" (19) "So what is the answer?" (*14*) "What is the output?" (*14*) "How do you know?" (*That is the value after the last function, so it is the output.*)

Repeat the same step-by-step process and questioning with the second row. (*10 ÷ 2 = 5, 5 + 2 = 7, 7 – 7 = 0*) Allow the students to do the third row by themselves, and then discuss any different answers or different strategies for obtaining the solution. (*8 – 5 = 3, 3 × 4 = 12, 12 + 7 = 19*) "Now look at the last row. What is different here?" (*Output and input are given. One of the functions is not.*) "How can we determine the missing function?" Allow a discussion to develop. There are several methods for determining the function, but the one that most students seem to choose is working backwards from the output. It is important when working backwards that the functions be reversed. The last function takes away 2 and leaves 3. When working backwards, we would start with 3 and add 2 back in to get 5. The next function divided a number by 2, and the quotient was 5. What number divided by 2 equals 5? It is, of course, 10. We can now look at the input of 6. After the function, it is 10. The function is +4. It is important to have the students describe the different methods they used to solve for the function. Their descriptions help them solidify their thinking and may help other students see the light.

Distribute the More Functions activity sheet. The students will determine outputs through several functions and determine missing functions.

Answer Key: *Part One:* 1. 17; 2. 24; 3. 22; 4. 25. *Part Two:* 1. +3, 9 + 6 = 15, 15 – 9 = 6, 6 + 2 = 8, 8 – 5 = 3; 2. – 5, 4 + 12 = 16, 16 – 7 = 9, 9 – 4 = 5, 10 – 5 = 5

Related Activity: Choose a number between 1 and 9. Multiply that number by 5. Add 3 and then multiply the sum by 2. Choose another number between 1 and 9 and add it to the product. Subtract 6. What is interesting about your answer?

Repeat the steps, choosing different numbers. Did you get an interesting answer? Why do you think this happens? Do you think it will happen every time? (×5 *and* ×2 *makes* ×10, *which moves the first number to the tens place. +3 and ×2 equals 6, and –6 makes it zero. The directions really say to multiply the first number by 10, then add the second number. It is much more exciting written in the original format.)*

■ **6-14.** *n* **TAKES THE PLACE (Learning Level)**

Objective: To determine the function for a variable

Materials: *n* Takes the Place activity sheet

Directions: Draw a horizontal table on the board. Label the top "Ears" and the bottom "Children." "How many ears does one child have?" *(2)* Write "2" and "1" on the chart.

Ears	2								
Children	1								

Fill in the rest of the values of ears for 2 children, 3 children, etc. "What function does this table show?" *(×2)* "I know how many ears these numbers of children have, but I want to know how many ears 20 children have. How would I do that?" *(20 × 2 = 40)* "Now I want to know how many ears 35 children have. How would I do that?" *(35 × 2 = 70)* "And now I want to know how many ears any number of children would have. Whatever the number of children, I want to know how many ears. How would I do that?" *(the number of children × 2)*

Write *n* on the board. "What does this letter mean in math?" *(It is a variable that means any number.)* "When we have a function, we can apply it to any number. We fill in the table and that gives us the input and output numbers, but not every input and output combination. We use the *n* to show the function for *any number*. I will use *n* to represent any number of children. What would I do to *n* to find out how many ears *n* children have?" *(n × 2)* "Any number times 2 will give me the number of ears." Have the students randomly call out some numbers. Take each number, multiply it by 2, and respond with the number of ears. "I now know the number of ears for any number of children. How many wheels are on a car?" *(4)* "How many wheels are there on two cars?" *(8)* "How many wheels are on four cars?" *(16)* "On five cars?" *(20)* "What is the function to find the number of wheels?" *(×4)* "How many wheels are on *n* cars?" *(n × 4)* "Now I can find the number of wheels for any number. I just substitute the number of cars for *n* and I can find the number of wheels."

Distribute the *n* Takes the Place activity sheet. The students will determine the function for a variable.

Answer Key: 1. $n × 4$; 2. 50, 80, $n × 2$; 3. number of bicycles $×2$; 4. $n + 2$; 5. 12, 102; 6. number of triangles $+2$; 7.

Ears	1	2	3	4	5	6	7
Cost	.15	.30	.45	.60	.75	.90	1.05

, $n × .15$; 8. $7.50, $15.00

Related Activity: Kanesha has chocolate chip cookies and oatmeal cookies in a bag. She says that she has twice as many chocolate chip cookies as oatmeal cookies. It is possible that Kanesha has 2 chocolate chip cookies and 1 oatmeal cookie. Construct a horizontal chart to show ten other possible combinations of cookies that Kanesha could have in the bag.

Answer:

Oatmeal	2	3	4	5	6	7	8	9	10	11
Choc. chip	4	6	8	10	12	14	16	18	20	22

Any that are in 2:1 are appropriate.

■ **6-15. REAL-LIFE FUNCTIONS (Challenging Level)**

Objectives: To solve problems using functions

Materials: Real-Life Functions activity sheet

Directions: "I am going to relate a story to you and I want you to identify and solve the problems in the story." Either write the problem on the board or on the overhead. "Daniel's father wants to be an informed person. Each day before school, Daniel goes to the store and buys five different newspapers for his father to read. What is the function that will tell how many newspapers Daniel has bought after *n* days?" (*n* × *5*) "Now let's see how we can use that function. How many newspapers did Daniel buy in 4 days?" (*20*) "How did you figure that out?" (*4 × 5 = 20*) "How many newspapers did Daniel buy in 9 days?" (*45*) "How did you figure that out?" (*9 × 5 = 45*) "How many newspapers did Daniel buy in 17 days?" (*17 × 5 = 85*) Continue on with several more numbers of days until you are sure that the students understand the concept.

Distribute the Real-Life Functions activity sheet. The students will solve problems using the functions.

Answer Key: 1. × $13; 2. $65, $130, $260; 3. number of lawns times $13; 4. × 28; 5. 112 miles, 196 miles, 280 miles; 6. number of gallons times 28; 7. × 9; 8. 72 beads, 135 beads, 225 beads; 9. number of bracelets times 9

Related Activity: Instruct the students to create two real-life problems that involve functions. They should use separate sheets of paper for each problem and include their names. When the students are finished creating, shuffle all of the papers and randomly distribute them so each student has two problems. They will work the problems and then confer with the creator of the problem to check the accuracy of the problem solving.

6-1. Choose the Best

Choose the best equation or equations for each picture (symbolic representation) shown below. Show your choices by drawing a line under the equations. Then state the reasons for your choices.

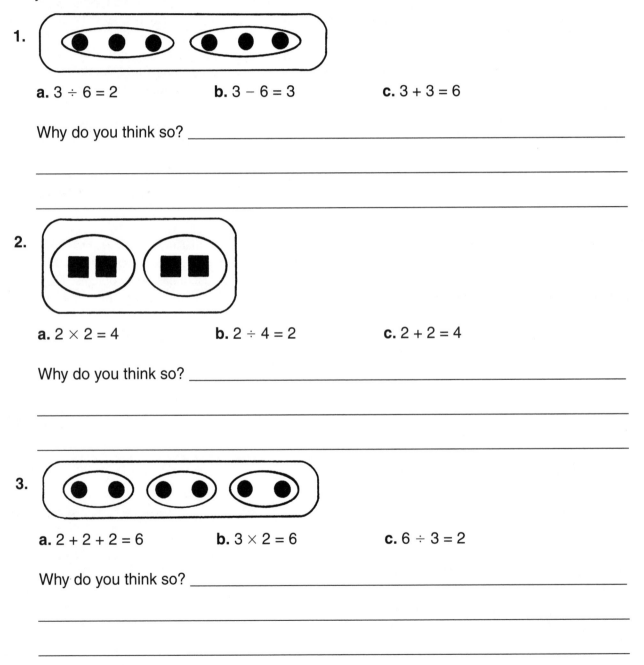

1.

a. 3 ÷ 6 = 2   **b.** 3 − 6 = 3   **c.** 3 + 3 = 6

Why do you think so? _____

_____

2.

a. 2 × 2 = 4   **b.** 2 ÷ 4 = 2   **c.** 2 + 2 = 4

Why do you think so? _____

_____

3.

a. 2 + 2 + 2 = 6   **b.** 3 × 2 = 6   **c.** 6 ÷ 3 = 2

Why do you think so? _____

_____

6-1. Choose the Best *(continued)*

4. Write three equations that could be shown by the representation below.

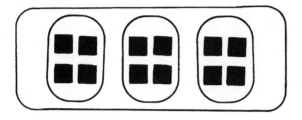

_____   _____   _____

5. Draw the representation that would best show the following equations:

$3 \times 5 = 15$ $5 + 5 + 5 = 15$ $15 \div 3 = 5$

6-2. Continue the Pattern

Lee and Kanesha drew some patterns, which are shown below. Follow the directions and answer the questions for each pattern.

○ ○ ○ □ □ ○ ○ ○ □ □

1. What figure would come next in the pattern? _____

2. If the pattern was continued, what would be the 13th figure? _____

3. If the pattern was continued, what would be the 22nd figure? _____

How do you know? _____

4. If the pattern was continued, what would be the 50th figure? _____

How do you know? _____

Find the next three numbers in these patterns:

5. 18; 15; 12; _____; _____; _____

6. 1,120; 1,024; 928; 832; _____; _____; _____

7. 4; 8; 16; 32; _____; _____; _____ Explain the pattern. _____

_____

8. 1; 3; 7; 15; _____; _____; _____ Explain the pattern. _____

9. Draw the next figure in the following pattern.

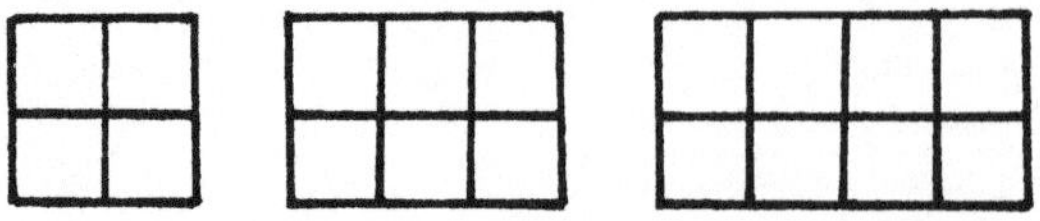

If the pattern was continued, how many small squares would be in the tenth

figure? _____ Describe how you figured out your answer.

_____

6-3. Reasoning

Mr. Gonzalez created some patterns for the students in his class. Think about the patterns below and answer the questions.

summer	fall	winter	spring	seasons	summer

1. If the pattern was continued, what would be the 14th word? _____ How do you know?

_____

2. If the pattern was continued, what would be the 31st word? _____ How do you know?

_____

3. Determine the pattern and then continue it.

S M T W T F S S ____ ____ ____ ____ ____ ____

4. Determine the pattern and then continue it.

J F M A M J J A S O N D J ____ ____ ____ ____ ____ ____ ____ ____ ____ ____

5. Add the next three figures to the pattern that Mr. Gonzalez created.

Describe the pattern in your own words. _____

_____

6. Study the pattern that has been started below and compare it to the T chart. There is 1 tile in the first row. The total number of tiles needed to construct the first row is also 1 tile. When row two was added, the total number of tiles in the pattern was 3 tiles. After row three was added, the total number of tiles in the pattern was 6 tiles.

Number of rows	Total number of tiles	Number of rows	Total number of tiles
1	1	6	
2	3	7	
3	6	8	
4		9	
5		10	

The pattern will continue until there are a total of ten rows. Complete the T chart to show the total number of tiles in the pattern after each row was added.

6-4. Patterns and Ratios

A ratio is used to show a relationship between two sets. Ratios can be written in different ways. One way is in a form such as 2 to 3. Another way is 2:3. The third way is in fraction form, $\frac{2}{3}$. A table is another way to show a ratio.

1. Each student in Juan's class has 4 books. The ratio is 1 student to 4 books (1 to 4; 1:4; $\frac{1}{4}$). Following the ratio, 2 students would have 8 books. Study the table below and fill in the missing quantities.

Students	Books
1	4
2	8
3	12
4	_____
5	_____
10	_____

2. When Keisha's soccer team practices, the coach provides 3 soccer balls for every 5 players (3 to 5; 3:5; $\frac{3}{5}$). Study the table below and fill in the missing quantities.

Soccer balls	Players
3	5
6	_____
9	_____
_____	20
_____	25
30	_____

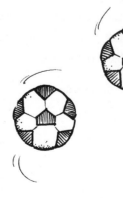

6-4. Patterns and Ratios (continued)

3. You can buy 2 apples for 25 cents at the fruit market. Write the ratio of apples to cost three different ways and then construct a table to show the cost of 4 apples, 6 apples, 10 apples, 16 apples, and 20 apples.

_____ _____ _____

4. Keisha, Hakeem, and Daniel found that their names have a vowel-to-consonant ratio of 3 to 3. List five other names or words that have an equal vowel-to-consonant ratio (2:2; 3:3; 4:4; or 5:5)

_____ _____

_____ _____

_____

5. Sometimes ratio tables are written in a horizontal form. Study the table below and fill in the missing quantities.

4	8		16		
5	10	15		25	

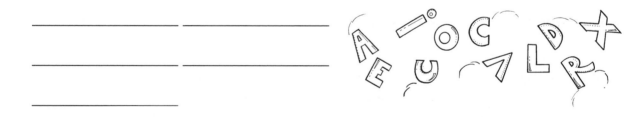

↑ **This means 4 to 5.**

Name two things that could be in a 4 to 5 ratio:

_____

_____

6-5. Properties

Part One: Answer these questions in your own words:

1. Describe the commutative property of addition and then give an example of that property.

   _____

2. Describe the commutative property of multiplication and then give an example of that property.

   _____

3. Describe the identity property of addition and then give an example of that property.

   _____

4. Describe the identity property of multiplication and then give an example of that property.

   _____

5. Describe the associative property of addition and then give an example of that property.

   _____

6. Describe the associative property of multiplication and then give an example of that property.

   _____

Part Two: Complete each equation and state which property you used.

1. $7 \times 3 =$ _____ $\times 7$ Which property? _____

2. $87 \times$ _____ $= 87$ Which property? _____

3. $5 + (3 + 4) = (5 +$ _____ $) + 3$ Which property? _____

4. _____ $= 9 + 0$ Which property? _____

5. _____ $\times ($ _____ $\times 8) = (5 \times 3) \times 8$ Which property? _____

Name _____   Date _____

6-6. Fact Families

When you use the same set of numbers to make related number facts, you have made fact families. Usually the number facts are made from a set of three numbers. The related facts can be either addition and subtraction, or multiplication and division.

Complete the fact family for each set of numbers. Then answer the questions.

1. 5, 7, 12

_____ + 7 = 12

5 + _____ = 12

12 − _____ = 7

12 − _____ = 5

2. 5, 7, 35

_____ × 7 = 35

5 × _____ = 35

35 ÷ _____ = 7

35 ÷ _____ = 5

3. Write a fact family for the following set of numbers: 7, 8, 56

_____ _____ _____ _____

4. Write a fact family for the following set of numbers: 8, 9, 17

_____ _____ _____ _____

5. What is the same about the fact families of the two following sets of numbers? 8, 8, 64 and 6, 6, 36

_____

6. What are six other sets of numbers that would make the same kind of fact families as 8, 8, 64 and 6, 6, 36?

_____

7. Roll a pair of dice and write the numbers you rolled with the dice: _____ _____
Use these numbers to make a fact family.

_____ _____ _____ _____

Roll again and write the numbers: _____ _____ Use these numbers to make a fact family.

_____ _____ _____ _____

6-7. How Much Do They Weigh?

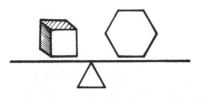

Ms. Rosa used three-dimensional shapes and a balance scale to create some math problems for her students. Study the shapes and the weights on the scale very carefully. Then answer the questions and explain how you got your answers. The weights of the shapes will be different in each problem.

1. The total weight on each side of the scale is 35 grams. The cube weighs 12 grams and the sphere weighs 8 grams. How much does the cylinder weigh? _____

   How do you know? _____

   _____

   _____

2. The total weight on each side of the scale is 16 pounds. Each cube weighs 5 pounds. Both spheres weigh the same. How much does each sphere weigh? _____

   How do you know? _____

   _____

   _____

Name _____ Date _____

6-7. How Much Do They Weigh? (continued)

3. The total weight on each side of the scale is 20 ounces. The cubes each weigh 5 ounces. If the cylinder weighs 2 ounces, how much does each sphere weigh? _____ However, if the cylinder weighs 4 ounces, how much does each sphere now weigh? _____ There are two more possible answers that could also be correct. Explain what the other answers could be.

_____

_____

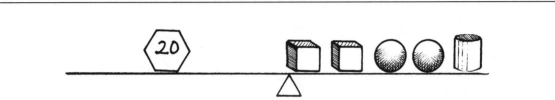

4. All the spheres weigh the same as the other spheres. Each cylinder weighs the same as the other cylinder. There are several different weights that would solve this problem. Look at the table. If each sphere weighed 1 gram, then each cylinder would have to be 12 grams to total 28 grams. If each sphere weighed 2 grams, fill in the table to show how much each cylinder would weigh so the total is 28 grams. Then fill in the rest of the table.

If each sphere weighs	Then each cylinder weighs
1	12
2	_____
3	_____
_____	_____
_____	_____
_____	_____

5. In your own words, describe what happened to the weights in the table.

_____

_____

Name _____   Date _____

6-8. Ms. Rosa's Challenge

Ms. Rosa used three-dimensional shapes and a balance scale to create problems that would challenge her students. Now it is your turn to take the challenge. Study each balance scale and figure out how much each shape could weigh. Remember that the total weight on each side of the scale must be the same so that it will balance.

For the questions, all the cubes must weigh the same as other cubes, all the spheres must weigh the same as other spheres, and all the cylinders must weigh the same as other cylinders. However, the value of each shape can be different for different questions.

1.

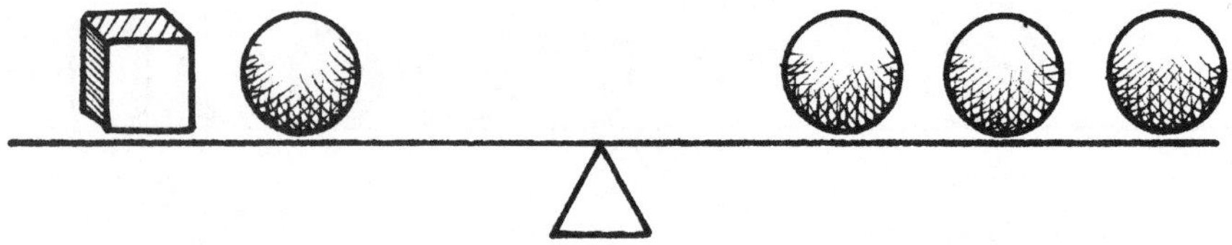

Each sphere weighs _____. The cube weighs _____.

Explain why your answer makes sense. _____

_____

_____

2.

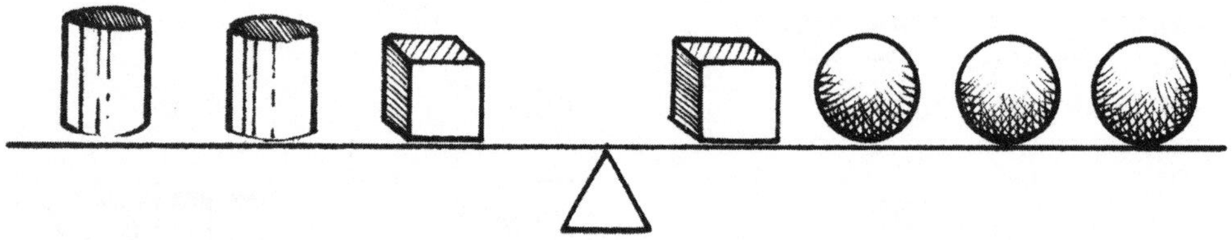

Each sphere weighs _____. Each cube weighs _____.

Each cylinder weighs _____.

Explain why your answer makes sense. _____

_____

_____

6-8. Ms. Rosa's Challenge (continued)

3.

Each sphere weighs _____. The cube weighs _____.

Each cylinder weighs _____.

Explain why your answer makes sense. _____

_____

_____

4. Decide the weight of each shape so both scales balance. All of the cylinders still weigh the same and all of the spheres still weigh the same.

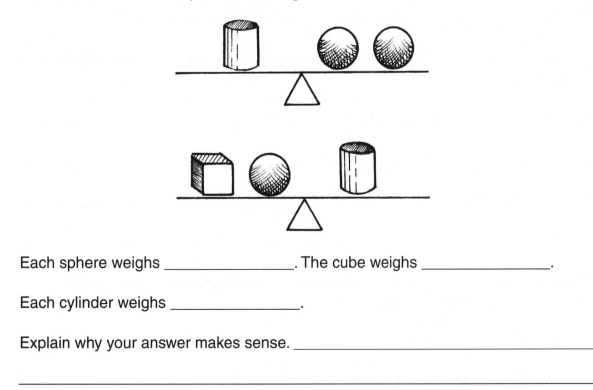

Each sphere weighs _____. The cube weighs _____.

Each cylinder weighs _____.

Explain why your answer makes sense. _____

_____

_____

6-9. Symbols

Part One: When comparing two numbers there are only three possible relationships. The two numbers are equal (=), one number is greater than the other (>), or one number is less than the other (<). Show the correct symbol and then complete the statement using one of the phrases below.

| "is equal to" | "is greater than" | "is less than" |

1. 7 ◯ 7   "Seven _____ seven."

2. 3 ◯ 9   "Three _____ nine."

3. 8 ◯ 2   "Eight _____ two."

4. 23 ◯ 16 + 7   "Twenty-three _____ twenty-three."

5. 9 + 8 ◯ 19   "Seventeen _____ nineteen."

6. 10 ◯ 4 + 5   "Ten _____ nine."

Part Two: Show the correct symbol and write the complete statement following the same form as above.

1. $10 + 17$ ◯ 7×5 _____

2. 7×7 ◯ 9×6 _____

3. 8×7 ◯ $23 + 23 + 8$ _____

4. 13×6 ◯ 7×12 _____

Part Three: Fill in a number to make the equation correct and then complete the statement in the same form as above.

1. $7 \times 6 < 30 +$ _____   _____

2. _____ $\times 7 = 10 + 10 + 1$ _____

3. $45 +$ _____ $> 9 \times 7$ _____

Name _____   Date _____

6-10. Words for the Operations

For each problem, locate the words for the operation, write the number sentence, and then solve the problem.

Addition	Subtraction	Multiplication	Division
plus	minus	times	divided by
sum of	take away	product	goes into
increased by	less than	groups of	quotient
added to	decrease	rows of	$\frac{1}{2}$ of
more than	comparison	sets of	$\frac{1}{3}$ of
greater than	difference	by	
		twice	

Let's do one together. "What is the sum of 2 and 3?" Which list of words contains "sum of"?

_____ Yes, it is addition. The number sentence would show 2 + 3. We would solve it and write 2 + 3 = 5.

The Vocabulary	Operation	Equation
1. the sum of 2 and 3	Addition	2 + 3 = 5
2. 5 take away 3	_____	_____
3. 4 sets of 6	_____	_____
4. 8 divided by 2	_____	_____
5. 7 increased by 3	_____	_____
6. 7 groups of 3	_____	_____
7. 4 less than 9	_____	_____
8. the quotient of 18 ÷ 9	_____	_____
9. twice the number 6	_____	_____
10. 3 more than 8	_____	_____
11. $\frac{1}{2}$ of 10	_____	_____
12. 12 decreased by 3	_____	_____
13. the product of 3 and 6	_____	_____
14. 5 greater than 9	_____	_____
15. multiply 5 by 4	_____	_____
16. the difference between 11 and 6	_____	_____

6-11. Discover the Rule

A function is defined as a rule that sets up a relationship between a first set of numbers, called the input, and a second set of numbers, called the output. For each input number there is only one output number. Look at the table below.

Input	Output
2	6
4	8
6	?

When 2 is the input, the output is 6. When 4 is the input, then 8 is the output. What is the

output when 6 is the input? _____ Yes, it is 10. The rule, or function, for this table is +4.

Part One: Study the tables below. Discover the rule, fill in all of the missing inputs and outputs, and write the rule or function for the table.

1.

Input	Output
6	12
8	16
	20
	24
14	

2.

Input	Output
12	7
14	9
	11
18	
	15

The rule or function is _____

The rule or function is _____

Name _____   Date _____

6-11. Discover the Rule (continued)

Part Two: Sometimes the rule or function involves more than one operation. Study the table.

The rule is ×3 and then +2. Each input number is multiplied by 3 and then 2 is added to the product to produce the output. Complete the following tables, which have rules that involve more than one operation.

Input	Output
2	8
3	11
4	14

1.

Input	Output
3	2
4	4
5	6
	8
	10
8	

The rule or function is _____

2.

Input	Output
10	15
12	16
14	
	18
	19
20	

The rule or function is _____

Part Three: Fill in some of the spaces in the tables below to show a rule or function. Exchange papers with a classmate and try to discover each other's rules.

1.

Input	Output

The rule or function is _____

2.

Input	Output

The rule or function is _____

6-12. Graph It!

Part One: We can use a function to complete a coordinate graph. Once the table is completed, the values are used for the coordinates. First, complete the table. One is done for you.

Function: _____

Input	Output
1	7
2	
3	9
4	
5	

Part Two: The next step is to graph the coordinates. Let the input be the *x* coordinate and the output be the *y* coordinate. The first set of coordinates is (1,7). Complete the rest of the coordinates: (1,7) (2,___) (___,___) (___,___) (___,___). Remember, run across the *x*-axis and jump up for the *y*.

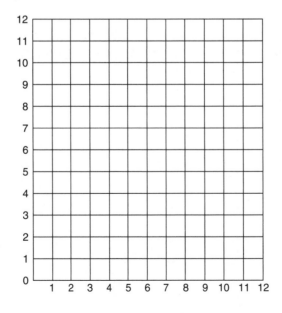

Connect the coordinates with a straightedge. What type of line did the coordinates make?

© 2004 by John Wiley & Sons, Inc.

6-13. More Functions

Part One: Follow the input number through several functions and record the output. Some are filled in for you to help you get started.

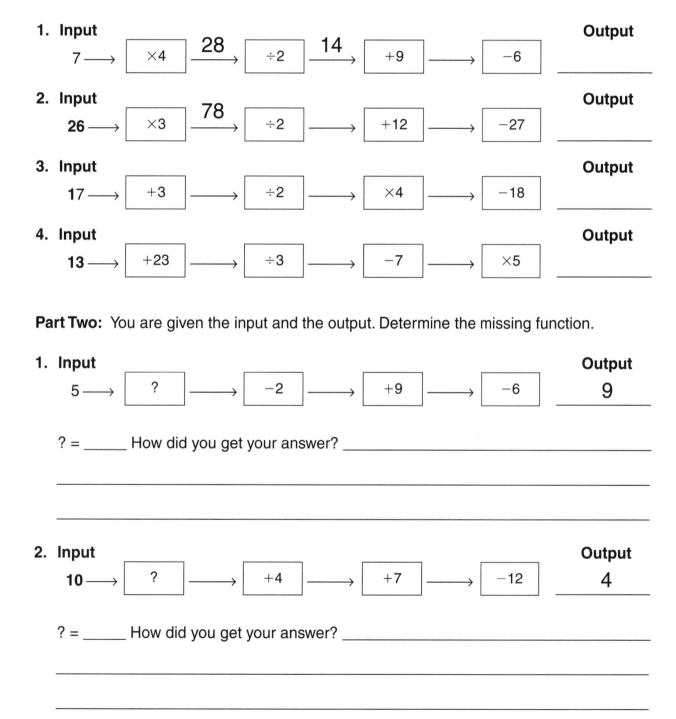

1. **Input**
   $7 \longrightarrow$ [×4] $\xrightarrow{28}$ [÷2] $\xrightarrow{14}$ [+9] $\longrightarrow$ [−6]   **Output** _____

2. **Input**
   $26 \longrightarrow$ [×3] $\xrightarrow{78}$ [÷2] $\longrightarrow$ [+12] $\longrightarrow$ [−27]   **Output** _____

3. **Input**
   $17 \longrightarrow$ [+3] $\longrightarrow$ [÷2] $\longrightarrow$ [×4] $\longrightarrow$ [−18]   **Output** _____

4. **Input**
   $13 \longrightarrow$ [+23] $\longrightarrow$ [÷3] $\longrightarrow$ [−7] $\longrightarrow$ [×5]   **Output** _____

Part Two: You are given the input and the output. Determine the missing function.

1. **Input**
   $5 \longrightarrow$ [?] $\longrightarrow$ [−2] $\longrightarrow$ [+9] $\longrightarrow$ [−6]   **Output** **9**

   ? = _____ How did you get your answer? _____

   _____

   _____

2. **Input**
   $10 \longrightarrow$ [?] $\longrightarrow$ [+4] $\longrightarrow$ [+7] $\longrightarrow$ [−12]   **Output** **4**

   ? = _____ How did you get your answer? _____

   _____

   _____

6-14. *n* Takes the Place

Variables are used to take the place of several values. A letter can be used to show a variable. The letter *n* is a common choice for a variable. When used as a variable, *n* means "any number." Study the data and then write an equation using the variable *n* to show the answer for any number.

1. One dog has 4 legs. Two dogs have 8 legs. Three dogs have 12 legs. The rule that we use to find out how many legs is *number of dogs* × 4.

   How many legs would *n* dogs have? _____

2. The table below shows the number of wheels on different numbers of bicycles.

Wheels	2	4	6	8	10	12	14	16
Bicycles	1	2	3	4	5	6	7	8

   How many wheels are there on 25 bicycles? _____

   How many wheels are there on 40 bicycles? _____

   How many wheels are there on *n* bicycles? _____

3. How do you know? _____

   _____

4. Each side of a green triangle pattern block is one unit in length. The perimeter of one triangle pattern block is 3 units. △ When another triangle is added, the perimeter is 4 units. ◁▷ The table below shows the perimeter of the shape when different numbers of triangle pattern blocks are joined.

Perimeter	3	4	5	6	7	8	9	10
Triangles	1	2	3	4	5	6	7	8

   What is the perimeter of *n* triangles? _____

6-14. *n* Takes the Place *(continued)*

5. What would be the perimeter of 10 triangles? _____ What would be the perimeter of

100 triangles? _____

6. How do you know? _____

_____

7. Corn is selling for $.15 an ear. Fill in the table to show the price of several ears of corn.

Ears of corn								
Cost								

The cost of *n* ears of corn is _____.

8. How much would 50 ears of corn cost? _____

How much would 100 ears of corn cost? _____

6-15. Real-Life Functions

Each problem below asks for information that can be found using a function. For each problem, study the data and determine a function. Then use the function to answer the questions.

> Antonio cuts lawns in his neighborhood. After he takes out expenses for the lawn mower, gas, and maintenance, he is left with $13 for each lawn that he cuts.

1. What function will show how much money Antonio has after cutting n lawns? _____

2. How much money would Antonio have after cutting 5 lawns? _____

   10 lawns? _____ 20 lawns? _____

3. How do you know? _____

   _____

> Christi and her family are going to drive to see some of their relatives. The family car goes 28 miles on each gallon of gasoline.

4. What function will show the family how far they have gone on n gallons of gas?

   _____

5. How far has the car gone on 4 gallons of gas? _____

   7 gallons of gas? _____ 10 gallons of gas? _____

6. How do you know? _____

   _____

6-15. Real-Life Functions *(continued)*

> Julie makes bracelets for the students in her school. She uses
> nine beads for each bracelet.

7. What function will show how many beads Julie uses to make *n* bracelets. _____

8. How many beads will Julie use to make 8 bracelets? _____

    15 bracelets? _____ 25 bracelets? _____

9. How do you know? _____

_____

Appendix

TEACHER RESOURCES

Section 1: SYMMETRY
- Symmetrical Pattern
- Asymmetrical Pattern
- Four Regions
- Flipped Words
- Mirror Lines and Figures
- What Comes Next?
- Find Those That Match
- Rotational Symmetry
- Will It? Frame
- Figures for Will It? Activity

Section 2: GEOMETRY
- Three Angles
- Circles and Angles
- Square and Rectangle
- Polygons
- Regular/Irregular
- Net 1 (Square Pyramid)
- Net 2 (Rectangular Prism)
- Net 3 (Cylinder)
- Net 4 (Cube)
- Net 5 (Cone)
- Rogs
- All That Gold Table
- Regions of a Circle
- Create a Graph
- Centimeter Grid
- ½-Inch Grid
- 1-Inch Grid
- Congruent Regions of Polygons
- Similar Figures I
- Similar Figures II

Section 3: MEASUREMENT
- Growing Squares
- How Long Will It Take? Clocks
- 24-Hour Clock
- Jogging Path

- Go for the Gold
- ½-Inch Coordinate Grid
- ¾-Inch Coordinate Grid

Section 4: STATISTICS
- Bicycles Ridden to School
- Picture Graph (Blank)
- Favorite Sports Graph
- Bar Graph (Blank)
- Growth of a Bean Plant Line Graph
- School Fundraiser Line Graph
- Line Graph (Blank)
- TV Watching Graph
- Pizza Crust Preferences Circle Graph
- Summer Trip Circle Graph
- Circle Graph (Blank)
- Protractor

Section 5: PROBABILITY
- 3-Region Spinner
- Paper Clip Spinner
- Two 3-Region Spinners
- Two 4-Region Spinners
- Dice Outcomes Matrix
- Heads and Tails
- Flipping Four Coins
- Two Bags

Section 6: ALGEBRA
- Set Rings
- Property Problems
- Scale
- The Challenge
- Operations
- Words for the Operations Practice
- Input/Output Tables
- Multiple Functions

Section 1: SYMMETRY

Symmetrical Pattern

Asymmetrical Pattern

Four Regions

II

I

III

IV

Flipped Words

Write the word correctly under the flipped word.

rectangle

_____

covering

_____

thrombus

_____

vertically

_____

Mirror Lines and Figures

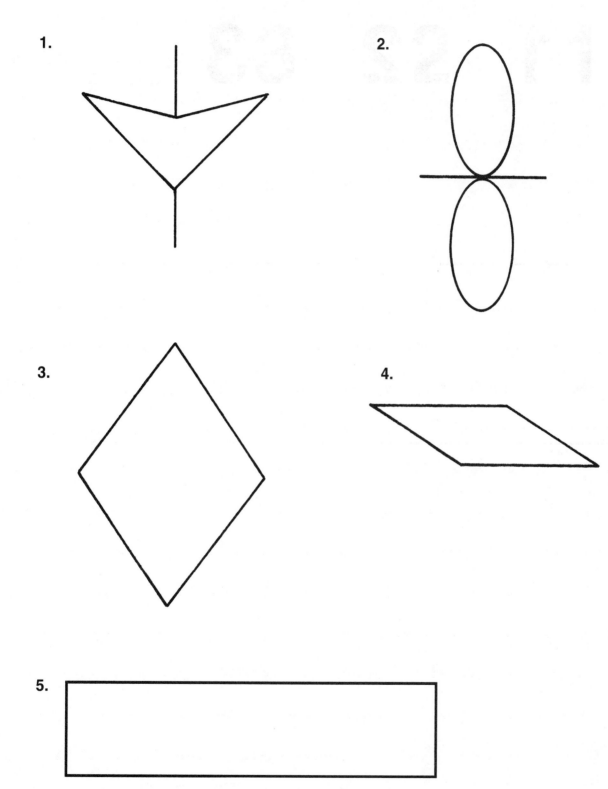

1.

2.

3.

4.

5.

What Comes Next?

� ᄅ2 ᘓ3 _____

_____ _____ _____ _____

_____ _____ _____ _____

Find Those That Match

In the 10 figures below there are 5 identical matches. The only difference is that one has been turned. Find the two figures that match each other and record them below.

Figure _____ matches figure _____.   Figure _____ matches figure _____.

Figure _____ matches figure _____.   Figure _____ matches figure _____.

Figure _____ matches figure _____.

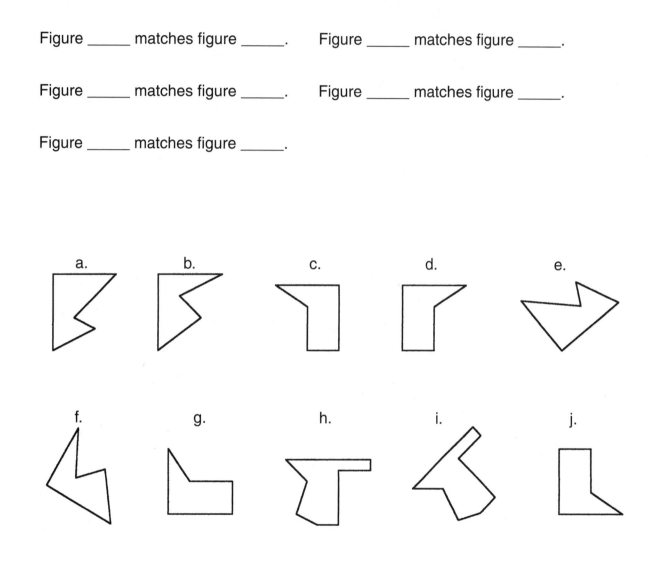

Rotational Symmetry

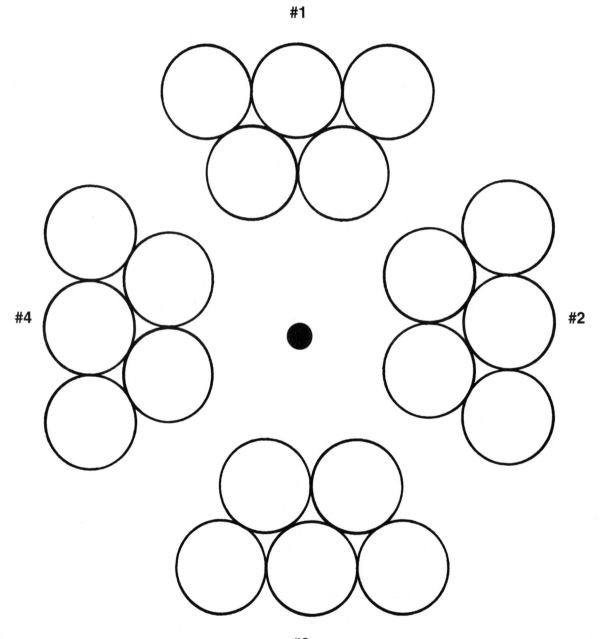

Will It? Frame

Figures for Will It? Activity

square

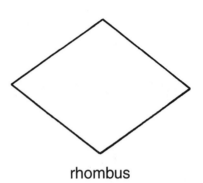

rhombus

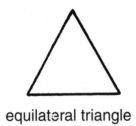

equilateral triangle

hexagon

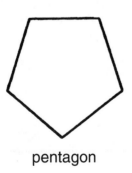

pentagon

Section 2: GEOMETRY

Three Angles

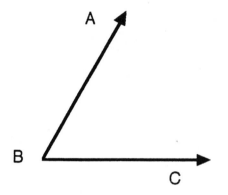

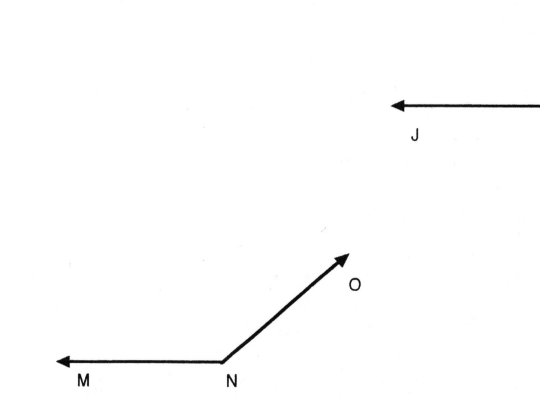

Circles and Angles

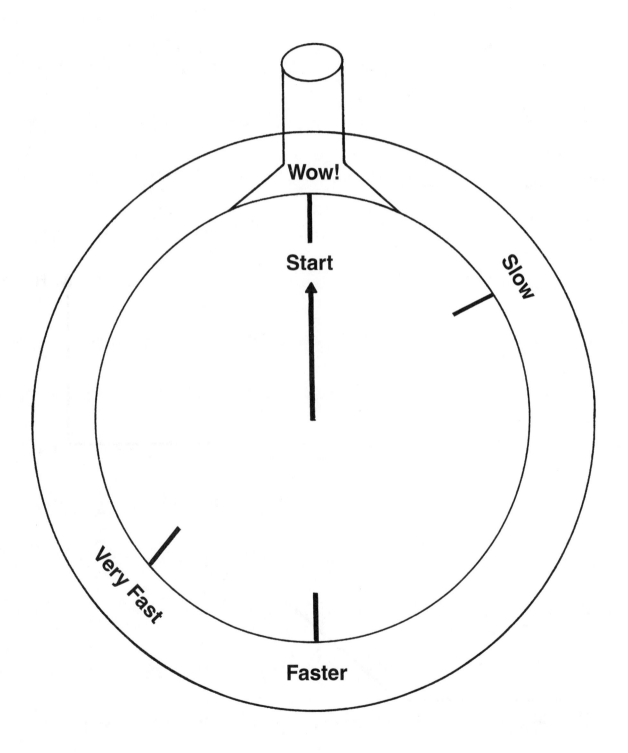

Square and Rectangle

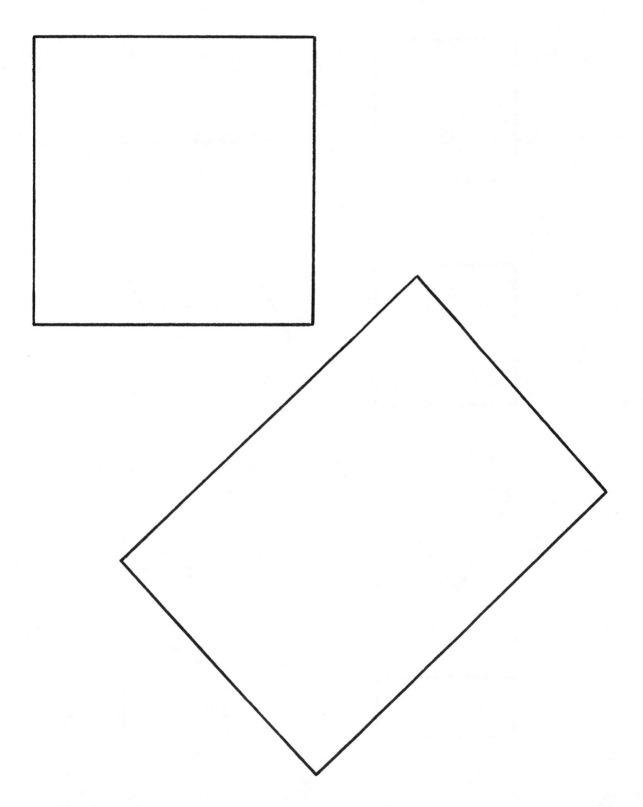

255

Polygons

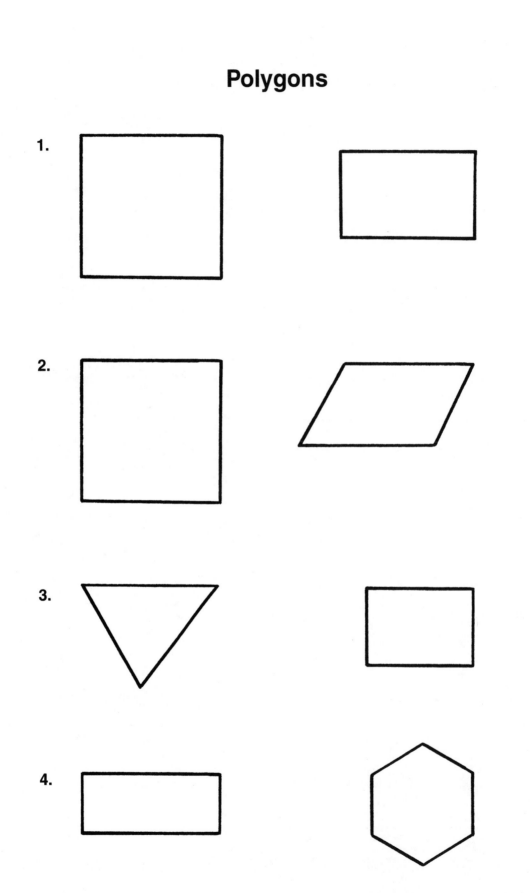

1.

2.

3.

4.

Regular/Irregular

Net 1 (Square Pyramid)

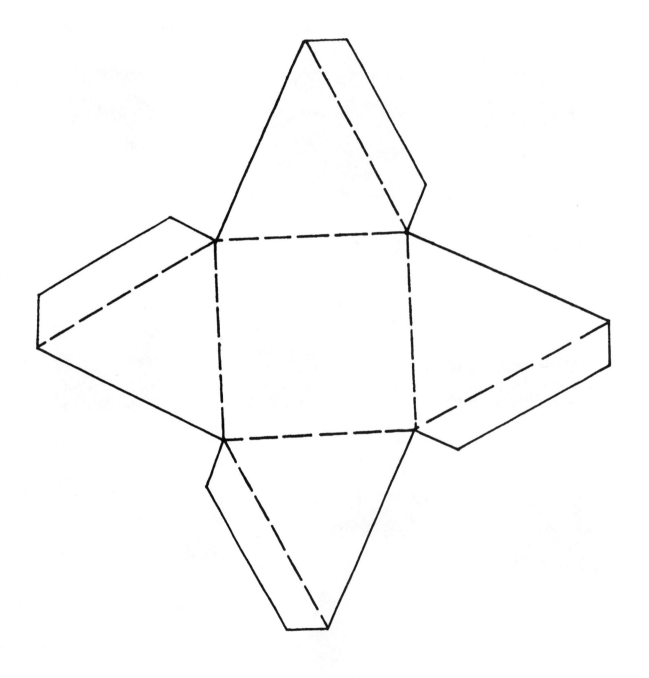

Net 2 (Rectangular Prism)

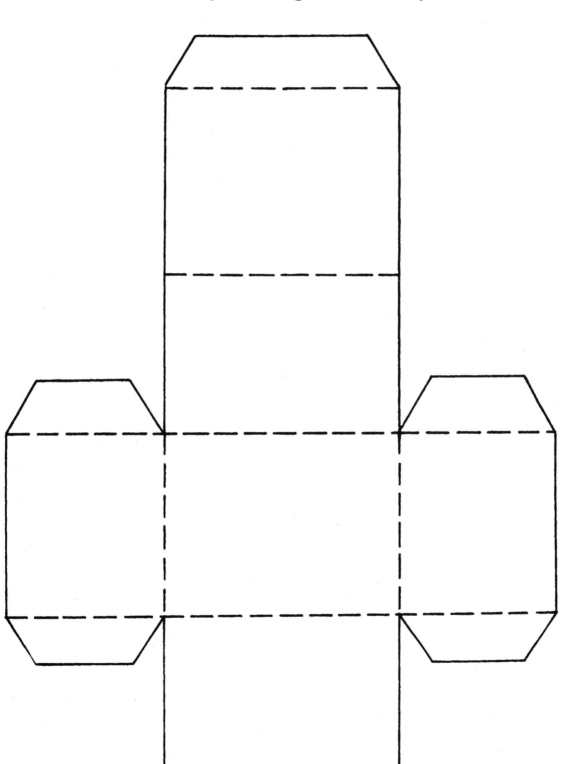

Net 3 (Cylinder)

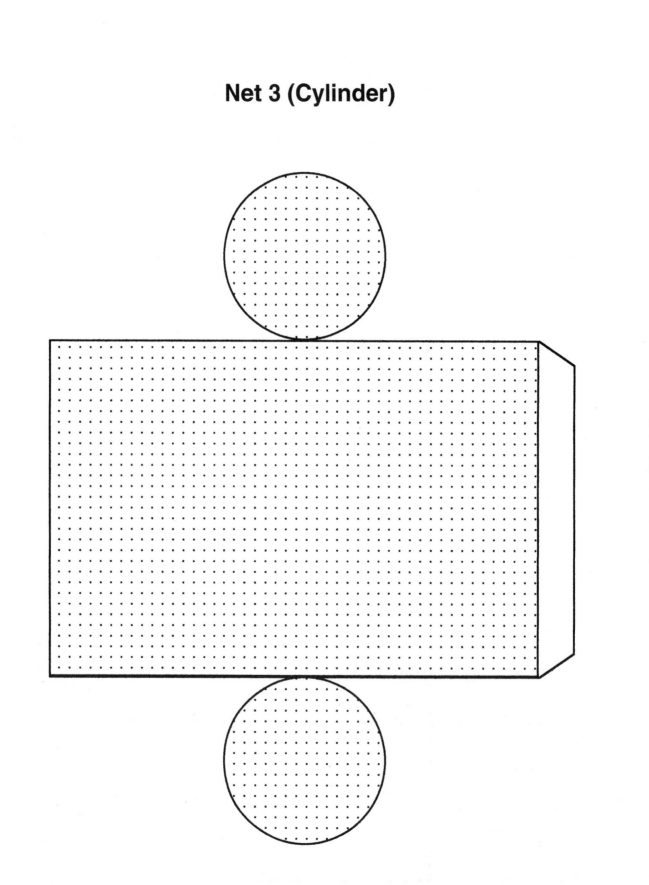

Net 4 (Cube)

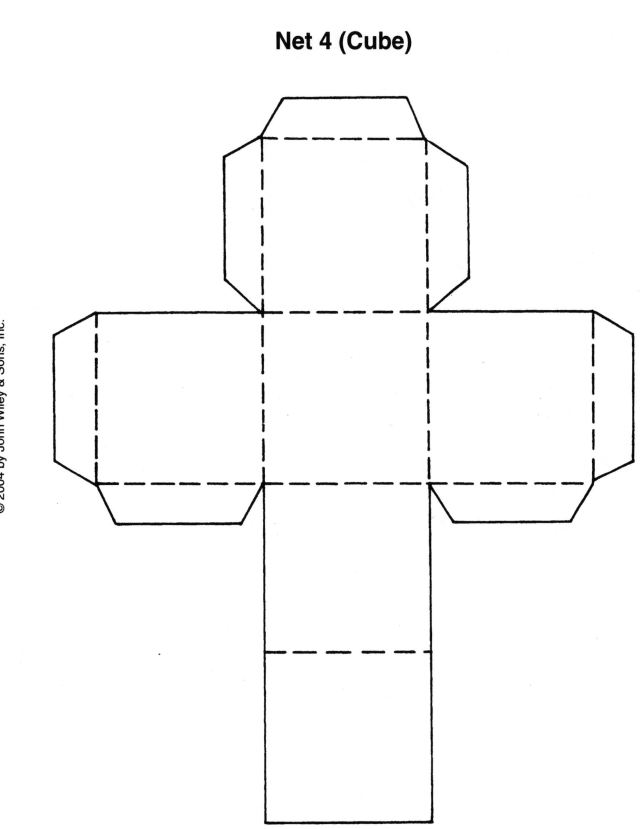

Net 5 (Cone)

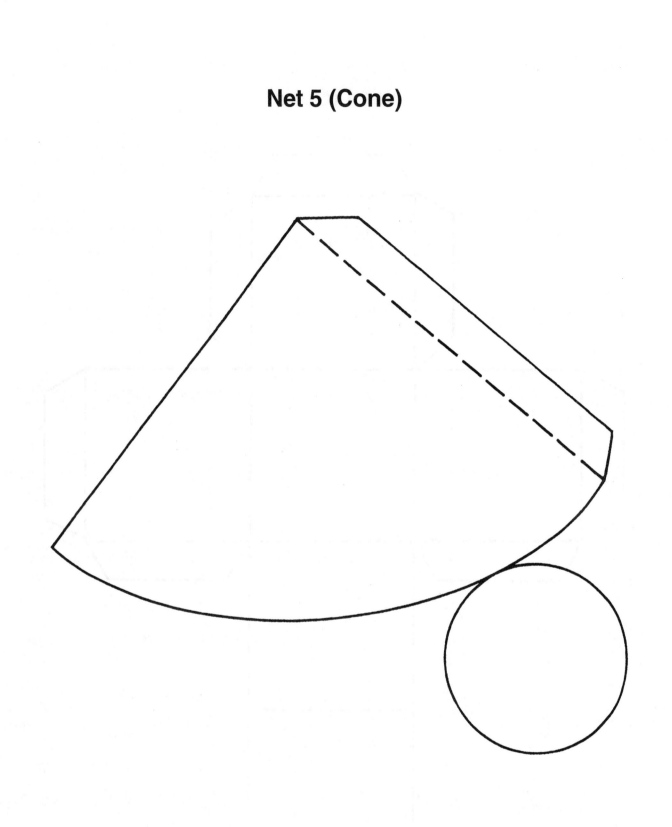

Rogs

These are Rogs.

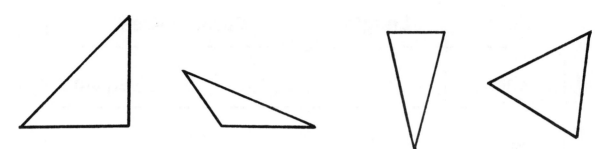

These are not Rogs.

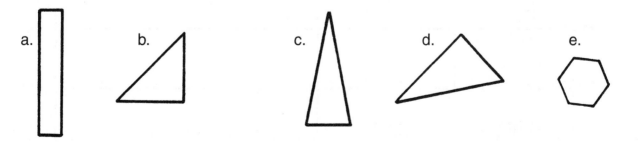

Which of these are Rogs?

a.   b.   c.   d.   e.

Describe the attributes of Rogs.

All That Gold Table

Rod	Length	Surface Area
white	1	sq cm
red	2	
green	3	
purple	4	
yellow	5	
dark	6	
black	7	
brown	8	
blue	9	
orange	10	

Regions of a Circle

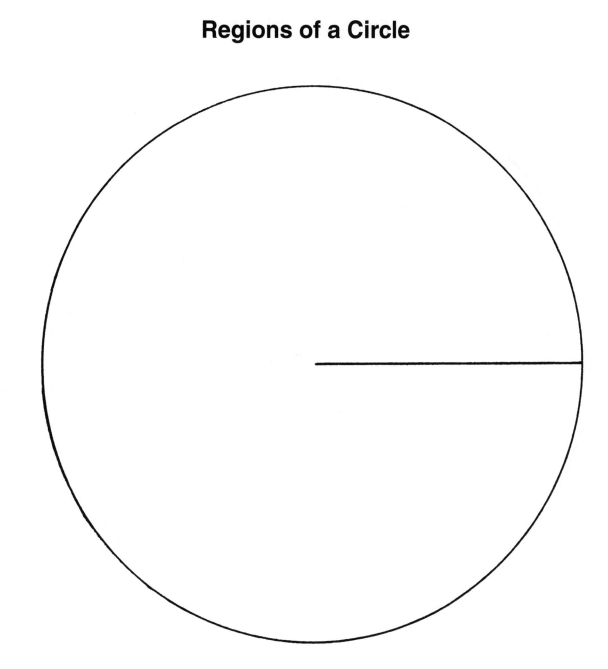

Cookie	Degrees
Chocolate chip	140°
Sugar	90°
Peanut butter	85°
Oatmeal	45°

Create a Graph

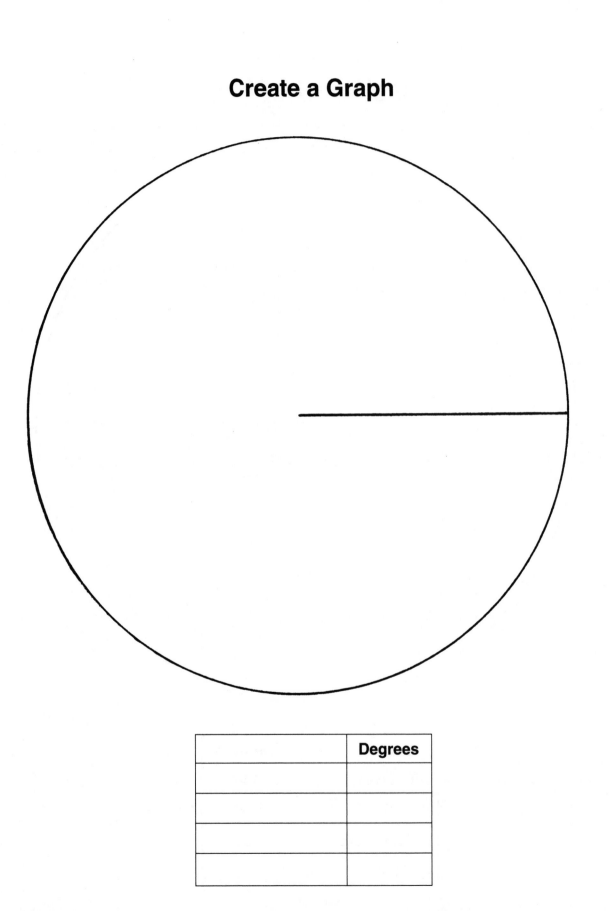

	Degrees

Centimeter Grid

½-Inch Grid

1-Inch Grid

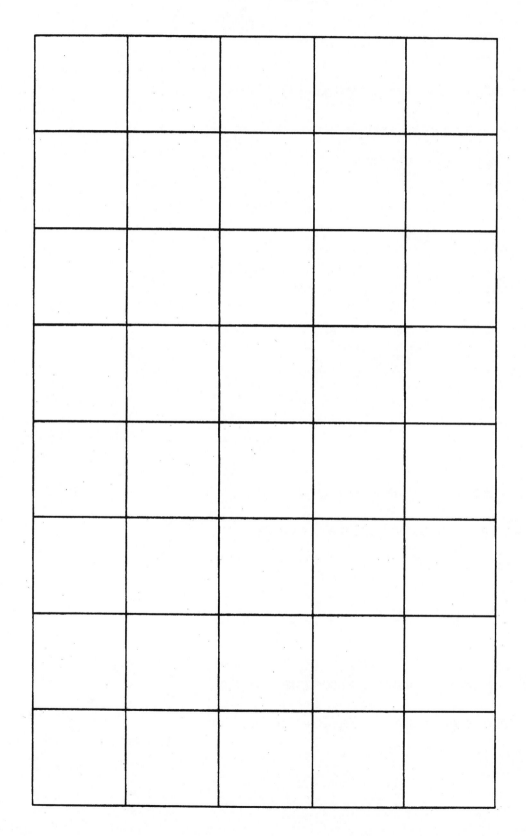

Congruent Regions of Polygons

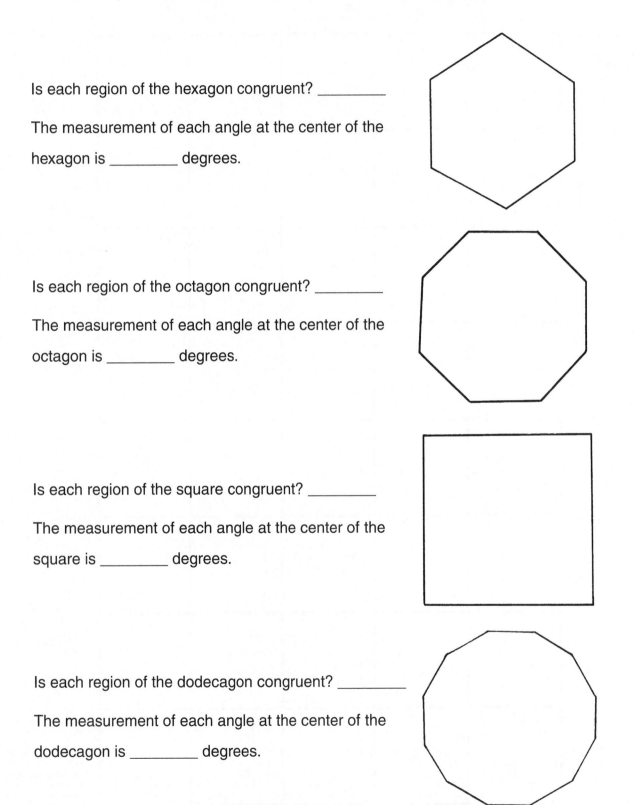

Is each region of the hexagon congruent? _____

The measurement of each angle at the center of the
hexagon is _____ degrees.

Is each region of the octagon congruent? _____

The measurement of each angle at the center of the
octagon is _____ degrees.

Is each region of the square congruent? _____

The measurement of each angle at the center of the
square is _____ degrees.

Is each region of the dodecagon congruent? _____

The measurement of each angle at the center of the
dodecagon is _____ degrees.

Similar Figures I

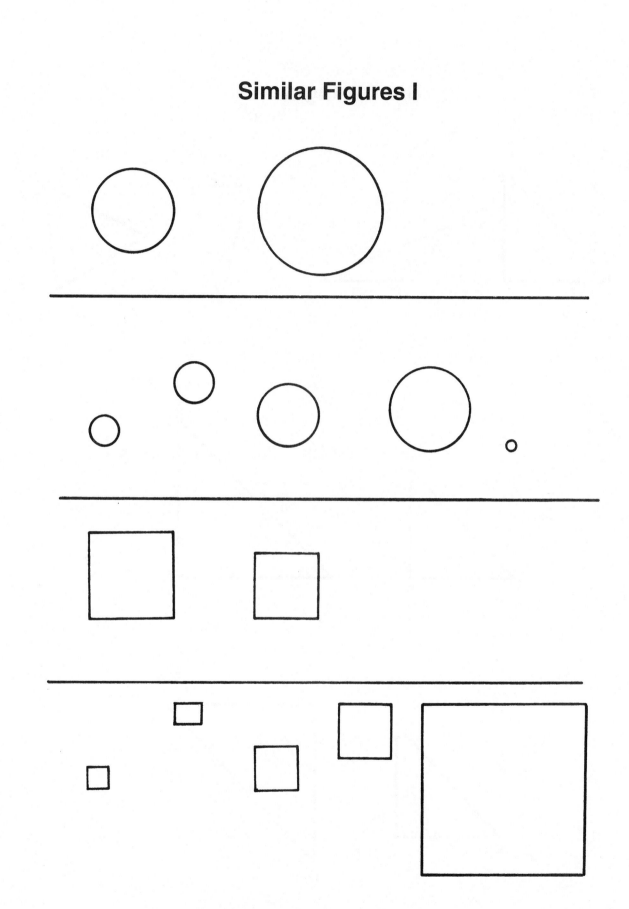

Similar Figures II

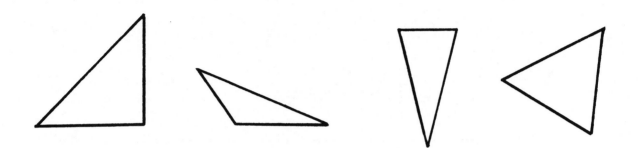

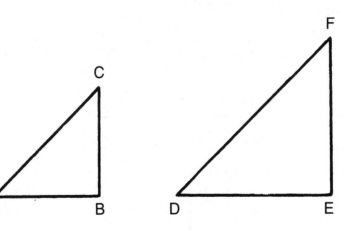

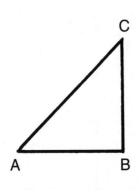
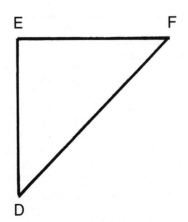

Section 3: MEASUREMENT

Growing Squares

Number of Squares	Area (square inches)	Perimeter (inches)
1	1	4
2		
3		
4		
5		

Describe the pattern for the area of the figure as the number of squares increases.

_____

_____

_____

Describe the pattern for the perimeter of the figure as the number of squares increases.

_____

_____

_____

How Long Will It Take? Clocks

Daniel's band practice begins at 4:00 and ends at 5:45. How long is Daniel's band practice?

_____

Hakeem arrived at his karate class at 7:00. It took him 10 minutes to walk to the bus stop and the bus ride took 15 minutes. What time did Hakeem leave his house?

_____

24-Hour Clock

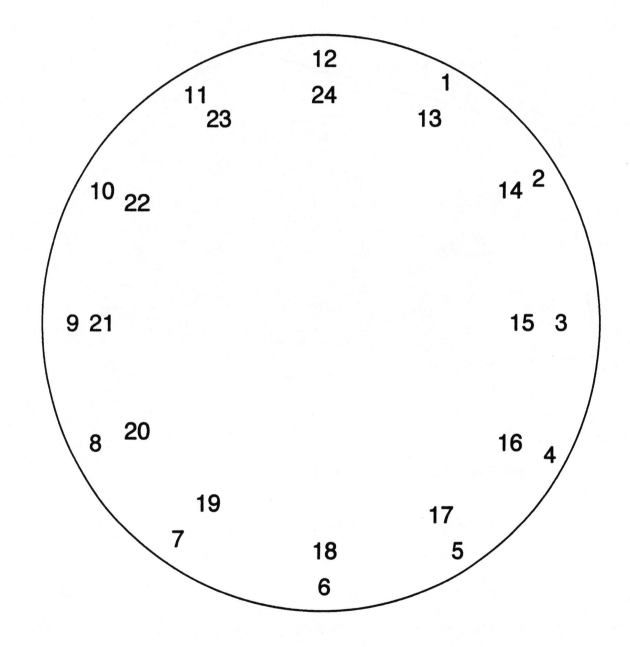

Jogging Path

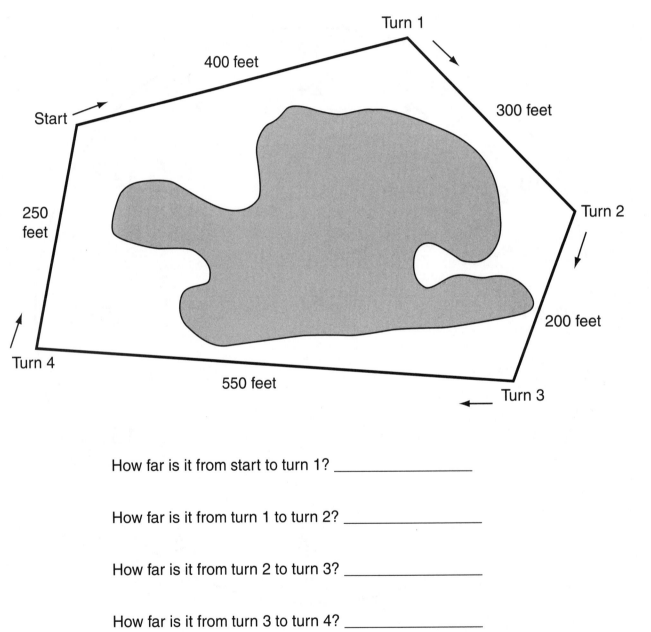

How far is it from start to turn 1? _____

How far is it from turn 1 to turn 2? _____

How far is it from turn 2 to turn 3? _____

How far is it from turn 3 to turn 4? _____

How far is it from turn 4 to start? _____

Go for the Gold

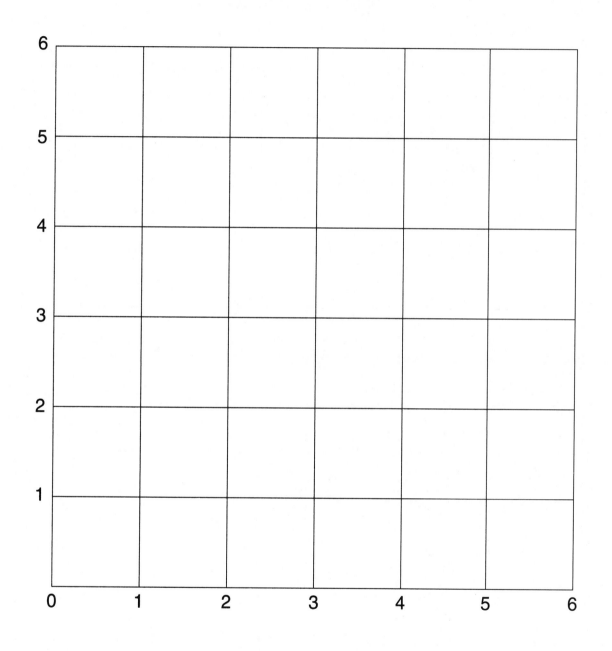

½-Inch Coordinate Grid

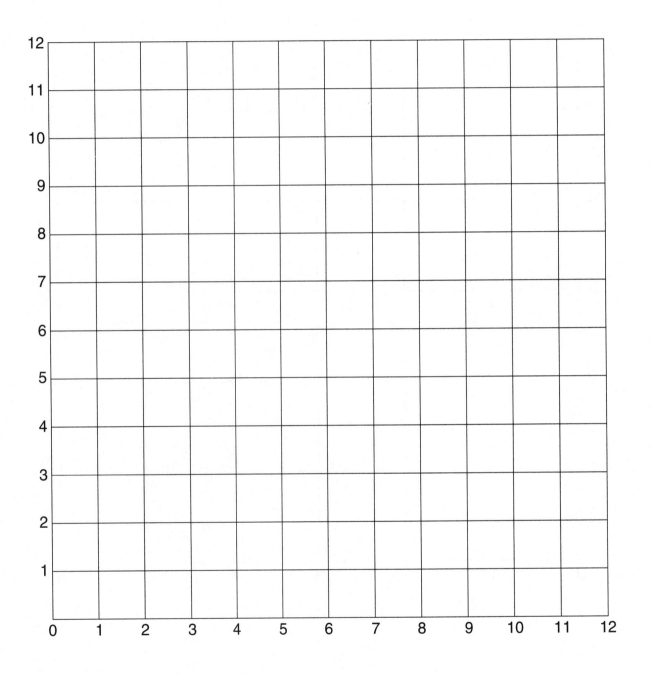

³/₄-Inch Coordinate Grid

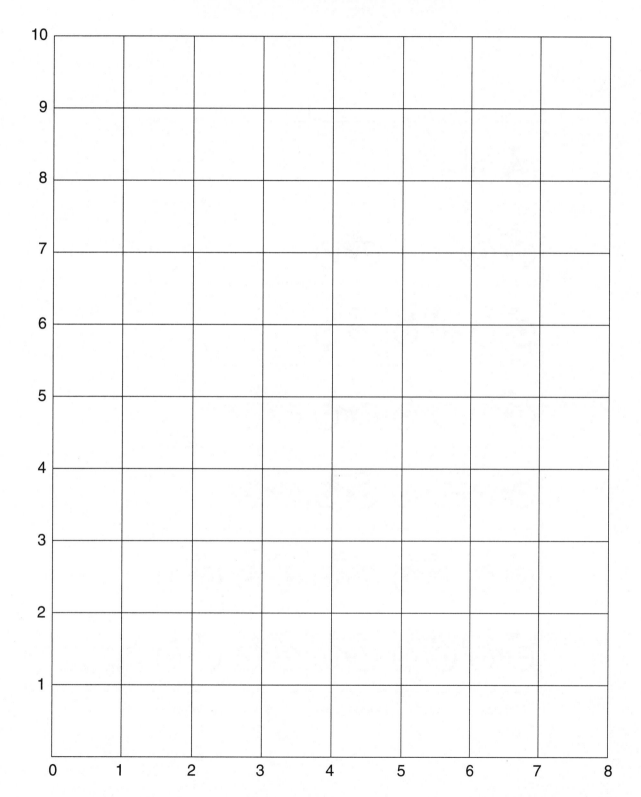

Section 4: STATISTICS

Bicycles Ridden to School

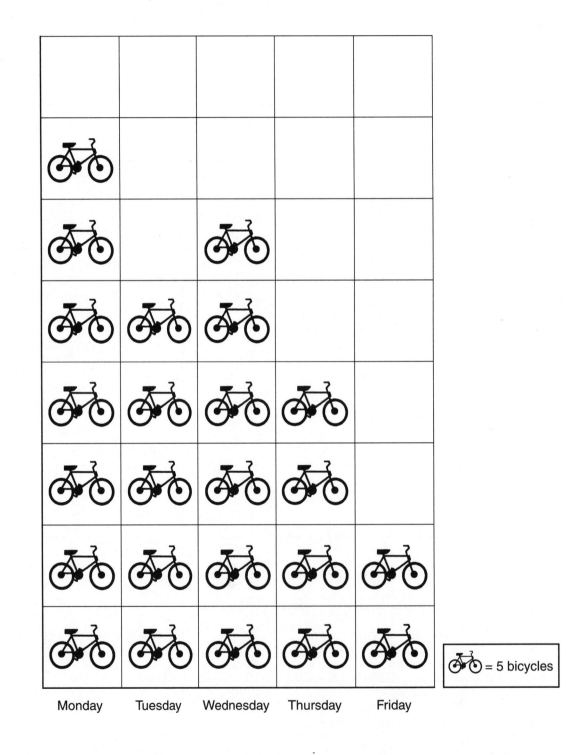

280

Picture Graph (Blank)

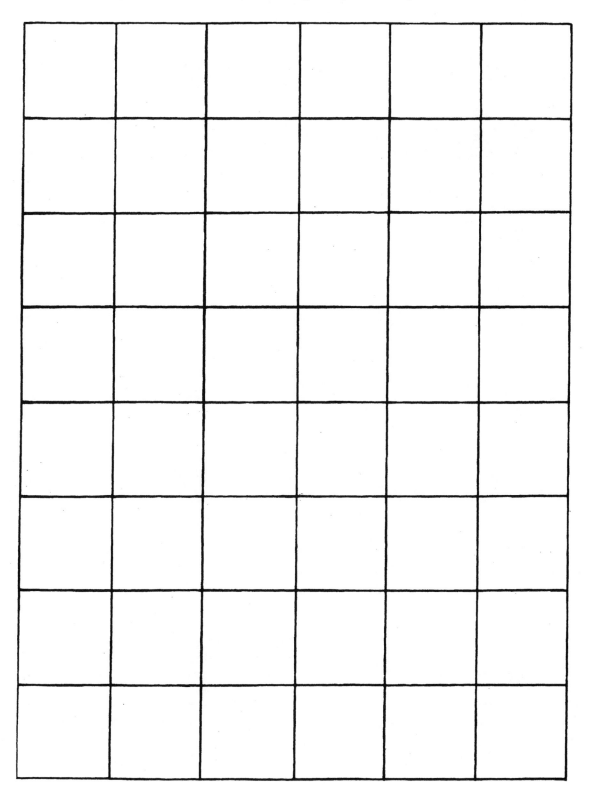

Favorite Sports Graph

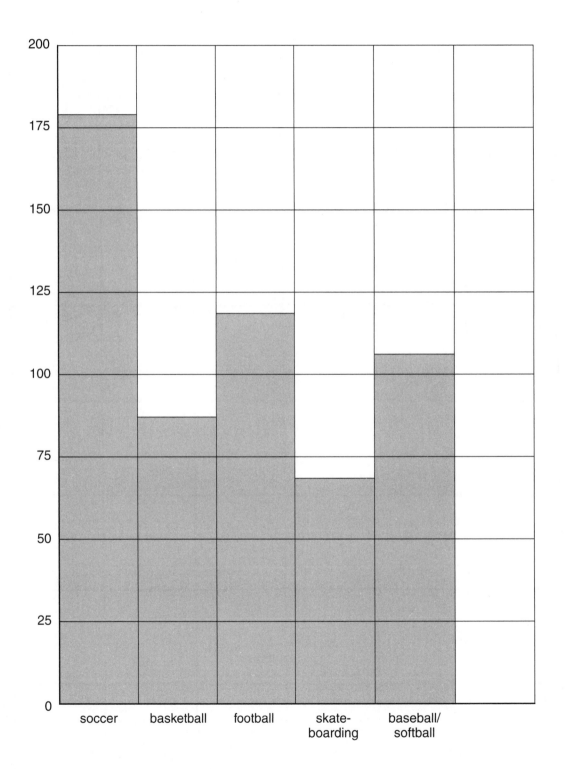

Bar Graph (Blank)

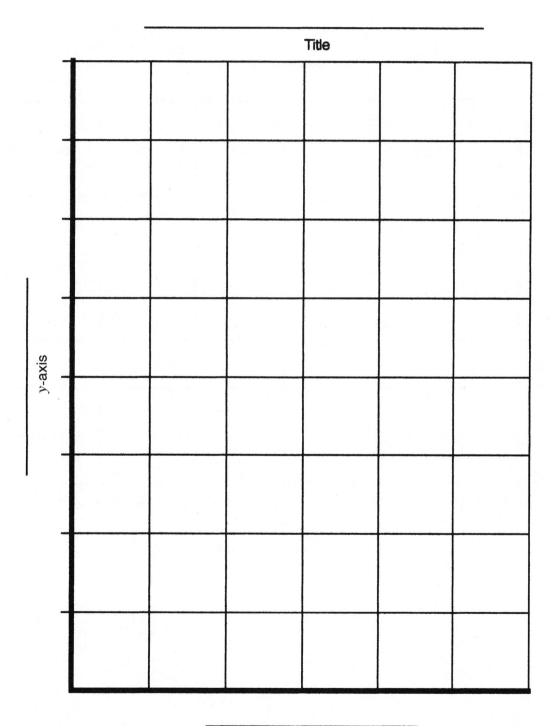

Growth of a Bean Plant Line Graph

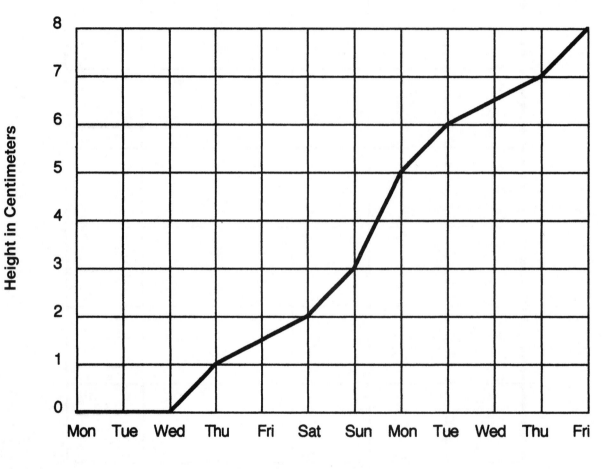

School Fundraiser Line Graph

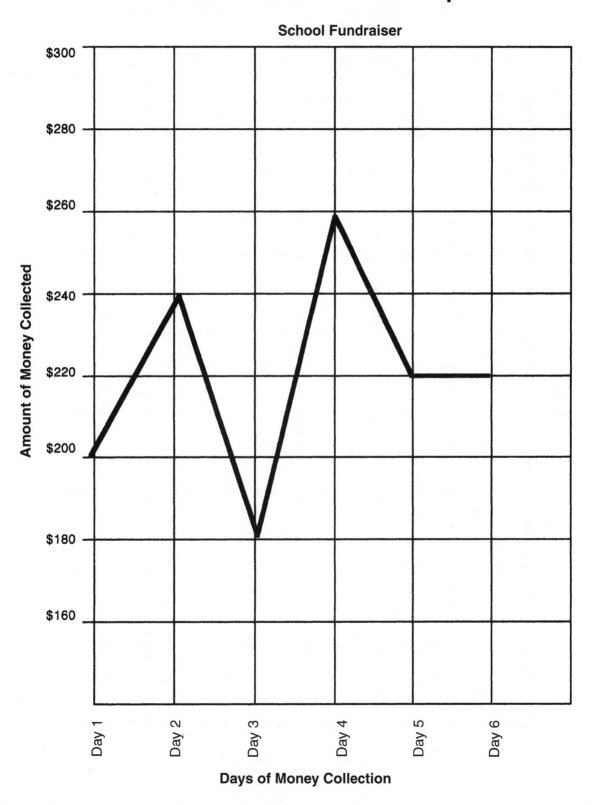

School Fundraiser

285

Line Graph (Blank)

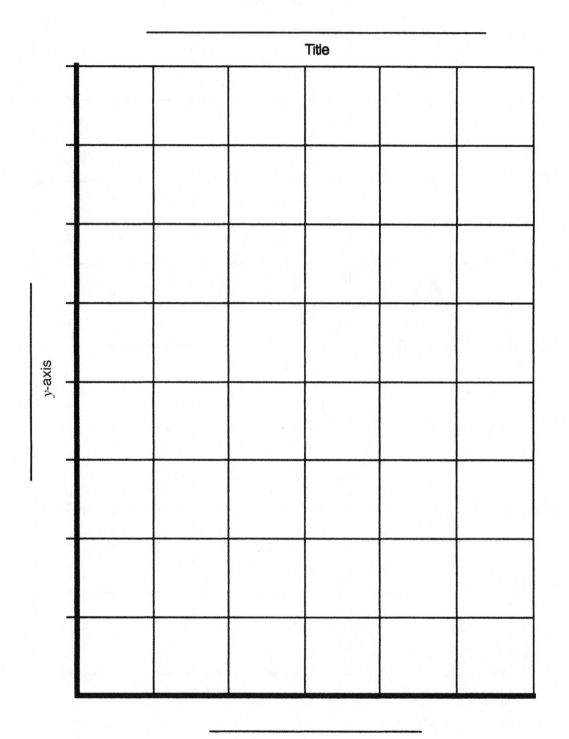

Title

y-axis

x-axis

TV Watching Graph

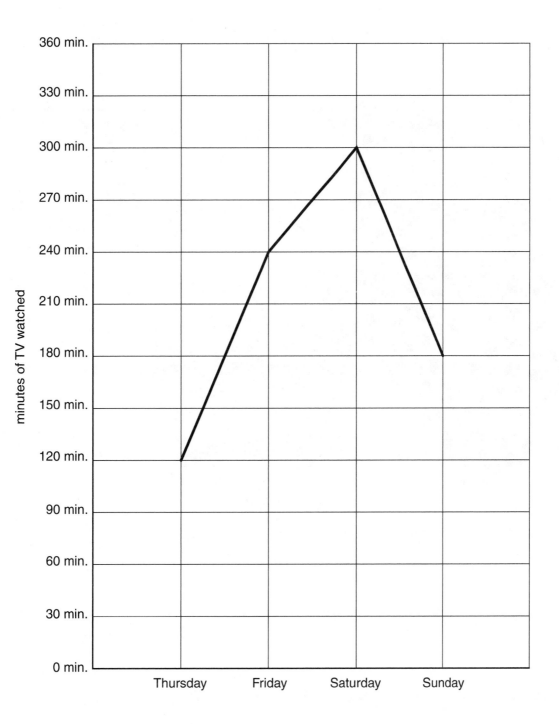

Pizza Crust Preferences Circle Graph

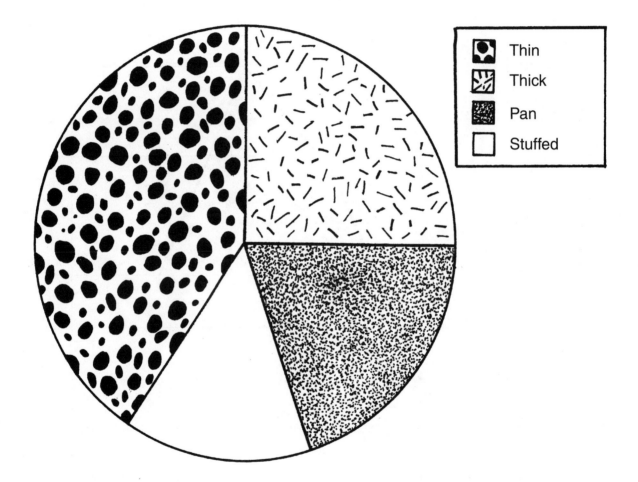

Thin
Thick
Pan
Stuffed

Summer Trip Circle Graph

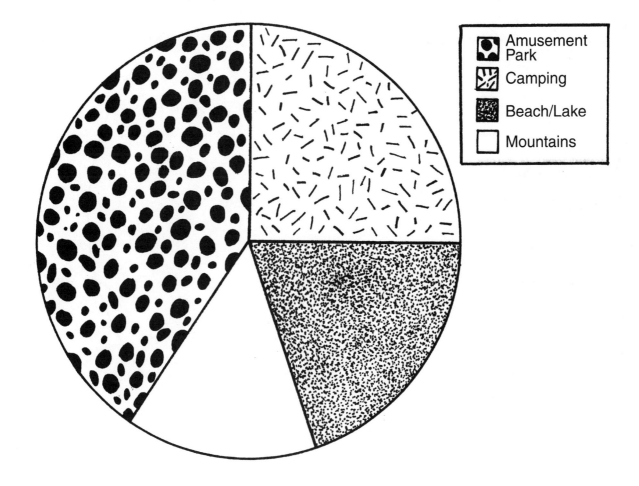

Circle Graph (Blank)

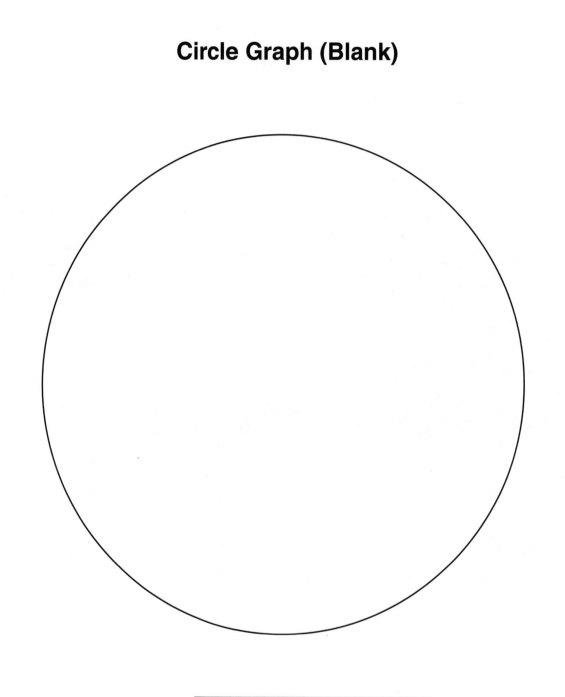

	Degrees

Protractor

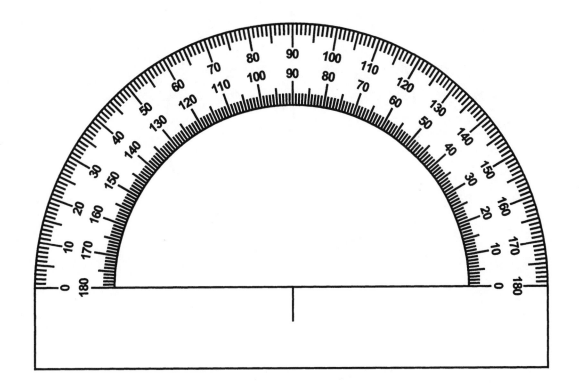

Section 5: PROBABILITY

3-Region Spinner

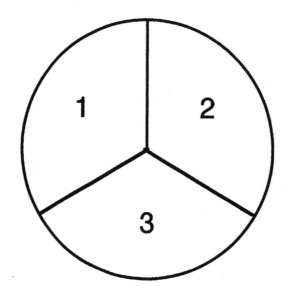

Paper Clip Spinner

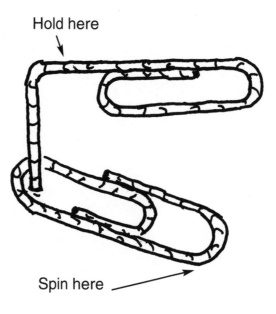

Hold here

Spin here

Two 3-Region Spinners

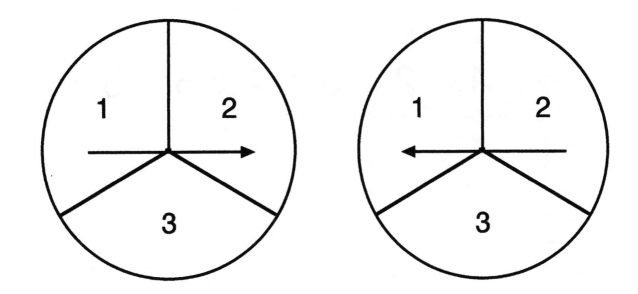

Two 4-Region Spinners

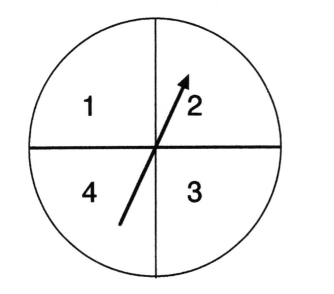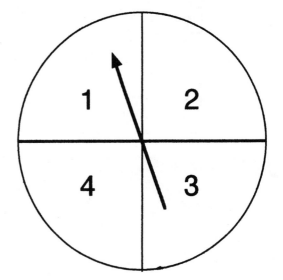

Dice Outcomes Matrix

+	1	2	3	4	5	6
1						
2						
3						
4						
5						
6						

Heads and Tails

Flipping Four Coins

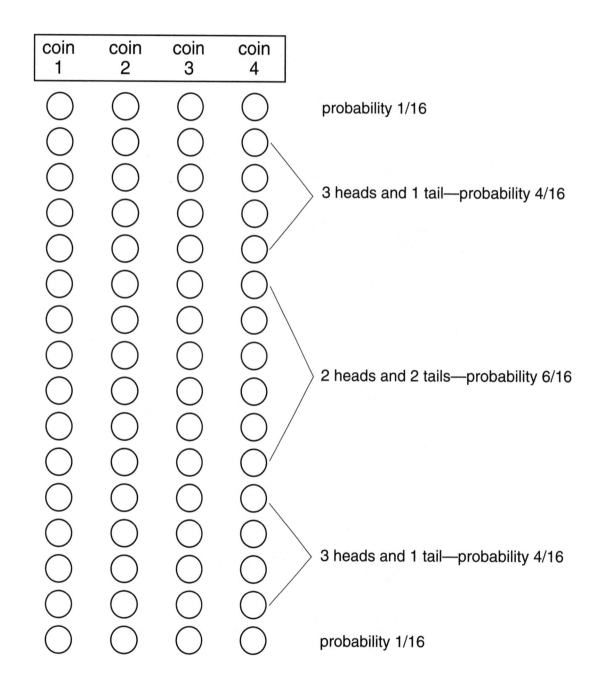

Two Bags

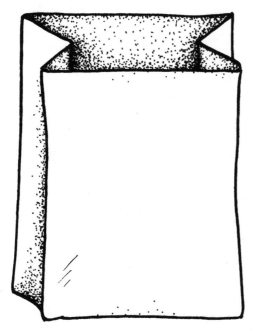

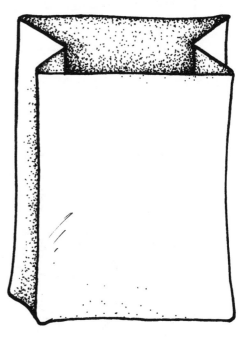

Section 6: ALGEBRA

Set Rings

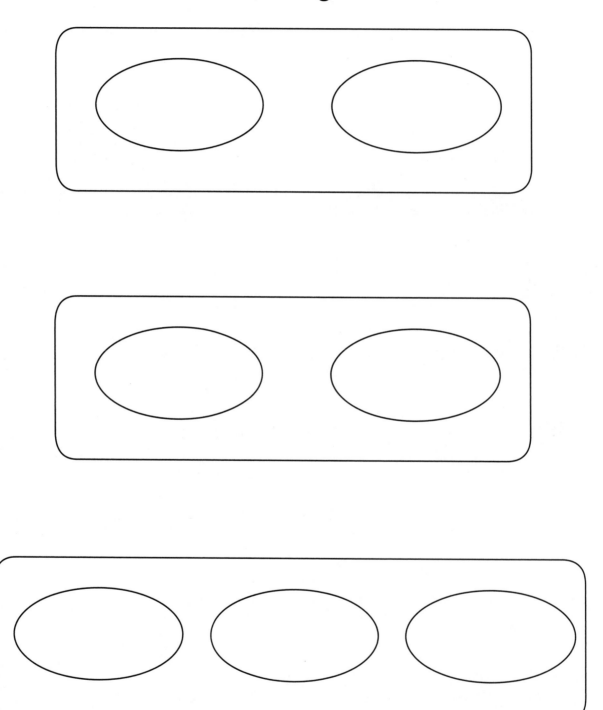

$3 + 3 + 3 = 9$ $3 \times 3 = 9$ $9 \div 3 = 3$ $9 - 3 = 6$

Property Problems

1. $5 + \boxed{} = 3 + 5$ Which property? _____

2. $13 + \boxed{} = 13$ Which property? _____

3. $(2 \times 3) \times 4 = 2 \times (\boxed{} \times 4)$ Which property? _____

4. Name the equation and the property for this representation.

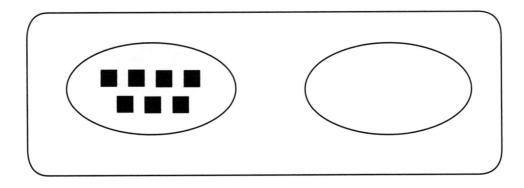

5. Name the equation and the property for this representation.

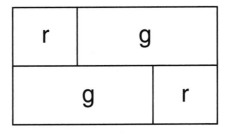

Scale

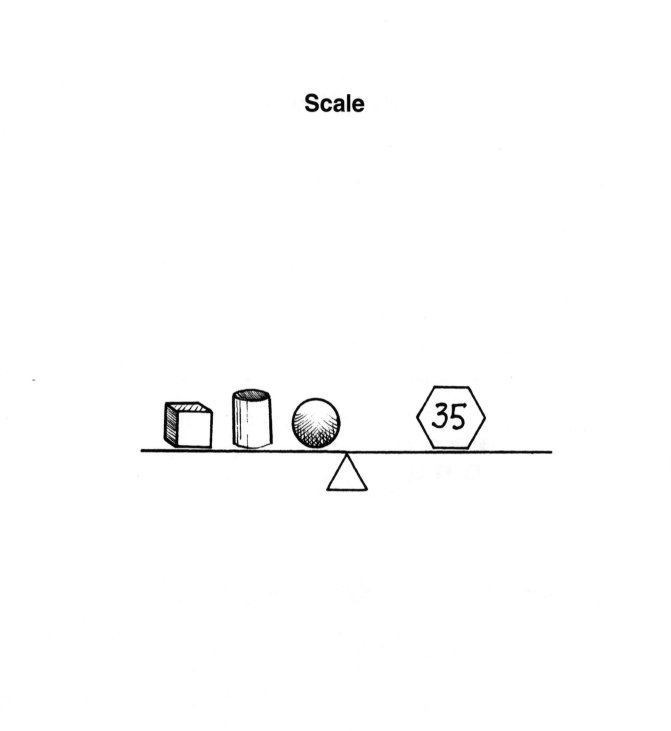

The Challenge

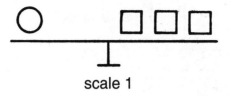

scale 1

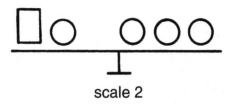

scale 2

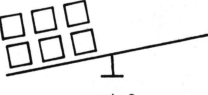

scale 3

Which one figure (square, circle, or rectangle) will balance scale 3?
Explain why your answer makes sense.

_____

_____

_____

_____

Operations

1. The sum of 4 and 3 is:

   $4 + 3 = 7$

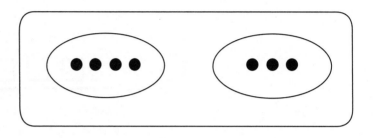

2. 8 decreased by 5 is:

   $8 - 5 = 3$

3. 4 rows of 5:

   $4 \times 5 = 20$

4. 2 more than 9 is:

   $2 + 9 = 11$

5. twice the number of 5:

   $2 \times 5 = 10$

6. $\frac{1}{3}$ of 18:

   $18 \div 3 = 6$

Words for the Operations Practice

Addition	Subtraction	Multiplication	Division
plus	minus	times	divided by
sum of	take away	product	goes into
increased by	less than	groups of	quotient
added to	decrease	rows of	$\frac{1}{2}$ of
more than	comparison	by	$\frac{1}{3}$ of
greater than	difference	twice	

Addition	Subtraction	Multiplication	Division
plus	minus	times	divided by
sum of	take away	product	goes into
increased by	less than	groups of	quotient
added to	decrease	rows of	$\frac{1}{2}$ of
more than	comparison	by	$\frac{1}{3}$ of
greater than	difference	twice	

Input/Output Tables

Input	Output
1	10
2	11
3	
5	
	19
	24

The rule or function is _____.

Input	Output
1	7
2	9
3	11
5	
	25
	29

The rule or function is _____.

Multiple Functions

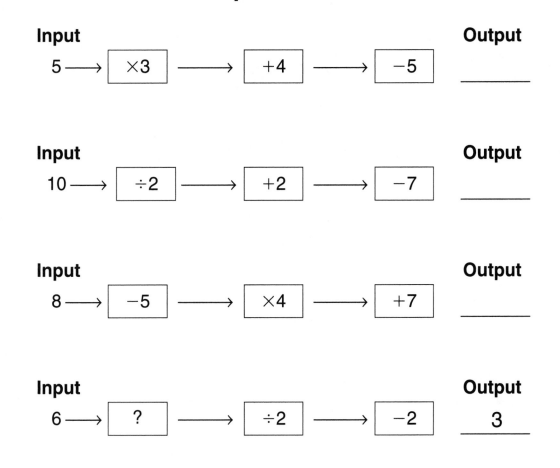

Input

5 ⟶ ×3 ⟶ +4 ⟶ −5   **Output** _____

Input

10 ⟶ ÷2 ⟶ +2 ⟶ −7   **Output** _____

Input

8 ⟶ −5 ⟶ ×4 ⟶ +7   **Output** _____

Input

6 ⟶ ? ⟶ ÷2 ⟶ −2   **Output** _3_

Glossary

Acute Angle   An angle that measures less than 90 degrees.

Addend   Each of the numbers to be added.

And   When specific events would be satisfactory.

Angle   Two rays that have a common point, the vertex.

Area   The number of square units within a closed curve.

Associative Property   When dealing with three or more addends or factors, how the addends or factors are grouped does not affect the sum.

Attribute   A distinct feature or characteristic.

Bar Graph (Histogram)   Displays data along a numeric scale. The numeric scale can be changed when necessary, but the intervals should always be the same size. Histograms are popular because it is easy to determine the most, the least, and those with the same number. It is common to display the variable on the horizontal axis of the graph. In addition, it is important to label each axis and to title the graph. Histograms are more suited for displaying discrete (countable) data such as cookies, children, pets, etc.

Bilateral Symmetry   Mirror symmetry or reflection symmetry.

Capacity   The largest amount a shape can hold.

Centimeter   A unit for measuring length in the metric system; $\frac{1}{100}$th of a meter.

Cell   The individual boxes formed by the lines of a graph.

Celsius   The scale for measuring temperature in the metric system.

Central Tendencies   How the data disperse or scatter. The measures of central tendencies are:

      Mean   (see page 309)

      Median   (see page 309)

      Mode   (see page 309)

      Range   (see page 309)

Chance   The occurance of an unlikely event.

Circle   A figure in which all points are the same distance from a point called the center.

Circle Graph   Uses sections of a circle to represent percentages of the data being shown. Circle graphs (also known as pie charts) are easy to read and interpret since the value of each section can be seen at a glance. However, knowledge of percentages and angles is necessary to construct and interpret the graphs, making them difficult for many students.

Circumference   The distance around a circle.

Closed Curve   A line that returns to its beginning point.

Commutative Property   The order of the addends or factors does not affect the sum or product.

Compare   To measure two objects to see if one is greater or if they are equal.

Cone   A three-dimensional shape with one circular base.

Congruent   The same shape and size.

Coordinate   An ordered pair of numbers.

Corner   The point at which three or more faces of a geometric shape meet.

Cube   A three-dimensional shape with six congruent square faces.

Cup   A unit for measuring capacity (volume) in the customary system; 8 ounces.

Cylinder   A three-dimensional shape with two congruent circles for its faces.

Diameter A line that connects two points on a circle and passes through the center of the circle.

Difference The result after subtracting an addend from the sum.

Digit Symbols used to show numerals; 0, 1, 2, 3, 4, 5, 6, 7, 8, and 9.

Duration The time it takes for an event to occur.

Edge The line formed when two faces of a geometric shape meet.

Equal Having the same quantity or value as another.

Equation A number sentence stating that two expressions are equal.

Estimate A reasonable approximation.

Event Something that occurs or happens.

Experiment A test or activity done in order to find out something.

Fahrenheit The scale for measuring temperature in the customary system.

Face Any surface of a three-dimensional shape.

Factor Each of the numbers to be multiplied.

Figure A two-dimensional closed curve.

Flip To turn a figure over.

Foot A unit for measuring length in the customary system.

Frequency The number of times a particular datum occurs.

Frequency Polygon *See* Line Graph.

Frequency Table A way to organize data that uses numbers to show how often something happens.

Function A rule that sets the relationship between two sets of numbers.

Gallon A unit for measuring capacity (volume) in the customary system; 4 quarts.

Gram A unit for measuring mass (weight) in the metric system.

Histogram *See* Bar Graph.

Hexagon A six-sided closed figure.

Horizontal Axis The horizontal line of the two lines on which a graph is built.

Inch A unit for measuring length in the customary system; $\frac{1}{12}$th of a foot.

Input The number to which a function is applied.

Intersecting Lines Lines that cross each other at a point.

Identity Element 0 for addition and 1 for multiplication.

Identity Property Shows no change to addition or multiplication.

Independent Events Events that do not depend on each other to occur.

Irregular Polygon A polygon whose sides and angles do not all have the same measure.

Key A text that shows the ratio of real objects to those represented in a picture graph.

Kilometer A unit for measuring length in the metric system; 1000 meters.

Likelihood The chance of a certain event happening.

Line A set of points that forms an endless straight path in two directions.

Line Graph (Frequency Polygon) Best suited for displaying continuous (measured) data such as feet, centimeters, temperature, ounces, etc., but can also display other data. Points are plotted to show related pieces of data and lines are drawn connecting consecutive points. The lines and points reflect changes in the data. Because of this, frequency polygons are usually not used to determine the most or least, but to show changes. It is important to label each axis and to title the graph.

Line of Symmetry   A line that divides a figure into mirror images.

Line Segment   A specific part of a line with beginning and ending points.

Liter   A unit for measuring capacity (volume) in the metric system.

Mean   The average, or normal, data for a given situation. The mean is calculated by dividing the sum of the measures by the number of measures. The mean is a reliable measure when the range is not too great.

Median   When the data are arranged in order of size, the median is the middle measure. In many cases, the median is part of the data set. Extreme ranges have little effect on the median.

Meter   A unit for measuring length in the metric system.

Mile   A unit for measuring length in the customary system; 5,280 feet.

Mode   The most frequently occurring measure in a data set.

Motif   A design.

Net   An unfolded and flat pattern of a three-dimensional shape.

Obtuse Angle   An angle that measures greater than 90 degrees but less than 180 degrees.

Octagon   An eight-sided closed figure.

Open Curve   A line that does not return to its beginning point.

Or   When any of two or more events would be satisfactory.

Order   To arrange from least to greatest or greatest to least.

Outcome   The result of an event or an experiment.

Output   The resulting number after a function is applied to the input.

Parallel Lines   Lines that do not intersect or cross each other.

Pentagon   A five-sided closed figure.

Percent   A ratio that shows out of 100, or for each 100.

Perimeter   The distance around a figure.

Permutation   Special arrangements when looking at order.

Pi   The relationship of the circumference of a circle to its diameter.

Picture Graph (Pictograph)   Uses pictures or representations to display data. The pictures represent values that are sometimes more than one. Picture Graphs usually compare data.

Prediction   Something that is stated or told in advance.

Preference   A liking for something.

Pip   The dot on a die.

Point   A specific location in space.

Polygon   A many-sided closed figure. Also a simple closed curve made from three or more lines.

Polyhedron   A three-dimensional geometric shape. Polyhedra is the plural term.

Prism   A three-dimensional shape whose bases are parallel.

Probability   The numerical measure of the chance that a particular event will occur, compared to the total number of events that could possibly occur.

Protractor   A tool for measuring angles.

Pyramid   A three-dimensional shape with one base and triangular faces that come together at one point.

Quadrilateral   A four-sided polygon.

Quart   A unit for measuring capacity (volume) in the customary system; ¼ of a gallon.

Range   The difference between the greatest and least measures.

Ratio   The numeric relationship between two numbers.

Ray   A part of a line that begins at a point and continues endlessly in one direction.

Rectangle   A closed figure with four sides and four right angles.

Rectangular Prism   A three-dimensional shape with six rectangular faces.

Regular Polygon   A polygon whose sides and angles all have the same measure.

Rhombus   A four-sided figure with two pairs of parallel sides and all sides the same length.

Right Angle   An angle that measures 90 degrees.

Rotational Symmetry   Turning symmetry.

Scale   A ratio that shows the relationship between drawings of different size.

Shape   A three-dimensional geometric form.

Similar   The same shape but not the same size.

Slide   To move a figure in one straight direction.

Sphere   A three-dimensional shape with all points the same distance from the center.

Square   A closed figure with four equal sides and four right angles.

Standard Units   Customary or metric units used for measurement.

Stem-and-Leaf Plot   A graph that shows the shape of a data set.

Survey   A question, or set of questions, that a specific group of people are asked. The results are the answers that the people give.

Symmetry   A characteristic of a figure or design that has balance or harmony.

Tally Table   A way to organize data that uses tally marks to show how often something happens.

Tessellate   To cover an area completely.

Tessellation   A figure that will cover an area.

Trapezoid   A four-sided figure with one pair of parallel sides.

Translational Symmetry   Slide symmetry.

Triangle   A closed figure with three sides.

Triangular Prism   A three-dimensional figure with two congruent triangular faces.

Turn   To rotate a figure.

Unit   An arbitrary measure.

Unlikely   Probably will not happen.

Value   A numerical quantity.

Variable   A symbol that can take on any of a set of values.

Vertical Axis   The vertical line of the two lines on which a graph is built.

Vertex   The point at which three or more faces of a geometric shape meet (corner).

Yard   A unit for measuring length in the customary system; 3 feet.